Journey of an Ex-Teetotaling Virgin

a memoir based on a true story

Fay Faron
Creighton Morgan Publishing Group
New Orleans, Louisiana

To Mom & Dad who never
stopped believing in my
teetotaling virgin within

Special thanks to my simply marvelous editor, Leann Logsdon. If she can't find it, it's not wrong. (Except for the part where I made changes after her editing...)

A Nasty Bit of Business *– A Private Eye's Guide to Collecting a Bad Debt*
Missing Persons*, a writer's guide to finding the lost, the abducted and the escaped*
Rip-Off*, a writer's guide to crimes of deception*

JOURNEY OF AN EX-TEETOTALING VIRGIN. Copyright 2021 © by Fay Faron. Printed in the United States of America. No part of this book may be used or reproduced in any manner whatsoever without written permission except in the case of brief quotations embodied in critical articles or reviews. For Information, address Creighton Morgan Publishing Group, 525 Pelican Ave., New Orleans, LA 70114

Library of Congress Control Number: 2021900936

ISBN: 978-1-7374306-3-6

Faron, Fay
Journey of an Ex-Teetotaling Virgin: a memoir based on a true story / by Fay Faron. – 1st edition
1. Travel stories
2. Humor
3. Women's Memoir

Table of Contents

1.	Five Years of Foreplay; Let the Games Begin	1
2.	My Boyfriend's Back & There's Gonna Be Laundry	7
3.	See Ya	23
4.	Been There, Born There	33
5.	When We Saints Came Marching In	51
6.	Jobs Even I Won't Take	67
7.	Rollin' on the River	77
8.	To Les-be or Not to Les-be	87
9.	When Teetotaling Goes Awry, Can Virginity be Far Behind?	99
10.	And So, We Drove On	109
11.	Sunshine & Showers	115
12.	Comeuppance of a Teetotaling Virgin	127
13.	My Big Fat Phony Sewing Machine Giveaway	141
14.	How I Spent My Summer Vacation	151
15.	Frozen in Place	165
16.	Blaze of Glory	181
17.	The Second Comeuppance	191
18.	The Back of Beyond	205
19.	The Newlywed Game	215
20.	The Sun Also Sets	227
21.	Masher of La Mancha	239
22.	Road to Morocco	247
23.	A Broad Goes Abroad—So You Don't Have To	263
24.	You're Never Too Old for Late-Onset Teenage Angst	271

Prologue

North End, Boston, 1974

I WAITED outside 121 Salem Street, averting my eyes from the lambs dangling in the window of Paesanti's Meat Market across the street. I busied myself with something inside my purse, but what I was really doing was waiting for somebody to come out although it didn't matter who because I didn't know anybody who lived there anymore.

I glanced around nervously, as I'd been doing these last couple of weeks. There were the usual suspects. An old Italian woman was perusing the fruit stand at Rinaldi's, her bright purchases in sharp contrast to her black dress and heavy veil. Three old men strolled past, towels strewn across their broad shoulders, chattering away in dialects of Rome, Naples and Sicily as they headed for the public baths. Boys in short trousers and checkered caps played marbles on the manhole cover outside the Brook Farm Egg Company.

Then, just my luck, Lennie the Cat came strutting out of Racupero Anna Tailors, looking all full of himself in his new pin-striped suit. Oh, great. All I needed now was to be spotted by the lovesick gangster.

A young mother exited 121 Salem St., her arms wrapped around a plastic laundry basket. I scurried in before the door sucked shut behind her and climbed the five flights to my old apartment. The 5th floor was just as I'd left it, completely vacant except for my bicycle and backpack, stashed outside Apartment #13.

I might be homeless, but at least I wasn't hall-less.

I snuggled into my flannel sleeping bag and tried to read but with the overhead bulb burned out, *Jaws* was just a blur. I tried to sleep but with another two hours before sunset, that was just a waste of time.

Well, okay, this was my punishment, I thought. I'd gone off in pursuit of earthly pleasures and now God had smited me Big Time. And this wasn't just some divine little slap-on-the-wrist warning smite, either.

Nope. This was a Full-Scale, Zero-Tolerance, Holy Shit Comeuppance.

Chapter 1
Five Years of Foreplay –
Let the Games Begin

January 20 to May 19, 1972

Vietnam: *55,000 American troops dead; Anti-war protests continue **In Other News:** "Bloody Sunday" marks the deadliest day in Ireland's "The Troubles" **On TV:** Me and the Chimp; Sanford and Son **At the Movies:** Cabaret; The Godfather **On the Radio**: Don McLean's "American Pie;" Neil Young's "Heart of Gold;" America's "A Horse With No Name"*

Phoenix, Arizona

I WAS BORN a teetotaling virgin.

Okay, let's face it, we all were.

The difference is I was expected to stay that way until the day I married the piano player at church—whoever that happened to be at the moment—and toasted my nuptials with sparkling cider alongside 350 of my parents' closest right-wing, fundamentalist Christian friends.

For my Bible-thumping patriarch, there was good and there was evil—and everything in between was evil. Still, Dad's world was fairly easy to navigate once you got the hang of it. Republicans were good, Democrats were bad. Baptists were good, Catholics were bad. Mormons were *really, really* bad. Sex outside of marriage was unthinkable—except if you happened to be the Virgin Mary, which Dad had no need to remind me I was not.

Teenage angst was strictly forbidden in our household. While my schoolmates were sassing back, shooting off guns in the desert, skipping classes, and doing wheelies out behind Pedro's Restaurant, I was tucked away in my travel poster-lined lilac bedroom watching

The Dick Van Dyke Show on a 13" black & white TV I bought for myself.

School was for education. Church for everything else.

Yet even in this insulated world, I was expected to be the best of the best, a beacon of light so that dazzling strangers would stop me on the street and say they wanted what I had. This would be my cue to whip out my Bible and save their sorry butts. I don't recall such an inquiry ever having been made, but I did memorize John 3:16 just in case.

I didn't want to go to college. Heck, I didn't want to go to grade school or high school either but look how that turned out. And then when I finally graduated Sunnyslope High in 1967, my parents made me go to college, a move I still believe borders on child abuse.

The first rung on my ladder of higher education was Glendale Community College, free to all Arizona residents. My thinking was (a) I wouldn't have to work for years paying off something I didn't want to do in the first place, and (b) I wouldn't have to drive very far to skip classes.

The next year, when all my friends transferred to Arizona State University, I did too. My social life there centered around Campus Crusade for Christ—an organization even more formidable than the 8th century Crusaders for which it was named.

Not into annoying proselytizing myself, I proceeded to use CCC as my own personal dating service. Almost immediately, I was ticking through boyfriends with Olympic speed. The problem was that all the guys were Good Christian Boys who'd never *think* of having premarital sex. Actually, they thought about it quite a bit. Unfortunately, every time they started feeling funny downstairs, they'd tend to pop the question.

I cannot tell you how many times a premature marriage proposal put the kibosh on a perfectly good romance. Sadly, should a girl nix a guy's generous offer to support her "'til death they do part" in exchange for a lifetime of nooky, he'd be off to the next girl. Nothing personal. That's just the way things are in the no-sex-before-marriage world.

The pressure only ratcheted up as the years clicked by, leaving coeds to watch the marriage pool being drained by a quarter every June, leaving them swimming in a tank full of half-dead fish.

Each Spring, "Take me!" "Choose me!" could be heard ricocheting from the Lang & Lit Building to the Student Union and back again. Life-long unions were sealed with a third-date kiss, chapels booked months in advance, and couples lucky if they could squeeze in a bit of pre-marital counseling before graduation day.

Like most girls, I envisioned myself in a white puffy dress, dodging rice and toasters as I glided down the aisle. In the Born-Again World, it didn't much matter who you married since everybody was taught the same things and therefore believed the same things. In fact, the only real decision was whether you wanted your kids to have brown hair or blonde.

But not me. I still believed in *The One*. My very own Prince Charming who God had created just for me. The boy whose job it was to love me.

As for finding *The One*, well, that was the conundrum. My first thought went to low hanging fruit. As it turned out, a real prince of my exact age already existed in the world—Charles, Prince of Wales. As for meeting him, that might be as easy as hanging around Hyde Park, enduring all the self-righteous pontificating until he wandered by in his bowler hat.

Still, what if Prince Charles wasn't *my* Prince Charming? He wasn't, after all, all that cute. What if our kids came out with those big ole Dumbo ears? And so, wise beyond my years, I relegated marrying Prince Charles to Plan B. Plan A remained smooching my way through college and marrying the very best kisser.

It wasn't long before I acquired a reputation as a kisser-and-not-marry-er. Abandoning the scorched earth of Campus Crusade, I searched out other Christian organizations on campus. I quit Student Mob—short for "Mobilization"—after finding the boys there irredeemably dorky. I lasted a bit longer at Faith Rests. But

Fay Faron

I finally quit there as well, after they flunked my homework assignment—writing a 10-page summary of the Old Testament—and then expecting I'd spend the entire weekend rewriting it.

By the second semester of my senior year, I'd taken every cushy course ASU had to offer. I hadn't seen my guidance counselor since my sophomore year when I'd showed up every other week to change my major. Back then, Mr. Todd told me to come back when my natural talents had shown me my true course in life.

"Oh, it's you," he said. "C'mon in."

"You look surprised," I said, entering.

"Actually, I am. I figured you'd have just dropped out by now."

"With my parents, not an option. Anyway, I made a list of all my classes and I wanna know what else I need in order to graduate."

I handed over my list: Physical Education. Coed Water Safety. Intro to Sociology. Personal & Social Adjustment. Survey of Musical Theater. Synchronized Swimming. Creative Writing. Composition. Prose. Clothing Construction. Clothing *Selection*. Geography of Europe. Family Relationships. Mass Communications. Magazine Writing. Advertising. And my personal favorite, Intro to Extreme Anal Behavior.

"What? No Trampoline 101?" asked Mr. Todd.

"They got that?"

"Kidding."

"Oh, look! You got an A."

"Really? Where?"

"Again, kidding."

Mr. Todd didn't say anything for a long while. *"Hmm,"* he said at last. *"Hmm, "Hmm."*

"What?"

"Well, here's the skinny, kiddo. College ain't like high school. You can't just hotdog it for four years and graduate. In college, you gotta actually major in something."

"I thought you might just bundle this into a major," I said. "You know, lemme know what I need to fill in the blanks."

"Ah, but these courses have nothing in common except they're all introductory. You need 30 hours in the same field in order to graduate."

This wasn't good. Not good at all. My parents had been forking over $69 in tuition every semester since community college. They expected me to graduate.

So, how do I get outta here?" I asked.

Mr. Todd and I stared at each other for what seemed like another three and a half years.

"Well," he said at last, "I guess you just quit."

Gee. You could've mentioned that sooner.

EXITING COLLEGE with no degree and no husband ticked off my frugal parents no end. And not just because they'd waisted $276 in tuition, but because there were no grandchildren in their foreseeable future.

Thankfully, I was able to present them with an alternative almost as enticing as the prospect of procreating—fulfilling my destiny as a World-Famous Creative Writer.

Except I didn't really want to be a Creative Writer. What I wanted to be was a Creative Live-er. And although more than a few famous authors had managed both, I had no intention of ending up like those rummies, Ernest Hemingway and F. Scott Fitzgerald.

Luckily, I had another mentor, fictional though she might be. Maisie Ravier was a fast-talking, curly-haired, ruffles-and-frills burlesque dancer portrayed by Ann Sothern in ten Depression-era films. Like me, Maisie was a teetotaling virgin. Unlike me, it had nothing to do with her parents and everything to do with the equally formidable Hayes Motion Picture Code.

Maisie's show biz career never lasted longer than the first few minutes in any one film. From then on, the showgirl with a heart of gold would find herself stranded in some exotic locale, taking one half-baked job after another, finding true love as easily as she found the funds to finance her travels.

In one film, Maisie was a barker at a midway shooting gallery where she fell in love with a Wyoming cowboy named Slim. In another, her little stowaway butt got booted off a steamboat in the Congo, where she proceeded to save her doctor-beau from "savages" with the aid of her sequined skirt and a conveniently timed thunderstorm. In another, the bubble-bath model helped her cutey cop boyfriend nab the scallywags who'd made off with her jewelry.

I could go on and on. Maisie certainly did.

But what I liked most about her movies was that each one was complete, with no reference to the true love that came before. No matter how perfect her "Happily Ever After," by the next film, she'd have acquired an endearing case of romantic amnesia, never pining for the Robert Young, George Murphy or Red Skelton she'd left behind. Always, effortlessly, finding another handsome / adorable / hunky / cute new boyfriend to take his place.

This was so me.

Or rather, who I aspired to be.

All my romances would be terribly meaningful, as long as they lasted. And when it was time to move on, there'd be no pining, no looking back, just a moment in time tucked away like a gem in a jewelry box. And then another boyfriend in another town down the road.

Faysie-Maisie.
Hmm.
I liked that.

Chapter 2
My Boyfriend's Back & There's Gonna Be Laundry

<u>May 20-31, 1972</u>

Vietnam: *Nixon says bombing won't stop until POWs released*
*****In Other News:*** *George Wallace paralyzed in assassination attempt* ***On TV:*** *All in the Family; The Sonny & Cher Comedy Hour; Mary Tyler Moore* ***On the Radio:*** *Roberta Flack's "The First Time Ever I Saw Your Face"*

Los Gatos, California

CONVINCING MY PARENTS I had to leave Phoenix in order to fulfill my destiny as a World-Famous Creative Writer wasn't all that difficult. Even they had to admit that although I was wildly talented, *nobody* was creative enough to find anything to write about in Phoenix. And so, they waved me off to Northern California to room with Cherie, my best friend from my camp counseling days in the Santa Cruz mountains.

By the time I arrived, Cherie had rented us an apartment in Los Gatos, arguably the jewel in a vast suburban wasteland where shopping center-centric cities like Sunnyvale, Cupertino, Campbell, San Jose and Santa Clara all melded together without personality or distinction.

Our converted two car garage apartment was separated from the main house by an interior wall, beyond which lived a couple in their mid-60s. And if their knock-out, drag down fights sounded like they were coming from the next room, it's because they literally were. More than once, I expected them to come crashing through the wall.

As for my roommate, Cherie and I had the same quirky sense of humor, love of life, fundamentalist Christian upbringing, and of course, teetotaling virgin ways.

Like me, Cherie was independently poor and consequentially thin. Unlike me, she had painfully pale alabaster skin, long blonde Mary Ann Faithfull hair and an untoned, lankiness Twiggy would have dieted for. In other words, Cherie was the perfect poster girl for the early 1970s.

I, on the other hand, was a lot like my taste in movies, stuck in the 1950s with my Esther Williams' curves and golden tan to match. As for my hair, I'd given up trying to iron it straight way back in high school and now I just let it go its own woofy way, a nod to Jane Fonda's Cat Ballou—although mine looked like it'd been styled in a wind tunnel.

And since no family is complete without pets, Cherie and I adopted a collie mix we called Chum, and a black and white kitty we named, "Telephone," because it cracked us up to go outside and yell her name.

"Telephone!"

Cherie graduated with a degree in Art History, which qualified her for a secretarial job in a San Jose law firm. Well, good for her because she could both type and spell.

Meanwhile, I found work at Cupertino High School, scoring the lofty position of "Cafeteria Supervisor," which paid an *astounding* $5 per hour, *three times* the minimum wage. Sadly, I only worked an hour a day, my sole duty making sure the kids put their trays away after lunch.

Still, I took my job very seriously, even chasing the little jerks out the door and across the campus, only to return to find their conspiring evil cohorts had left me with a room full of dirty dishes to pick up.

And even though my $100 per month income easily covered my half of our $70 monthly rent, I took an afternoon job driving a good humor ice cream truck. My commissions there ranged from $12 to $17 per day, depending upon the neighborhood and the weather. Most days, I drew the far-flung route of Milpitas, a town so empty of residents it left me wondering if the Rapture might've happened and I was the only one not taken.

Five months of Northern California and, well, I was ready to move on. It wasn't that I didn't like Los Gatos. I mean, what was not to like? Within a 100-mile radius was Santa Cruz, Monterey, Carmel, the Gold Country, the Sierra Nevada's, San Francisco, Sonoma, the Russian River and the beautiful, albeit always foggy, Bodega Bay, site of Alfred Hitchcock's, *The Birds*.

But if Northern California was this great, what must the rest of the country be like?

New Orleans! Florida! Appalachia! New England!

I wanted to see it all. Heck, I wanted to live in it all.

It took almost nothing to convince Cherie to come along. And then, just as we were packing up to leave on what I'd begun calling, "Our Grand Adventure," everything changed.

"GET UP," said Cherie, "I sold the bed."

I rolled over onto the shag carpet and a couple of guys yanked up the mattress and walked it out the door. I was trying to go back to sleep, but with Chum licking the lotion off my legs, good luck with that.

"Hey! You still want that old underwood?" asked Cherie, nudging me with her toe.

I knew she'd try something like this. Which was why I was using it for a pillow.

"We get to keep one thing, remember?"

"*Harrumph.* I've never even seen you type."

I found it amusing that Cherie never actually harrumphed, she just said the word instead.

"You'll see me type in Phoenix!" I called after her.

"Yeah? And then I'll never see you type again!"

I turned over and went back to sleep. The dream always began the same.

Fay Faron

Pearly Gates, Heaven

I peered through the ornate gate at the empty mansions lining the deserted golden streets. There was nobody inside. Not a sign of life. Not so, for the two lines waiting to get in.

There was one sign that said, "Long Line," and next to it, another reading, "Express Line." Both stretched back as far as the eye could see. Neither seemed to be moving.

In the Express Line were the rosy-cheeked virgins. Brides and grooms nuzzling each other's noses like Eskimos. Young parents cooing at their infants. Gray-haired grandmas and grandpas gazing lovingly into each other's eyes. Secretaries with tee-shirts that bragged, "I married the boss!" And the Twelve Disciples who'd you'd think would've gotten into Heaven by the end of the 2nd century, at least.

In the Long Line were the unwed mothers with their squawking babies. Lesbians with bad haircuts. Long-haired hippies passing stubby, hand-rolled reefers. Teenage boys guzzling Schlitz out of paper sacks. Flappers fresh from Prohibition. Society dames who'd dropped dead, mid-martini at the Copacabana.

And, of course, Hitler.

"Excuse me!" I said to the pretty blonde angel, the spitting image of Glenda the Good Witch. She was holding a clipboard, had a Bic pen behind her ear and a wingspan so wide she had to turn sideways to walk.

"Can you tell me which line I should be in?"

Celeste gave me a long, hard look. She made a swirly motion and I dutifully twirled. She eyed my backpack with a scowl that turned to disgust when her eyes dropped to the third finger of my left hand, ringless as it were.

Celeste gave me the hairy eyeball, the likes of which I had never seen on Planet Earth. And by the time I died, I'd seen a lot of hairy eyeballs.

"Back of the Long Line," growled the angel, walking away.

Los Gatos, California

BY THE TIME I meandered out to our dwindling garage sale, Cherie was splayed out on an aluminum lawn chair, her shorts hiked up on her painfully rosy thighs, her eyes laser-beamed into Irving Wallace's, *The Word*.

"I'm hungry," I said.

"My. Body. Does. Not. Require. Food," said Cherie in her annoying robot-voice.

"I'm not like you. I faint."

"Taco Bell?" she sighed. As if we ever ate any place else.

We dragged the rest of our stuff out to the driveway, plopped a big "Free!" sign on top, and took off for the home of the 6-item, 19¢ menu.

We returned to find a large malamute behind our screen door.

"There's a dog inside our apartment," I whispered.

"What's a dog doing inside our apartment?" Cherie whispered back.

"Looks like Perfect's dog."

"What would Perfect's dog be doing inside our apartment?"

"Should we call the fuzz?"

"And say what? There's a dog inside our apartment?"

We entered to find not only Micah inside our apartment, but Perfect as well. My old college crush was lounging on his overstuffed backpack, looking all Marlboro Manish in his straight-legged jeans and denim jacket.

That was the good news. The bad news was, he was munching his way through our grocery sack of cherries meant to last a week. Meanwhile, Micah and Chum were crouching and pouncing, slobbering all over each other as they tugged at each other's ears.

Cherie and I hadn't seen Perfect since we'd hitchhiked 225 miles to surprise him a couple of months before. (Sure, we both had cars. What we didn't have was money for gas.)

Ever since I'd moved to Northern California, Cherie had been waxing poetic about Lake Tahoe, a body of water she called so undefinably blue it could be described as cobalt, turquoise, aquamarine, indigo, or sapphire, depending upon the time of day and the weather. Of a lake so cold, water skiers had to wear wetsuits. Of slopes so sunny, snow skiers whooshed down them in shorts and tee-shirts. There were casinos where free cocktails were served at the slot machines, and the Von Trapp Family Singers warbling at a Swiss chalet on the strip.

It took Cherie and me eleven hours and seventeen rides to get to South Lake Tahoe. Which as it turns out, is nowhere near North Lake Tahoe. It took another hour for Perfect to drive over the icy roads to come fetch us. And yet another to haul us back to his little yellow cabin in the woods.

Upon our arrival, we poured Telephone out of her pillowcase, at which time she shot up onto the refrigerator where she stayed all weekend, screeching her little lungs out, as a smitten Micah panted at her from below. Cherie took one look at Perfect's Jesus hair, Dr. Zhivago mustache, Sundance Kid smile, and Rhett Butler dimples, and did a little panting of her own.

"Perfect," she purred.

"Told'ja."

When I returned from changing into my red-and-white striped flannel onesie, Perfect had peeled down to his tee-shirt and boxer shorts, and Cherie was practically Nudesville, wearing nothing but her panties and an oversized San Jose State tee-shirt.

I scanned the room.

One bed. One couch. One floor.

One him. One her. One me.

Perfect would get the bed, of course.

Pah-leese. I got this!

I leapt onto the sofa and flashed my pal a triumphant grin. And then to my horror, Cherie vaulted onto the bed and shot me a triumphant grin all her own.

Dang!

And then, Perfect climbed in beside Cherie and turned off the friggin' light!

"Nighty-night," he called out to me.

"Don't let the bed bugs bite!" Cherie sang out.

Gee willikers. Never saw that coming.

"I SAW HIM FIRST," I hissed as we laid out our sleeping bags that first night Perfect came to live with us.

"Bummer for you," said Cherie, "Since 'first dibs is not a covenant I feel compelled to honor, given it's not in Leviticus, let alone any other obscure Old Testament tome."

I wasn't surprised. I hadn't learned much in college, but one thing I did know. There was no honor among bridesmaids.

The next morning, Cherie schlepped off to work off her two weeks' notice, a compulsion I did not share since (a) Cupertino High School had let out for the summer, and (b) as it turns out, quitting the ice cream truck driving business requires no notice whatsoever.

Every day, Perfect and I would go out exploring. The first day, we checked out the Garden of Eden, a clothing-optional, hippie swimming hole deep in the Santa Cruz Mountains. The next, we picnicked at the Old Covered Bridge in Felton, followed by an afternoon hike down the narrow gage railroad tracks through the redwood forest. The next day, we waded through the big, holed boulder at Natural Bridges State Park, watched the surfers riding the 10' waves and then swam back through the boulder after the tide came in.

Another day, we hung out in Santa Cruz, gliding over the boardwalk in a gondola, and then meandered down to the Old Cooper House to listen to the street musicians. And yet another, we rode our bikes from Santa Cruz to Capitola, had coffee on a balcony overlooking the pastel Venetian bungalows lining the lagoon and then strolled the footpath beside the creek side cottages.

Every day, we'd talk, and talk, and talk.

About how the FBI was bugging John Lennon's phone. And how the Chicago Seven's convictions were being overturned. And naturally, the spate of skyjackings ever since D.B. Cooper had parachuted out over the Oregon wilderness with $200,000 in ransom money. And all the while, Perfect's dazzling dimples would be dancing in his face, as if the flawed human condition was the most hilarious thing on earth.

Evenings would find Cherie and me flirting outrageously behind each other's backs while Perfect remained as unreadable as 4-point italic type. He could be into either of us or neither of us, it was impossible to tell.

Nighttime was the worst. Our sleeping arrangement became three little soldiers—girl, boy, girl—in a smart little row. Each of us careful not to bend an arm or a leg that might inadvertently touch another.

Every night I'd wait for Cherie's gentle breath of sleep, then expand and contract my chest in a silent dog-whistle which proved so faint even Micah and Chum slept through it.

ONE DAY I came home to find Perfect nowhere in sight.

His van was there. Micah was there, leaping and pouncing, slobbering all over Chum. Telephone was on top of the refrigerator screeching her little lungs out. But as for Perfect, well, he was MIA.

I was searching for our grocery bag of cherries when an old friend called to say my ex-boyfriend was getting married—not six months after I dumped his sorry butt.

My first thought was, "How rude!"

My second was, "I gotta pray for that girl."

"Sorry. what were you saying?" I said to my friend.

....

"Well, I don't give a good gahoot who the jerk marries, as long as it's not me. Besides, I've moved on."

....

"Yep! I'm seeing a guy."

Okay, not at the moment.

....

"Well, I don't know if you'd call him my boyfriend *exactly*. But, yeah, we *are* living together.

....

"Okay, not *living*-living together, but sleeping together."

.........???!!!!

"Okay, not *sleeping*-sleeping together, not shacking up or anything, but—"

I kept walking around, pulling the long, curly, telephone cord behind me, searching for Perfect.

Or, failing that, at least, the cherries.

....

"Yeah, of course, I like him. Truth be told, I *lurve* him. The problem is my cruddy roommate's bonkers over him too."

Right about then, it occurred to me how odd it was for Micah to be there. And for Perfect's van to be there. And for Perfect *not* to be there.

I pulled the pink princess phone over to the screen door and peered out. Yup. His van was there, alright. The cord trailed behind me to the bathroom door. It was partially open, so I knocked lightly and peeked inside.

No Perfect.

Even more distressing, still no cherries.

And that's when I saw the accordion doors to our wall-kitchen pulled shut. That was odd. Cherie and I never closed those doors. But he couldn't possibly be in there. The entire kitchen—stove, fridge, cabinets, countertop—were all shoved up against one wall. With that door shut, there wasn't even room to stand.

"Later-scater," I whispered, hanging up.

I tiptoed over and slowly pulled open the folding doors. And there was Perfect. Sitting on the countertop. Boots in sink. Munching away on our nearly depleted bag of cherries.

"Processing," he grinned.

Eugene, Oregon

"EXCUSE ME!" I called to Ethel, our gum-smacking waitress. "Where *are* we?"

"The It'll Do Diner, hon. Folgers?"

"Please. But what *country?*"

"Uh, America?"

"The *continent* of America? Or the *United States* of America?"

Perfect slid the menu across the Formica table and pointed out the Eugene, Oregon address.

Un-friggin-believable.

It had taken us thirteen hours to come 200 miles. Meaning our freight train had been galloping toward Canada at the breakneck speed of 15 mother-lovin' miles per hour.

And to think I was worried we'd overshoot.

Still, I couldn't believe I'd talked Perfect into hopping a freight train to Canada.

"It'll be like *It Happened One Night*," I'd enthused. "Except with hobos!"

With no train tracks running through Los Gatos, our plan had been to hitchhike to the freight yard in San Francisco and hop a train from there. Instead, our first ride took us all the way to Mount Shasta, 300 miles to the north.

And while I'd arrived at the majestic snow-capped peak looking *mighty fine*—what with my woofy curls spilling out of my Ali MacGraw *Love Story* woolen cap—after a night of slamming through freight yards, enduring the screech of metal wheels on tracks, tree limbs scraping against the boxcar like ghosts trying to get in, and the stench of diesel fuel as we thundered through the tunnels, by the time we stumbled out of the boxcar at dawn, I looked like I'd aged seven years.

In doggie years.

Now what they don't tell you—and by "they" I mean the authors of the bestselling freight-hopping guidebooks—is to go potty before vaulting onto the first boxcar you see. And that's because while a freight train might indeed reach speeds up to 100 miles-per-hour, it's normally up and down within the same four inches. And if you're sharing a mummy-style sleeping bag with a guy you haven't even made out with yet, a bursting bladder is sure to put the kibosh on that romance.

At first, I thought rolling over might alleviate the situation. That turned out to be a complicated maneuver which required us to tumble over in unison like a couple of sumo wrestlers locked in a death grip. Eventually, I had no alternative but to wriggle out of our cozy cocoon and teeter over to the farthest, darkest corner of the boxcar to relieve myself.

I had completed the task and was preparing to teeter on back, when I heard Perfect yell, "I'm gonna do you one better! I'm doin' one out the boxcar door, going 100 miles an hour!"

Which brings me to another thing the bestselling, "How to be a Hobo" guidebooks don't tell you. Apparently, human pee does not evaporate when the temperature drops below freezing. Instead, it forms a small, yellow frozen pond, which shows no sign of thawing until your hobo's hobos have hobos.

And another thing. Just try finding one of those helpful, "Welcome to Wherever" signs like they have at the fancy-schmancy Amtrak stations. Instead, you are let off in the middle of nowhere, and have no way of finding out where you are without tromping across a sooty, snowy field to some dive like the It'll Do Diner.

In the restroom, freshening up, I saw what Perfect and Ethel had been too kind to mention.

Naively, I'd pictured my appearance something akin to Perfect's, looking all dapper in his fur-lined denim jacket, with one dramatic stripe of black soot slicing across his chiseled features.

But *nooo*.

Instead, I looked like I'd stumbled out of Pompei in 79 AD. Or more accurately, been dug up 2,000 years later.

By the time I arrived back from my cold-water cleanup, Perfect had learned the next north-bound freight train wouldn't be leaving until 6 p.m. As for thumbing north from here, as it turns out, hitching is illegal in Washington State. Thankfully, lounging beside the roadway is not, just as long as you keep your thumbs in your mittens. Which was fine by me since I had no intention of taking my thumbs out of my mittens until the summer solstice.

Blaine, Washington

REBUFFED BY eagle-eyed Canadian Mounties—always on the lookout for Vietnam draft dodgers, and diesel fuel-smelling undesirables—Perfect and I had little choice but to clean ourselves up and try again the next day. Considering our financial circumstances, I suggested bedding down in the all-night bus station.

But *nooo*.

Perfect wanted to check into an actual motel. Which would've been fine if he was offering to pay.

But *nooo*.

He expected us to go halfsies.

We were mid-squabble when he yanked me into a dingy little motor inn. He rang the tin bell and a very large, very white bear of a man ambled out in a wife-beater tee-shirt.

"We'd like a room," said Perfect.

"No, we would not," I informed the clerk.

"Smoking or non?"

"Neither!"

"She meant 'either.' What's cheaper?"

"Don't make no never mind, kiddos. One bed or two?"

"We are *not* shacking up," I informed the clerk. "I am not that kind of girl."

"None of my bee's wax, lady. Eight smackers. Take it or leave it."

"Eight dollars! American? That's outrageous! Motel 6 is only $6. And they leave the light on for ya!"

"Shut up and give me your purse," said Perfect.

"We'll give you five," I told the clerk.

"This ain't no swap-meet, toots."

I was about to go up to $5.50, when I heard the door jangle behind us. I turned to find a blurry-eyed sailor with a robust, blonde-haired lady draped over him like a fox stole.

"We'd like a room," purred the tart. "Wouldn't we, honey-bunchkins?"

"One left," said the clerk. "Assuming these folks here don't take it. Twelve bucks."

"Twelve *dollars?* What happened to eight?"

"Supply and demand."

I watched in shock as the hooker wriggled her john's wallet out of his pants pocket. She was still counting out the ones when I realized Perfect had dumped the contents of my purse, and was separating the quarters, nickels, dimes and pennies from the tampons and whatnot.

"Twelve bucks!" said Perfect, adding his paper money to my pile of coins. "We'll take it."

We had only just stepped into the room before rethinking the whole bus station option. And that's because, although I'd once thought Cherie was the peskiest thing on earth, it was only because I hadn't met any bed bugs yet.

Fleeing the scene in search of diner, we weren't a block down the street before being forced into a telephone booth to escape a thundering sleet storm. Forty minutes later, we were still there, cold, starving, cranky, and so bored we started perusing the telephone directory in search of names to poke fun at.

There were a lot of Smith's, Johnson's, and Turner's, most with ordinary first names like John, Richard, and Harold. The closest we found to anyone sounding remotely interesting was a guy named Jack Easley.

And so it was that we decided to send our new pal, Jack Easley, a postcard from Canada the next day—assuming we could pass the hygiene test to get in.

Which is exactly what we did.

Canadian Border

THE NEXT morning, we crossed into Canada without incident. We tarried just long enough in Peace Arch Park to pick out a postcard for Jack Easley before heading back to Los Gatos.

Almost immediately, we caught a ride in a converted milk truck headed all the way down Interstate 5 to the Mexican border. Our driver was Matt, a 22-year-old recently divorced guy tooling around America in hopes of healing his broken heart. Thrilled with our good luck, we told Matt to let us off in Patterson, just 80 miles across the mountains from Los Gatos.

It wasn't long before Matt started stopping for every long-haired hippie alongside the roadside. And even though the milk truck was packed tighter than a Mexican jail cell, Matt stopped for one last thumb-bum. And so, with the addition of "Moonbeam," a 15-year-old waif with chopped yellow hair, Daisy Duke shorts, and a fake fur-lined parka, Matt's broken heart was broken no more.

Perfect and I snuggled together on the long sleeping bench, averting our eyes from the near naked hippies coupling, uncoupling, and recoupling with a variety of partners on the floor below us.

"I may never have sex again," I groaned.

"You've had sex?"

"Well, no. But now, I never will."

It was past midnight when we rolled across the border into California. I'd drifted off into a sort of half slumber, soothed by the lullaby of hushed voices and the soft rumble of the engine, when suddenly I felt myself falling. Like I was in an earthquake in the air. No, like in a clothes dryer with a bunch of pots and pans. And then—*bam!*—I landed in a pile of wriggling snakes. Snakes with elbows.

It was only after the truck came to a stop that I realized the long, terrifying screech I'd heard had been the van scraping the asphalt as it swirled in circles down the highway.

"Faybo!"

"Here!"

Perfect reached down through a jumble of backpacks and body parts, thankfully all still attached, and yanked me out of the human stew.

Gagging on the stench of gasoline mixed with the sweet smell of weed, we crawled toward the lone shaft of light streaming from the driver's door. Perfect pushed me up and out. I landed on the wheel and shot directly onto the freeway. He was right there, dragging me to safety.

One by one, hippies dropped onto the shoulder of the road beside me. Good Samaritans stopped, directed traffic around the crash site, even located Matt 200 yards back, unconscious, but thankfully, alive.

But where was Perfect?

Then I saw him. Cross-legged on the top of the truck, his bandana tied bandit-style over his mouth to escape the fumes, reaching down, pulling out stoned and stunned hippies one by one.

It was a good half hour before an ambulance arrived to cart Matt off to the hospital in Chico. The rest of us crammed into a second ambulance, shaken, but all heads accounted for.

Except for one. Little Miss Moonbeam.

It was in en route to the hospital that we finally pieced together the cause of the crash. It seems Matt had been standing up, switching places with Moonbeam, teaching her how to drive, when he lost control of the milk truck. As for the little runaway, it seems she'd caught a ride out of there with the first car to leave the scene, never waiting to see if the rest of us had lived or died.

Fay Faron

Chapter 3
See Ya

<u>June 1 - 14, 1972</u>

***Vietnam:** Navy Seals rescue 2 POWs ***At the Movies:** Butterflies are Free ***On the Radio:** Sammy Davis Jr.'s "The Candy Man"

Los Gatos, California

I CRAMMED all Cherie's and my things—whites and darks, jeans and undies—into an industrial-sized washing machine, while Perfect shook and sorted every garment, read every label, and placed every color-coordinated pile into its own machine.

An hour later, I was sitting on a cardboard box of wrinkly clothes, waiting while he slid wire inserts into his straight-legged Levi's so they'd have a crease down the front.

I am so not making this up.

I couldn't believe this guy. And not just because of his weird laundry habits. We were leaving first thing in the morning and Perfect had missed every opportunity to jump my bones. Not in our little side-by-side position each night, as Cherie snored contentedly beside us. Not in the frigid boxcar, smished together tighter than a couple of Siamese twins. Not even in the Bed Bug Motel, where he insisted we go halfsies.

And then, in his most egregiously missed opportunity, that very morning when we'd hiked up to the secluded eucalyptus grove in the Stanford Hills, and there in that most romantic of settings, nestled between the Farallon Islands to the west, Mount Diablo to the east, San Francisco the north and San Jose to the south, what does the guy do?

Nothing. Absolutely frigginglutely nothing.

And then, halfway down the hillside, in a wide open meadow—the kind of landscape for which "The Golden State" was named—Perfect tosses his silver space blanket onto the prickly yellow reeds and proceeds to pounce.

I had but a nanosecond to enjoy the moment when that scene in *From Here to Eternity* flashed before my eyes—you know, the one where Burt Lancaster and Deborah Kerr are necking in the surf, and it looks like so much fun except you just know she's going to be washing the sand out of her privates for, well, an eternity.

But then I thought of something Deb obviously had not.

If we could see from here to eternity—or in this case, the Town & Country Village in Palo Alto—then everyone in the Town & Country Village of Palo Alto, could see us as well. Along with any random hiker / peeping Tom / pervert that happened by.

"The nice, secluded glen wouldn't do?" I asked, softly.

It wasn't meant to be a deal-breaker. I wasn't asking him to stop. I was just negotiating the venue.

WE ARRIVED BACK from the washateria to find Cherie cross-legged on the floor, swaying gently to "Brandy (You're a Fine Girl)" on her transistor radio. As soon as Perfect went out to change his oil, Cherie pulled a bottle of Southern Comfort from behind her back.

"Left over from the old tenants," she giggled.

Since Cherie wasn't much of a giggler, I could only assume Southern Comfort does not lose its potency with age.

She took a swig, wiped its neck, and passed the bottle to me. An hour later, with our inhibitions as loose as our lips, we finally addressed the elephant outside swabbing bird poo off his windshield.

I'm a little fuzzy on how the whole thing came down because there was a lot of Southern Comfort involved, but I do remember us fussing about who Perfect loved the most. And that's when I sensed Perfect standing in the doorway behind me.

"Oh, Lordy," he moaned.

I turned to see him taking in the scene. Cherie and I knee-high in laundry and three sheets to the wind.

"You need to choose," Cherie informed him, a bit on the slurry side. "It's her or me, Mr. Man!"

"You're giving me an ultimatum?" chuckled Perfect, in spite of himself.

It was pretty ridiculous. First thing in the morning, Cherie and I would be off on Our Grand Adventure and Perfect was headed to a remote island off British Columbia, where he'd be spending the summer helping a friend build a cabin in the woods. There was a good chance neither of us would ever see him again.

I don't remember much of what happened after that, because there was, after all, a lot of Southern Comfort involved.

I do recall Cherie disappearing into the bathroom. Emerging in nothing but her bra and panties, and then swaying seductively in the dim light of the doorway like she was in a private production of *Cat on a Hot Tin Roof*.

What she expected from this, I do not know. But perhaps reading the room, the next thing I knew, she was careening around boxes, grabbing her car keys and then was out the door. There was the screech of her Honda as she backed onto busy Los Gatos Almaden Road, leaving Perfect and me in stunned silence.

Eventually, he and I settled into our usual sleeping spots, girl/boy/girl except with a missing girl bookend on the far side. We lay there in the darkness, my thoroughly fuzzy self throbbing with the possibilities, and yet afraid that Cherie might return at any moment. And she could be quite stealth when she wanted to be.

And then, finally, silently, Perfect inching closer, until I could feel his warm breath on my face.

Could this be it? Was it really happening?

The thought was barely out of my noggin when a thin shaft of light spread across the floor beside us.

There was the quiet squish of feet on carpeting, the whoosh of my roommate sinking down onto her usual spot beside Perfect. Or rather where Perfect should have been.

And then finally, mercifully, eventually, came her rhythmic breath of sleep. Only then did he quietly, gently, roll back into place.

Leaving me to sigh—Goodnight, sweet prince.

Or more likely, goodbye.

Los Gatos to Phoenix

CHERIE WAS AS glad as I was to be driving our own cars as far as Phoenix. It was there we would leave my parents' old Rambler station wagon, Bessie, and continue on in her Honda Z.

Had the previous night's showdown happened a few days earlier, we might have just called off the trip altogether. But thankfully, when 7 a.m. arrived, we just got up and went.

The most traveled route from the Bay Area to Phoenix was a 17-hour trek down highway 101 to Los Angeles, and from there, Interstate 10 on into the Valley of the Sun.

It was not a fun trip.

Even if you left first thing in the morning, you'd arrive in L.A. smack in the middle of an afternoon commute that turned Los Angeles into an eighty mile long parking lot. Once out of L.A. proper, Interstate 10 became a 4-lane road which meandered thirty miles out of its way to pass through the tiny town of Wickenburg, Arizona, then spilling onto the streets of Sun City, Surprise, Peoria, and Glendale before joining up with Black Canyon Highway, Phoenix's only freeway, located on the extreme western side of the city.

Instead, we chose to skirt Los Angeles to the north, then follow Route 66 to the Colorado River, before dipping down to join I-10 on into Phoenix.

All day long, Cherie and I hop-scotched down 101, stopping only for gas and postcards for our new pen pal, Jack Easley.

Whereas, initially, Cherie had been excited about prolonging the prank, now she was quite obviously so pissed at me that she sulked every time I stopped for postcards in the designated sight-seeing spots along Highway 101.

Castroville, the "Artichoke Capital of the World." Gilroy, the "Garlic Capital of the World." Salinas, the "John Steinbeck Capital of the World." Soledad, the "Prison Capital of the World." And King City, the "Stockyard Capital of the World."

Our singular glimpse of the ocean came at Pismo Beach, before turning east for the tortuous climb over the Sierra Madres. Dipping down into the desolate Cuyama Valley, we endured eighty miles of scrubby wasteland before reaching the 40-mile long mountain pass known as The Grapevine.

Our uphill climb was a series of frustrating attempts at passing one slow moving truck after another without the engine power to do so. And then, finally, we crested the top of the hill, reveling in the *whee!!!* as we tumbled down the other side—only to be shot down by a killjoy of a state trooper with a radar gun.

From the tiny town of Gorman, we took Highway 138 through the high desert, beneath a setting sun in shades of saffron, tangerine and flamingo.

And then, the world melted into blackness.

There were no towns, hence no streetlights.

No farms, hence, no house lights.

No moon, no nothing. Not even a danged UFO.

Just fifty miles of florescent stripe, lighting the way a hundred feet at a time.

Lulled by the monotony of the 2-lane road, I suddenly realized I'd lost sight of Cherie's taillights up ahead. I raced to catch up, only to have them disappear at the next dip in the road. Bessie's speedometer rose from 50 to 80 as the old Rambler shuddered in protest.

"She must be going a hundred miles an hour," I muttered to Chum's little puppy dog head, asleep in my lap.

Now with Perfect a thing of the past, I longed for Cherie and I to be best friends again. Boyfriends come and go, I told myself. Girlfriends are forever.

It took fifteen minutes to catch up to "Cherie." Except it wasn't Cherie. It wasn't even a Honda. We passed the coupe and sped up to the next set of taillights. Still not Cherie.

"She must be going 100 miles per hour," I told Chum, in case she hadn't heard me the first time.

I zoomed up to the next set of lights. Again, not Cherie.

Dadgummit!

She couldn't be *that* mad. Ticked off enough to ditch me? Pissed of enough to drive all the way to Phoenix all by herself? Irked enough to hide until I passed on by, then turn around and head back to Los Gatos?

I spent forty minutes ripping through the warm night, chasing one set of taillights after another. Finally, I came to a "T" in the road, a spot so desolate, the only sign of life was the one that read Mojave: twenty miles to the north and Lancaster, five miles to the south.

Really, Cherie? Really?

Why wasn't she waiting for me here?

We'd agreed to stop in Lancaster, but how could I ever find her in a town neither of us had ever been?

I pulled over and let Chum out to pee.

I was fishing Telephone out from under the seat when a pair of headlights sliced through the Rambler. A car screeched up, spewing gravel everywhere, turning Telephone into a ballistic furry windmill.

"Son of a motherless goat!" Cherie screamed, sprinting toward the Rambler. "You must've been going 100 miles an hour!"

Phoenix, Arizona

"YOUR MAIL'S on the table," said Mom. "Oh, and some guy called."

"Harry?"

"Nope, not Harry.

I found the page torn from the inspirational calendar Mom kept by the phone. On it was Perfect's name, along with a seven-digit number.

"Mom? The area code?"

"Didn't say—602?"

It couldn't be. Area code 602 spanned the entire state of Arizona. The last time I'd seen Perfect, he was in 408, headed north into area codes unknown.

Vintage Perfect. Had to be mysterious.

I dialed the 7-digit number.

"Faybulous!"

"Hey. You're in Phoenix?"

"Dropping off some shit at my folk's. I didn't say? Well, it was a bit nutso there at the end. Anyway, just called to say 'hi.'"

"Uh, okay, hi."

"Well then—See ya!"

And then, he hung up.

You gotta be friggin' kidding me.

So, now what?

Knowing Perfect, he'd just show up at my parents' house. Maybe today, maybe tomorrow. Certainly, without calling first. Meaning I couldn't go anywhere. I'd have to sit by the phone and wait.

I didn't even bother telling Cherie he'd called. She was still smarting from the whole showdown lollapaloosa our last night in Los Gatos. And knowing Perfect, he might show up at all.

Two days came and went without so much as a phone call from the See-Ya Later Jerk.

By Day 3, I'd about lost my marbles. Cherie and I were friends again, so that was good. And I dutifully put in some time at the typewriter so my parents remained convinced I was still on track to becoming a World-Famous Creative Writer. Still, Cherie and I were leaving the next day, and Perfect didn't even know that. Like he even cared.

Oh, I know! He's waiting for me to make a move. Of course, he is. After all, if he showed up here, there'd be the problem of Cherie. It was up to *me* to make this happen.

And so, I came up with a plan.

Six a.m., I shook Cherie awake.

"Hey, wanna go for a bike ride?"

"Get stuffed." she mumbled, turning over and going back to sleep.

Yahoo!

Now, all I had to do was pedal down Dunlap, past short, squat Sunnyslope Mountain—with its giant "S" whitewashed each year by incoming freshman—then bike up Central Avenue to Glendale Avenue, follow Lincoln Drive past Barry Goldwater's house on the hill, and then on into Perfect's Arcadia neighborhood. No big deal. Just as long as I got there by 9 a.m., when the temperature was sure to rise above 100.

Perfect would open the door and there I'd be, all *tan* and *buff* and *thin*, given a very flattering case of dehydration which would've sucked every ounce of water weight from my body.

Knock. Knock.

Ding-dong.

Pant, pant.

"Oh, Lordy."

Perfect was staring at me like I'd just stumbled out of Donner Pass without a big breakfast of friend first. His mother gave me a glass of water and made me lie down on the couch. She wanted to call an ambulance, but Perfect said I'd probably be okay.

I pretended I *was* okay, blathering on, feeling the words falling from my mouth like a broken kaleidoscope, then giggling and trying again with no more luck. And then for an encore, falling asleep in the middle of a sentence. I awoke to find Perfect and his mother off in the kitchen, quibbling about whether I was too young to be considered eccentric or if I might still pass for quirky.

When I hauled myself into the bathroom, I saw what they saw. A sopping mess of lanky, sweat-soaked hair framing a beet-red, mascara-streaked face. I washed, went back out, breathed in the cool air conditioning and fell back asleep on the couch.

It must have been 3 o'clock when Perfect hauled me and my bike back to Sunnyslope. Dad led me past a startled Cherie into my lilac room, where I slept the rest of the day and most of the night.

The next morning, Telephone took one look at Cherie's Honda Z, clawed her way out of my arms and raced back into the house where she hid herself so expertly, it would've taken the Gestapo to find her. Mom suggested Telephone come to live with them—as had all my pets since college—and Cherie and I happily agreed.

And then, we were off on the start of Our Grand Adventure.

Fay Faron

Chapter 4
Been There, Born There

June 15 - August 1972

Vietnam: *Photos published of "Hanoi Jane," (AKA, Jane Fonda) & South Vietnamese children running from napalm* ***Watergate:*** *"White House Plumbers" break into DNC headquarters* ***In Other News:*** *Billy Graham's Texas rally draws 75,000; Pilots strike for better security; U.S. median income is $10,285* ***At the Movies:*** *Deep Throat; Deliverance* ***On the Radio:*** *Gilbert O'Sullivan's "Alone Again (Naturally)*

Kansas City, Missouri

EVEN BEFORE Cherie and I left Los Gatos, we were determined there were three things we needed to make ourselves happy.

Apartments, jobs, and boyfriends.

We called it The Holy Trinity.

Place to Live

MY 83-YEAR-OLD grandmother still lived alone in my childhood home, high on the hill overlooking the old airport.

Hawthorne Circle was a cul-de-sac of five houses with zero fences to restrict dogs and kids roaming between them. My family moved there in 1950, the year after the house and I were both born. Like most post-World War II families, my parents lived with their parents until they could afford a home of their own.

Gram's house was designed by Mom, adding to the legend there was nothing my mother could not do. The simple 3-bedroom, 2-bath floor plan had a glass porch overlooking the street, and a built-in china cabinet to display Gram's collection of hand-painted plates, mother of pearl tea sets, Havilland china, and sterling silver decanters.

My parents had been begging Gram to come live with them for years, but she preferred to stay in her own home with her soap opera families.

As a kid, I watched the soaps with her. For years I thought this was one long program where the characters came and went throughout the day. Thanks to Gram, I was so hooked on daytime dramas that I set up a voice recorder to tape *The Guiding Light*, *Love of Life* and *Search for Tomorrow* when my college classes conflicted with their time slots.

No less addicted by summer, Gram wrote me long letters when I worked as a camp counselor, chronicling the slow-moving, blow-by-blow action, logging each character's questionable decision, and/or disturbing behavior. Her letters were a great source of amusement to my fellow counselors, including Cherie, who'd invariably would gather around as I read them aloud.

Visiting Gram brought back all my childhood memories. My fourth birthday when I made a crown out of construction paper and wore it next door to "Aunt Casey's" to announce, "Bet'cha don't know why I'm wearing this crown!" Only to have my cuteness rewarded with a homemade peanut butter cookie. Then, there was the old lady across "the big street" who had no grandchildren of her own so she bought toys so the neighborhood kids would come play at her house. There was the field where my daddy helped me catch fireflies and put them in Mason jars with holes punched in the lids. And where he clapped and clapped as I rolled down the long grassy hill toward the creek.

We got the first Chum dog toward the end of her life, and not in the usual way. Dad was working at Sears and sold a refrigerator to a man who'd stopped paying. With his commission in jeopardy, Pops went to collect. Seeing the man's dire circumstances, Dad offered to make his payments in exchange for the old collie dog leashed in the back yard. And with that, Chum became a treasured member of our family.

Chum was twelve when we got her, which made her 84 in doggie years. I was four, which made me 28 in doggie years. That made Chum kind of like my doggy-grandma. And like any good grandma, I had only to hold onto her collar for her to lead me home when Mom whistled each evening at dusk.

My best friend, Kathy, lived on the cul-de-sac down the hill. We got in all manner of trouble together, for which everyone invariably blamed me. Like the time I was teaching her how to make flaming crepe suzettes and her mother's kitchen curtains caught fire.

Now really, how was that my fault?

Or the time we were in Gram's basement, cutting out Betsy McCall paper dolls out of the magazine, and decided it would be *even more fun* to paint the cement floor white. And then, just at the very moment when the paint can fell over and paint went everywhere, Gram stuck her head down the stairs and hollered, "Girls! Don't touch the paint!"

The only fly in my childhood ointment was my brother, Daniel, who was quietly, behind the scenes, trying to kill me.

My parents had prayed to have a boy, and then a girl, reasoning the older brother would look after his treasured little sister. Their prayers were answered when Danny was born first, and then me, two and a half years later. Guess God didn't stick around long enough to hear Part 2, because the only looking-after my brother ever did was over his shoulder to make sure nobody was watching while he was trying to snuff out my tiny little life.

Danny had always been the prince in his kingdom ever since Mom almost lost him when she was six months pregnant. Dr. Stipe came over and confirmed the baby was still there, but since Mom had flushed the toilet, he couldn't be sure there hadn't been a twin.

Despite Mom being on bed rest, Danny arrived three months early, weighing in at 3 ½ pounds, so small in fact, that Dad could hold him in the palm of his hand. From then on, everyone, most especially Grandma, considered Danny a Gift from God.

Well, that worked out just great for Danny. That is until I came along and *ruined everything*. The exact opposite of my fragile older brother, I showed no signs of exiting the womb until I could be fitted for my prom dress. By the time I was finally coaxed out six weeks past Mom's due date, I weighed 9 pounds 3 oz.

Born at home, 3:15 on a Sunday morning—forever after referred to as "in time for Sunday school"—I got there before Dr. Stipe did. Our beloved family doctor's first words were, "Oh, look! This time you've got a little girl!"

Gram's first words were, "Look, Jerry, she's got a dimple!"

Danny's first words were, "Let's frow that baby out the winder!"

Actually, he didn't say that until a little bit later. According to my plush pink baby book, Danny was "thrilled" to find out he had a baby sister, "for whom he had been impatiently waiting," wrote Mom. "He immediately went and got his bottle and a pair of outgrown socks and gave them to the baby, along with a big kiss."

Before the week was out, Dad's eight brothers and sisters, my cousins in tow, all arrived to check me out. As legend had it, I awoke to find the entire clan gathered around my crib. I studied each face in turn, then gave a mighty sigh, put my head down and went to sleep.

My mother carefully chronicled every adorable "first" in my baby book. How at five months, I wasn't crawling but rolling over to my destination. How I'd swat away Daddy's newspaper so I could sit on his lap. How I'd walk on my tippy toes, "as if she can hardly reach the ground." About how my teeth came in, one by one, all over my mouth. And how I wanted to quit kindergarten after a week because they hadn't taught me to read yet.

But, alas, my life wasn't as idyllic as my baby book would suggest. My big brother was, after all, trying to kill me.

From the time Danny had lips and I had ears, he'd been lying to me. For a while I believed everything he said, but eventually I caught on that everything that came out of my big brother's mouth was a big fat lie.

Once Danny had me properly set up, then came the payoff. Mom and Dad were at work, Grandma was—I don't know where—and Grandpa was supposed to be watching us. Danny and I were playing in the back yard on a new swing set that had not yet been cemented into the ground. My brother was swinging, and I was watching the poles slide up and down into their holes.

"Hey, Dummy!" called Danny.

"Uh-huh?"

"If you stick your big toe under that, it'll cut it off."

"Will not!"

"Will to!"

"Will not!"

"Will to!"

So I did, and it did.

My screams summoned Grandpa, who grabbed my severed toe and called Dr. Stipe, who met us at the hospital and sewed it back on. Forever after, Mom referred to it as my "$40 toe."

Danny got in trouble for telling me the truth so naturally he went back to lying to me since he'd never gotten punished for that, not even once.

And so, it all began again. Fib after fib. Lie after lie. Danny kept it up until I was once again lulled back into the assurance that everything my big brother said was the opposite of being true.

Then came Easter Sunday. Danny and I were standing at the back of the station wagon, waiting for our parents to stop talking to every single person they'd ever met in their lives, along with a bunch of people they hadn't. I was all dressed up in my frilly pink dress and what Mom called my "Margaret O'Brien" straw bonnet, looking mighty cute, I might add. Danny and I were chatting nicely for once when my brother said—

"Hey, Dummy."

"Uh-huh?"

"If you stick your face in that exhaust pipe, it'll turn it black."

"Will not!"

"Will too!"

"Will not!"

"Will too!"

So I did, and it did.

After that, Danny was barred from telling me the truth for an entire week.

The funny thing was however naughty my brother was, I always felt like Grandma loved him more than me. I think it was because everybody had spent so many hours praying for him to live while I came out practically a toddler. But the even funnier thing was that even though I knew Gram loved Danny best, I still loved her more than almost everybody else in the whole world put together.

I was nine when my dad's insurance company transferred him to St. Paul, Minnesota. The giant ponds in, "The Land of 10,000 Lakes," had barely frozen over before my dad developed a severe case of rheumatoid arthritis, reducing his 6'3" hulk to that of a cripple. My mother watched in anguish as Pops withered away, his hands and feet becoming as gnarled as tree roots. The day he couldn't get out of the bathtub was the day Mom flew into her usual take-charge manner, hauling him off to Mayo Clinic in Rochester.

The doctors were stumped. Aside from him being in the right age group, forty to sixty, Dad didn't fit into any of the other high-risk categories. He wasn't a woman. He had no family history of the disease. He didn't smoke, wasn't obese, and had never been exposed to toxins like asbestos.

So, why now? What had caused this robust man to suddenly waste away? It might be the climate, the docs agreed. After all, Minnesota was even more humid than Kansas City, if that was possible. The driest places on Earth, they agreed, were Phoenix, Arizona, and Cairo, Egypt. I was outvoted three to one and so our family moved to Phoenix when I was in the 5th grade.

We'd barely driven over the state line when Dad's joints began to move again. By the time we got to Phoenix, he was visibly better. My parents fell in love with the state, as did my brother and I, since it was notably void of snow, mud and mosquitoes.

I MOVED INTO the bedroom across from Gram's, the one with the glass porch overlooking the street. Fifteen years earlier, my grandpa had died there after spending three years in a semi-conscience state while Gram spoon-fed him, changed his bedpan, and held back his tongue during the epileptic seizures he failed to mention until after they were married.

Cherie took the front bedroom, the one where Mrs. Nadeau died. The old lady was no relation to us but she had heard what a kind-hearted soul my grandma was and came a'knockin' with the offer to leave Gram all her money if she'd take care of her until she died. What Mrs. Nadeau failed to mention was that she'd live long past when her money ran out, all the while ringing her little silver bell for Gram to come shoo away the flying chimpanzees in the tree outside her window.

Before that, Cherie's room was occupied by my 102-year-old great grandfather, "Poppie," who suffered a fall at 99 and came to lie in bed there three years there before he died. And before that, Gram's sister, Dode, who passed away there in 1952.

It wasn't what you'd call a lucky room.

But there was life in that house as well. Not only did my family live there for the first five years of my life, but Gram's younger brother, who I called, "Uncle Jim," came along with Poppie when they closed up the farm in 1954. With no rooms left, he slept on a cot in the dining room. And then, there were Grandpa's three free-loading, free-spending, free-wheeling sisters who crashed there between husbands. I have no idea where everyone slept or how many of them were there at once, but I do know Grandma had someone in bed, sick or dying, for over two decades.

Gram liked living alone, even though it was becoming challenging. Having never learned to drive, once a week she'd call the same cab driver who'd drive her down Briarcliff Road to the grocery store and then help her haul her bags up the thirty stone steps to the house. Naturally, Cherie and I took over those duties for the summer.

Grandma grew up on a farm, milking cows and churning butter, but her 83 years of healthy living changed the day Cherie and I arrived home with McDonald's 25¢ hamburgers. Gram was so excited she gave us $2 and told us to buy as many as we could so she could freeze them and pop one in the oven whenever she was hungry.

Now, that's a shut-in.

Jobs

WITH OUR HOUSING situation so easily solved, Cherie and I tackled the employment front. Cherie took an assignment from Manpower, working as a secretary. As for me, I gravitated toward "people-person" jobs, which I thought I liked at the time, but found out later I hated.

My dream had always been to work at Macy's, the downtown department store where my mother had worked as Assistant to the Silver Buyer when I was a little girl. Truthfully, I'd always had warm and fuzzy feelings about Macy's ever since I got married there at the age of five, a sacrificial bride in a Tom Thumb wedding put on to promote the Silver Department.

In fact, Mom had choreographed a similar event two years earlier for her friend's engagement party. Back then, Danny had been the groom, I was the flower girl and my handsome, hunky 4-year-old neighbor, Vernon, was the ring-bearer. But at seven, my brother was too old to be getting married again, so this time he played preacher, Kathy was a bridesmaid, and I was the bride.

My second bridesmaid was the most beautiful little girl in the entire kingdom—a dark-haired, ivory skinned, pint-sized version of Snow White. This exquisite creature was someone I'd never have chosen to stand beside me since she was a thousand times prettier than I was. In fact, in the real world, Vernon would have been marrying Snow White instead of me. But since it was my mama who was the casting director, good luck with that.

Grandma made our dresses out of soft satin, identical except for their color. Kathy got to wear a pretty pink, and Snow White was decked out in a lovely light blue, which complemented her long, dark, fat Scarlett O'Hara ringlets. As for mine, it was a boring beige, perhaps an early premonition I'd never qualify to wear white if I ever got married for real. Preacher Danny wore a white choir gown, and the Men's Department found a tiny tuxedo for Vernon, while the Flower Department contributed his carnation boutonnière.

Mom had everything planned out, except for the part where Kathy and I were jumping on some old bed springs the day before and I busted my lip wide open. Dr. Stipe came to stitch me up, but still I cried and cried because how could I get married the next day with a big fat lip? Mom said to just keep my veil down and nobody would notice.

So there I was, my preacher-brother making faces at me as I slow-walked down the aisle while my rosebud-throwing flower girl stole the show, and Kathy smiled fondly at me, even as Vernon proceeded to make googly-eyes at Snow White—which I found particularly annoying since the girl had no personality to speak of, primarily because with her looks she didn't need one. But all that was about to change. Because in just moments, "Miss Penny-Pincher" would kiss "Mr. Moneybags" so magnificently that he'd forget all about Snow White's doe-eyes and Bambi lashes and decide he just might want to make this for real.

"I now pronounce you man and wife," said my preacher-brother. And with that, I grabbed Vernon and smacked him upside the lips right through the veil I'd been instructed not to lift.

Needless to say, the marriage didn't work out.

WHEN I WENT to work at Macy's, I was kind of hoping to be made Assistant to the Buyer like my mom, or perhaps some other lofty position where I could flounce about in the perfect lighting and thinning mirrors and live the glamorous fashionista life for which I was born.

But *nooo*.

Instead, I was stuck in a 6th floor stockroom, filing index cards for every deadbeat who'd ever stiffed Macy's out of a set of Jacks. I didn't even get to make nasty phone calls er nuthin'.

My initial plan had been to bike to work each morning, given it was only six miles from Grandma's house, down the long, steep

Briarcliff Road, through North Kansas City, past the old airport and over the heavily trafficked bridge into downtown. By Day 2, I'd traded that dream for a 20-minute bus ride, which left me a half hour to linger over a cup of Folgers at the Katz counter while I waited for Macy's to open.

Given I only worked Mondays, Wednesdays, and Saturdays, I went looking for a second job.

"STUDENTS," read the ad in the *Kansas City Star.*

> *"Yes, There's Still Time! Summer Employment.*
> *Must be 19 or over.*
> *Jobs available for enthusiastic young people.*
> *Salary $105."*

I attended a 30-minute presentation explaining how to "give" a family a set of encyclopedias *for free,* and then charge them $488 when they weren't looking.

Here's how that worked. Yes, the set was "free," but the customer was obligated to buy a $48 update each year for a decade. We were to emphasize that this was the dealer's cost, and the company didn't make a dime.

When the presenter asked for questions, I asked what would happen if too many events happened in a single year to fit into just one volume.

I don't remember the answer to that one.

Second question: If the company was selling the books at cost, where were they getting the $105 to pay me?

"Any other questions?" asked the presenter.

I raced through the questionnaire, checking off boxes willy-nilly. In the comment box, I scribbled down some random thoughts. I handed in my paper and was *this close* to making a clean getaway when I was told to sit down and wait for my interview.

Big hairy gulp.

Ten minutes later, the company president was reading my comments, filled with words like, "shyster," "hoodwink," "wheeler-dealer," and "scam." Words I'd just so recently been proud to write. He then spent a good half hour telling me (a) how wrong I was, (b) how too honest I was, and (c) how poor I'd be my entire life if I kept this up.

"So," he said. "When can you start?"

Aghast, I asked if he really wanted someone who wrote something like that working for his company.

"With the proper training," he said.

THE AD READ:

> *"Good Morning!*
> *We are looking for young energetic, enthusiastic, hard-working, reliable, responsible, team-oriented people to join our family for full and part-time positions.*
>
> *Become a waiter or waitress, or assistant waiter or waitress, or hostess or cook, at Kansas City's most unique, happy, enjoyable, busy family restaurant. Come see us at the one and only Washington Street Station. 900 Washington St. Have a nice day!"*

Nine hundred Washington Street had once been a powerhouse for the Kansas City Cable Railway Company before that structure met its fiery demise in 1901. In keeping with the railway theme, the waitstaff all wore striped overalls and engineer's caps as we scurried about in the turn-of-the-century town created in the rebuilt cavernous space. The menu featured eleven different combinations created by swapping pastas and sauces. Plus, an unlimited salad bar with hot crusty bread, along with a scoop of spumoni all for $2.95. Patrons could eat in a cable car, or in Grandma's Garden, or on her Front Porch, or in the Governor's Mansion. They could sip cocktails in the Barber Shop Saloon or be serenaded while they dined in a booth fashioned out of a bedstead in the Brass Bed Cocktail Lounge.

One night I was serving a party of eight. Everything was going fine until dessert. The problem was the large round cardboard container of spumoni was still frozen solid in the center and sloppy-soft around the edges. I scooped up the mushy parts first, mining the last four dishes from the unforgiving slab in the center. Arriving back, I slid the bowls onto the table, their contents ranging from a mountain of melting pastel to tiny turds of pink and green.

"Excuse me," said the dad, with a twinkle in his eye. "How come some people get a lot of ice cream and others get so little?"

"Well, sir," I said, "sometimes, that's just the way life is."

Anywhere else, I might have been fired. At Washington Street Station, I got a big tip.

EVEN WITH CHERIE'S fulltime job and my two part-times, we still needed more, more, more money to move to New Orleans in the fall. And thankfully, the 1972 presidential election provided us with just such an opportunity.

On July 13th, the Democratic nominee, George McGovern, announced Missouri Senator Thomas Eagleton as his running mate. It didn't take long for the national press to discover what many locals already knew. A decade earlier, Eagleton had been hospitalized for nervous exhaustion, even receiving electric shock treatments. McGovern pledged to keep Eagleton on the ticket, but *The Kansas City Star* still wanted to know what readers thought. Should Eagleton bow out? Should McGovern dump him?

For three nights, Cherie and I took turns at Gram's black boxy phone, dialing registered voters to see what they thought. And then, the study was never even published because on July 25th, less than two weeks after the brouhaha began, Senator Eagleton bowed out of the race.

Boyfriends

Place to Live. Check.
Job(s) Check.
Boyfriends—*hmm.*

Okay, I already had a boyfriend, now didn't I? But he was in Washington State, sawing his little heart out. To his credit, Perfect had been writing faithfully all summer, keeping me more informed about the progress of his friend's log cabin than the trajectory of our so-called romance.

Fayster,

Now at Island. Just incredible. Sea and lush green. Cliff looking out at sunset and moon over water. Very nicey. Poured pilings for deck & stairway up the rocks. Otherwise, lots of work & very busy. Gotta go. People waiting on me now.

Hey, what the hell are you doing? Your dummy postcard said nothing. Running. Bye. Hello to the appropriate companions.

I spent hours analyzing his terse prose, eking out as much passion as I could. It took a lot of Creative Reading.

The problem was I didn't have a boyfriend in the entire 816 area code. And it was a really big area code. Plus, I didn't even need that great of a boyfriend either since I'd obviously dump him should Perfect miraculously show up. Besides, given I was only going to be in Kansas City for a few months, if I dawdled, our first date might also be our last.

Efficient as usual, Cherie hooked up with a law clerk at her Manpower job. As for me, I started dating my Macy's coworker, Vince, a grad student living with his parents in their upscale Tudor-style home on a manicured street, protected not only by a gate but a security guard.

Shortly after we met, Vince quit Macy's, declaring it was only a matter of time before we'd all be replaced by computers.

Yeah, right.

Still, it turned out to be a good move, even in the short term, since TWA paid $3.10 an hour, almost twice the minimum wage.

"That young man is going places," said Gram, and she wasn't just talking about the $98 passes he could buy to Rome, London, and Paris. Ever practical, she was talking about TWA's full health and dental coverage. But what Gram liked best about Vince was that he had red hair and freckles, just like her. Meaning our children would have red hair and freckles, just like her.

But, of course, Vince had a Major Flaw.

The concept of the Major Flaw is fairly simple. Every guy is perfect except for one thing you just can't get around. It might be that, like the real "Perfect," he lives 1,800 miles away. Or like my foreign exchange high school crush, he doesn't speak English. Or, like Robert Redford, he's already married. Or Gene Kelly, who's a year younger than my mother. He might like boys more than girls. Or boys just as much as girls. Or he's an inch shorter than you are, dooming you to never be able to wear heels, not just on your wedding day, but for the rest of your life. All these qualify as Major Flaws. Basically, a Major Flaw is that one thing that cannot be ignored in an otherwise perfect guy. It's the deal-breaker.

Vince's Major Flaw was that he was Mafia. Okay, maybe not *Mafia*-mafia, but Mafia as defined by Gram, meaning he was Italian. Thankfully, Gram didn't know Vince was Italian because his red hair and freckles threw her off.

As for me, I had no idea all Italians were in the Mafia until Grandma told me. In fact, I clearly remember the day she met me at the door with "terrible news."

"What is it, Gram? Has Chum run away? Did Mom die? Is a tornado touching down in the living room?"

"Some Italians have moved next door." said my grandmother.

"I know, Gram. But what's the terrible news?"

"Some Italians have moved next door!"

To give Gram her due, Kansas City did have a pretty impressive gangster history. Political corruption. Racketeering. Illegal gambling. Bootlegging. Shady real estate deals. Power plays between rival families with names like Binaggio, Civella, Spero, and Bonadonna. One godfather hopscotching over another until they got machine-gunned down or went to prison for tax evasion.

The most hated mob boss of my parent's generation was Thomas Pendergast, a Democrat who controlled city government from 1925 to 1939. One of his proteges was Harry S. Truman, who went from being a bankrupt haberdasher, to judge, to senator, and finally to U.S. president. In fact, it was this decades-long marriage of local Mafia and city government that turned Dad from a lifelong donkey into an eternal elephant.

One night, Vince took me to dinner in North Kansas City, the compact little town wedged between Gram's house and the real Kansas City across the river. As soon as we parked, a freak storm came out of nowhere. Ninety mile an hour winds raged for over an hour, rocking Vince's 1965 Mustang convertible like a sea saw. We huddled together as a nearby warehouse thundered into collapse. So fast moving was this storm, it eluded the weathermen's radar. There wasn't even a warning blast, because those were reserved for tornados, which this was not.

The next day, *The Kansas City Star* reported that fierce winds and high pockets of rain had cut a mile and a half long swath, six miles through the area. Houses flooded, mobile homes crumbled, a bridge got washed away, and everyone within a 75-mile radius was without power for eighteen hours.

Which only goes to show, when God doesn't want you dating an Italian, He's not all that concerned about collateral damage.

Filley, Missouri

WITH SUMMER ENDING, there was one place I still wanted to visit before we moved on. Our old family farm in South Missouri.

My grandmother was born in a tiny town called Filley, midway between El Dorado Springs and Stockton. Some of my favorite childhood memories involved visiting there before Uncle Jim and Poppie came to Grandma's house to die. The white farmhouse with the green gabled roof was a simple two-story structure, four rooms stacked atop four others. Given these rooms were used for various purposes, they didn't have names like, "living room," and "bedroom." Instead, they were called "the east room," or "the north room," depending upon their location. The house had no electricity, and our water came from a bucket which when lowered deep into the earth, came back with the coldest, tastiest liquid on the planet. There was an outhouse down by the "crik," a big iron bell used to call "the hands" in from the field, and a black cauldron that'd turned many a pig into lard.

Invariably, Kathy would come along with us to the farm since anytime my family went somewhere, she'd come, just as I'd be invited along whenever her family went somewhere. We slept upstairs in Uncle Jim's room, our shared twin bed crammed under the eaves, causing us to hit our heads every time we turned over.

Kathy and I spent a lot of time on the front porch swing, playing hand-clapping games and finding animals in the clouds. Afternoons, we'd go down to the chicken coop, taking care to skedaddle before Uncle Jim came to wring one of their necks for dinner. After that, we'd accompany him out past the crik, to call the cows in for their dinner.

"Comjer!" Uncle Jim would bellow. "Comjer!"

One day I asked Uncle Jim which cow was Comjer, figuring it must be his favorite since it was the only cow he ever called. As it turns out, Uncle Jim was yelling, "Come Jer!" as in, "Come, Jersey cow." Still, I thought Comjer was a fine name for a cow, and I vowed if I ever got one, I was going to name it Comjer.

By the time Cherie and I visited Filley, the house had been vacant for two decades. In the meantime, itinerant hippies had moved in, and then out again, when the rooms they'd defecated in became unlivable, even for them. There were sticky cobwebs, and scurrying spiders, and roaches darting across the floor. Without electricity or running water, there was no relief from the suffocating Missouri heat.

Admittedly, I had visions of Cherie and me staying there awhile, perhaps growing our own vegetables and living off the land, just as my ancestors had done a hundred years before. In my girlish delusion, I even thought Perfect might come live with us, because hey, look how well that turned out the first time. I sent him pictures of the house and barn, asking him what he thought it would take to make it livable. This is what I got back.

"Faybo,

The structures appear sound. Not that they wouldn't require work, but all uninhabited farmhouses have sagging roofs (at least porch roofs.) Both house & barn appear well-supported. External conditions are less promising.

The sky is a horrendous gray. Note the thick white, indicating no storm nor rain, nor even the possibility of a breath of air stirring. Only a thick wetness which requires a human to develop gills in order to survive.

Further, the vegetation is brown—very good for planting and then developing one's religious inclinations in daily pleas for rain because God never intended man should live in such country.

Likelihood of survival in 94-degree weather with a relative humidity of 87%...

* *Vegetation: 18%*
* *Livestock: (cattle, chickens, etc.) 9% - But only if the well is in working order.*
* *Wildlife (quail, pheasant, etc.): 90% - but only through migration to more habitable regions.*
* *Insects (mosquitoes, fleas, wasps, chiggers, etc.): 99.7%.*
* *Humans: .028%."*

And just in case there was any misunderstanding that he might be enticed into my hair-brained scheme, Perfect added—

"While it is true God provides sanctuary for all his creatures, He assumes the most intelligent of them will keep themselves the hell out of the domains of others. Clearly the mosquito is king in South Missouri."

Fay Faron

Chapter 5
When We Saints Came Marching In

<u>September 1 - 14, 1972</u>

Vietnam: Paris peace talks stall ***In Other News:*** Palestinian terrorists attack Munich's Summer Olympics ***On TV:*** Maude ***On the Radio:*** Looking Glass' "Brandy (You're a Fine Girl)"

New Orleans, Louisiana

"GRANDMA, I'm in New Orleans!" I yelled into the phone outside the Café du Monde.

To which she replied, "Oh dear! How did you ever find New Orleans?"

I guess in her little shut-in mind, you just wandered around until you found a place. Which was pretty much what we did. Had we taken the most direct route, Cherie and I would have passed through just three states, a journey of 884 miles. Instead, we opted for a 170-mile detour so Jack Easley could receive postcards from a total of seven states.

Like most tourists, our first stop was the French Quarter. We scored a parking spot outside the Wildlife and Fisheries Building on Royal, a marble structure that took up an entire square block. The ornate building was fashioned in the likeness of those built for the 1933 World's Fair in Chicago, the first of many that were to replace the entire French Quarter with similar structures. That is until activists saved the crumbling neighborhood and turned it into a first-class destination.

Finding no "No Parking" signs, we checked the curb.

"Is that red?"

"Not anymore."

A tow truck ambled by, the driver giving us a wink and a nod before driving on. Taking this as a thumbs-up, Cherie and I headed on over to Café du Monde for beignets and cafe au laits.

"Scratch out 'luxury,' 'fabulous,' 'gracious living,' *blah-de-blah-blah,"* I said, reading the *Times-Picayune* upside down from across the table. "'Above Canal'? 'Below Canal'? What's that?"

"Basement apartments?" asked Cherie. How come Canal's the only place with underground apartments?"

"Beats me."

A tiny Asian waitress arrived to take our order. We paid in advance which she said we needed to do, because she had to buy the *beignets* inside and then sell them back to us. Hoping she actually worked there, we forked over 75¢ and were relieved when she returned with our chicory coffees and three squares of fried dough. She plopped down the plate and a puff of powdered sugar exploded upwards.

"S'cuse me," said Cherie, grabbing the waitress by the arm. "Where's that?" she asked, pointing to an apartment listed on Tchoupitoulas Street.

"St. Thomas projects. You no wanna go there. That Tremé," she continued, jabbing at another address. "That Faubourg Marigny. No way, Jose. That Bywater. Not there. That one, Uptown. That okay, but you no Uptown ladies."

She pushed up her rhinestone reading glasses and bent down for a closer look. "Central City, no. Mid-City, maybe. The Vieux Carre okay, but no Decatur."

"Aren't we on Decatur?"

"We good block. That bad block."

Okay, sure, we wanted to live in the French Quarter. Who wouldn't? The problem was our tourist map didn't show any streets outside the tourist section, so we had no idea where any of these places were. And that's when God used the classified section of the *Times-Picayune* to indicate He wanted us to live on Canal Street.

How did we know this?

Duh!

Because Canal was the only street name we recognized. See how easy it is to follow God's plan for your life?

THE AD READ:

Looking for an Apartment
WITH EVERYTHING?
Spacious comfortable apts
1036 units...Bellman...24-hour security
Most convenient, most central location
in the city
On-site covered parking
Spacious lobby, dark walnut paneling & terrazzo flooring
Maid, switch board & message service available
Look No Further! Come See Us!
CLAIBORNE TOWER APARTMENTS
1732 Canal St.

"When pigs fly," I sighed. "Look for one with less stinkin' luxuries."

"Trust in Him," said Cherie, looking skyward, displaying the kind of confidence only a True Believer can pull off.

It was just a few short blocks to our car. Or rather where our car should've been, had the Wink'n a Nod tow truck driver not returned to haul it away. And so, we tromped up St. Louis Street, each block sketchier than the last, across Rampart, around an above-ground cemetery and five more blocks of urban blight, until we reached the auto pound beneath the Claiborne St. Overpass.

"How ya doin', my babies?" asked the Black lady in the barred cage, wiping her greasy fingers on a sack of Popeyes Mighty Good Chicken.

"Just bitchin'," said Cherie, beaming her plastic smile, which in no way matched the somber-as-a-judge mug shot on her driver's license. The lady recounted our $75 worth of $1 bills and called for someone to come unlock the chain link gate.

"Have a blessed day!" she called as we drove off.

THANKFULLY, the auto pound was mere spitting distance from the Claiborne Towers, meaning we wouldn't have to walk very far every time we got towed. We parked beneath the sign at Meal-A-Minit, informing customers they had, "Seating for 10,000 – Ten at a time!" From there, we led Chum into the block-long, block-wide 17-story fortress. The opulent premises looked more like a 5-star hotel than an apartment complex. There were 1,036 air-conditioned units accessible by a bank of Otis elevators, and a lobby ringed by a beauty salon, a barber shop, a Walgreens, the Cafe Carnival, and the Golliwog Lounge.

We found the rental office on the first floor, and waited in cool, comfort until the rental agent came out to greet us.

"Sorry, girls, no pets," said Miss Sally, sounding genuinely sorry.

"Oh, she sleeps in the car," lied Cherie. I shot her my, "She never sleeps in the car except with us" look, but Cherie's inscrutable lying face gave away nothing. Certainly not that she owned a bag big enough to stuff Chum inside, which she did whenever she wanted to sneak the pooch in somewhere.

Miss Sally did a bit of harping about how great the Claiborne Tower Apartments were and then got right to the dealbreaker.

"And all that for just $130 a month."

"For a two-bedroom?" asked Cherie.

"A studio."

Cherie and I just shrugged and got up to leave."

"We do have another complex," said Miss Sally, quickly. "It's, well, off campus, one might say."

"How far off campus?" asked Cherie.

"About a half a mile. Just past where they're building the Superdome. Eighty-five dollars a month. Two bedrooms, unfurnished. Pets, no problem."

"Super!" we yelped in unison.

"Meet me in the parking lot," said Miss Sally, rising. "Oh, and bring the dog. You're gonna need it."

We followed the rental agent over to 24 square blocks of nearly identical brick buildings. A virtual city within a city. We parked on a cement slab, displacing a half dozen Black basketball-playing teens who stared at us like they were Mardi Gras Indians, and we were pesky French explorers. We walked across blocks of green—well brown, mostly—to one of the 4-story buildings, some of the windows with bars, others with air conditioners dangling precariously out of them.

"How many peeps live here?" asked Cherie, stepping over a mama breast-feeding her baby on the iron stoop.

"Fifteen hundred—"

"People?"

"Families."

The 4th floor apartment was, by anyone's standards, dark, grimy and suicidally dingy. Miss Sally admitted it needed a paint job, a task she said which would take several days.

"But we need an apartment today!"

"Before the sun goes down!!"

"And our bikes get stolen off the top of the car!!!"

Miss Sally agreed to let us move in that very afternoon if we agreed to paint the unit ourselves.

"First month, $85," said Miss Sally. "And a hundred for the security deposit. Cash only, I'm afraid."

Cherie and I each pulled out our half and handed Miss Sally $185.

"Do we get a receipt or something?" asked Cherie.

"Come in Monday and I'll write ya'll out somethin'."

"Is there a lease?"

"Nah. We trust you," Miss Sally winked. "Just as long as at least one of you has a viable source of income."

Cherie and I just looked at each other. What the heck was a "viable source of income?"

"A job," Miss Sally clarified.

"Oh! No problemo," said Cherie. She explained how she'd worked for Manpower in Kansas City, so she'd simply go down that very afternoon and pick up an assignment. The rental agent smiled and handed over the keys.

Our first day in New Orleans and we were down nearly a quarter of our summer savings.

THAT NIGHT we drifted off to the melodic strains of mamas singing the blues to their babies on the fire escapes—which might've been quite restful had it not been punctuated by the occasional burst of gunfire.

The next morning, Cherie took the bus to her temp job at One Shell Square and I went to work scrubbing mud off sheetrock it would have taken an archeologist years to find. What I hadn't counted on was the heat and humidity, still stifling in early September. I scoured the same danged wall all danged day and was still getting buckets of Mississippi mud rolling off my sponge.

By 5 o'clock, Chum and I were sitting on the curb beneath the "Watch for Falling Bullets" billboard, waiting for Cherie's bus to bring her home. To the south, downtown rose out of the humidity like a gleaming Emerald City, full of adventure and promise just out of my reach.

"Fay-bay-bee!" a jubilant Cherie sang, as she tumbled off the bus. "Isn't life grand?" Cherie was still warbling, "You Know What It Means to Miss New Orleans," as she skipped across the compound. Chum and I were panting to catch up as she bounded up the staircase and began shoving keys into our triple-locked door.

The reason for Cherie's elation was a young lawyer named Walt, who was teaching her everything there was to know about "N'awlins," as she was now calling our new home. Like how in the classifieds, "Below Canal," meant downriver from Canal Street, and "Above Canal," meant upriver. About how locals called the French Quarter, the "Vieux Carre," and the Central Business District, the "CBD."

And how nobody in New Orleans told directions by north, south, east or west because the streets all followed the curve of the river. So instead, places are either "upriver" or "downriver;" or "lakeside" or "riverside."

"In fact," said Cherie, "the Mississippi twists and turns so much that the sun actually rises over the Westbank."

As happy as I was to learn all these tidbits, I had to admit the gushing over Walt got old fast. Even more depressing, Cherie having a life while I was not. I felt like a housewife waiting for her husband to come home, only to hear him crow about his secretary. And if there was one thing I never wanted to be, it was a housewife. Or, failing that, a secretary.

THREE DAYS LATER, I was still scrubbing the same danged wall, and Chum was chasing the same danged cockroach around the living room. I spent three sweltering afternoons waiting for Cherie's bus beneath the billboard warning of falling bullets. Endured three days of Walt-centric gush-fests. And three mosquito-riddled nights listening to mamas singing to their babies on the fire escapes.

Finally, I could stand it no longer. And so, I put on my least damp dress and answered the following ad in the *Times-Picayune*.

Earn $2.25 PER HOUR
helping the Times-Picayune deliver newspapers.
Route experience helpful, but not necessary.
For information, see Mr. Nickolaus at 3800 Howard Street.

God wanted me to have this job! Of course, He did. I'd be working for a newspaper, just like Mom always wanted. No matter that I'd be delivering them instead of writing for them, she'd get over that just as soon as I made editor.

Mr. Nickolaus spent a long time staring at my application, his black, wiry, Groucho eyebrows twitching quizzically around on his forehead.

"How long y'all been on the dole?" he asked.

"The dole?"

"Public assistance."

"We're not on public assistance," I bristled. "Cherie and I are hardworking, tax-paying, career-oriented hippies."

"Are ya now?" grunted Mr. Nickolaus. "Hmm. So how long y'all been stayin' Backatown?"

"Pardon?"

"The Cally-ope Housing Project."

"I think it's pronounced, 'Ca-li-o-pee,'" I said, trying not to embarrass Mr. Nickolaus for his obvious lack of education.

"Sorry, dawlin', it's *Cally-ope*. *Ca-li-o-pee's* the music comes off'a the rivah. No need to get all Frenchy with the street names 'round here. Like it's '*Kor-an-dah-let*,' not *Kor-an-dah-lay*.' And '*So-krats*' not 'Socrates.' You gonna deliver papers in the parish, ya gotta know this stuff."

"So, I get the job?"

"No way, lil' dumplin'."

"I *don't* get the job?"

Mr. Nickolaus pulled out a big city map and slid it across the desk. "See all them big, yellah squares?"

"Yes, sir."

"Well, them's the sixteen neighborhoods where the TP delivers newspapers."

"Okay."

"And see them big pink squares."

"Yes, sir."

"Them's the eleven districts we don't deliver newspapers to 'cause iff'n we did, no paperboy would make it out alive. So, look at where y'all been stayin'."

It took a minute to pinpoint our apartment smack in the center of one of the eleven pink blocks where the brave boys of the *Times-Picayune* dared not go.

"Well, we can't move," I told him.

"Why the heck not?"

"Because God wants us to live on Canal Street."

It took about a minute for Mr. Nickolaus to pick his jaw up off the floor and shove it back onto his face.

"Well," he said at last. "Then, for Chrissake, Get yer gol-dern butts on over to Canal Street!"

CHERIE POPPED off the bus, chirping about having an *"envie"* for a satsuma snow cone. She continued trilling all the way up the iron staircase and through the arduous task of unlocking our triple-locked door. Once inside, I shoved her into the bean bag chair and told her everything Mr. Nickolaus had told me.

Fact No. 1: The Calliope Housing Project—which is what he called the "Black ghetto slum" where we lived—was the most dangerous of the city's "Big Four" housing projects. The reason was its layout. Multiple blocks of three and four-story buildings with no streets between them, making it impossible for cops to patrol.

Fact No. 2: Since we had, quite obviously, not filled out the mountain of paperwork necessary to qualify for public assistance, we were essentially squatting in the federally funded facility. As for what happened to our rent money, it was undoubtedly pocketed by scam artists at the Claiborne Tower Apartments, in cahoots with the Housing Authority of New Orleans.

"So, said Cherie. "When we couldn't afford the luxury apartment, they shuttled us on over here?"

"Looks like it."

"And we're paying $85 a month for what everybody else is getting for free?"

"'Fraid so."

Still, I expected a fight. God didn't make mistakes after all, Cherie would argue. The problem was Cherie was a far better Christian than I ever aspired to be. It was no secret God talked to her a whole lot more than He ever talked to me. Plus, He told her really specific stuff, whereas He pretty much let me step in doggy do-do all over the place. I just had to convince my roomie that *just this once,* God had made a mistake. I just hoped she wasn't going to give me a bunch of malarky about God's will and all kinda crap like that.

"You know," said Cherie. "I have always wanted to live in an integrated neighborhood. I just never pictured I'd be the only one integrating it."

THE NEXT MORNING, we grabbed a newspaper and a couple of *cafe au laits,* climbed the levee behind the Café du Monde and watched the sun rise over the Westbank. There, we found the following ad.

> BEAUREGARD SQUARE APTS.
> 1801 Hector, Gretna.
> Walking distance
> to Oakwood Shopping Center
> & 15 min. from downtown New Orleans.
> 1 bdrm., kitchen, drapes, carpet, 2 pools
> $113 unfurnished

The Beauregard Square Apartments turned out to be everything the Calliope Housing Project was not. Nestled in a meadow of Spanish moss-draped live oaks, the Mansard roof complex looked like somewhere Hansel and Gretel might live. The apartments all had fluffy white carpeting, freshly painted walls, central air and heat, and as advertised, *two* swimming pools. Best of all, the complex was just a mile-long bike ride to the free ferry that delivered you to the foot of Canal Street.

We slapped down first and last, and spent the rest of Saturday alternating between sneaking our stuff out of the Calliope Housing Project—so as not to offend our Black neighbors—and lounging around the pool, plotting how to get our money back.

"I got it," said Cherie. "Remember how Miss Sally said the only way she'd rent to us was if one of us had a 'viable source of income?'"

"Yup."

"*Soooo*, what if the little lady came to believe I didn't work for Manpower at all."

"But you do."

"Stay with me, here. If she were to think I *didn't* work for Manpower—*had never* worked for Manpower—then she'd wanna break the lease, right?"

"Yeah, except we don't have a lease. We never got one."

"It's implied. Anyway, if *she* broke the lease instead of us, then she'd *have* to give us our money back, right?"

"I guess so. So, what'da we do?"

"Just leave it to me," said Cherie.

MONDAY MORNING, I dropped Cherie off downtown and drove over to our old apartment where I waited patiently for Miss Sally to come evict us. At 4 o'clock, the rental agent still hadn't shown up, so I drove over to the Claiborne Tower Apartments to make it easy on the old gal since she was pushing fifty, after all.

Finding the office closed for the day, I slipped into Meal-A-Minit for a 35¢ cup of chicken and mushroom soup—although I'd have preferred the bacon-wrapped filet mignon for $1.75, and maybe even a 50¢ shot of whiskey, since waiting around to get evicted can be quite stressful. At 5 o'clock, I drove over to One Shell Square to pick up Cherie.

"I don't wanna talk about it!" she growled, shoving herself into the driver's seat, leaving me to scramble over the gear shift knob and onto Chum.

Cherie was still seething as she careened across the bridge, honking her way around a bus that was clearly taking up one and one-tenth lanes. I was still searching for my seatbelt—which Cherie had extravagantly purchased as an option on her Honda Z—when she slid off the Mississippi River Bridge onto the street-level Westbank Expressway.

"So, I called Miss Sally," said Cherie, who apparently wanted to talk about it after all. "And I told her, 'Hey there, Miss Pittypat from Manpower here.'"

"Wasn't she in *Gone With the Wind?*"

"That was *Aunt* Pittypat. I was going for a Southern name. So, I said, 'You know that girl, Cherie? Well, she doesn't even work for us! And we at here at Manpower are *really* pissed, 'cause she's using us as a reference to score apartments and drugs and stuff all over town.'"

Jumpin' Jiminy! I sure hope Miss Sally doesn't drop a dime on us for scoring drugs and stuff. That wouldn't end well.

Cherie scooted around a bus stopped outside the Oakwood Mall, almost knocking down an old lady in the process. The old woman banged the hood of the Z with her umbrella, gave Cherie the finger and shuffled on.

"So," said Cherie, "Miss Sally says, 'Oh no, there must be some mistake! Cherie and Fay are such lovely girls.' So, I say, 'No, they're not! They're *horrible* girls! That Cherie's nothing but a big fat liar. And that friend of hers, Fay, well, she's no saint either.'"

"Good. I'm glad you let her have it."

Cherie screeched to a halt outside our apartment and dug around for her bug spray.

"So," I said, 'You should evict Cherie and that no-good friend of hers, Fay, too. Toss 'em in an eddy for all I care!'"

"Did you mention us getting our bread back?"

"No wait, you're going to love this. 'So,' Miss Sally says, all sweetie-poteetie like, 'Oh no, there must be some mistake. Fay and Cherie are *delightful* girls.' So, I say, 'No, they're not! They're *terrible* girls!'"

"So, Miss Sally loves us?"

"Miss Sally wants to marry us and have our babies."

"YOUR TURN," Cherie announced the next morning as we were bumping each other out of the line of sight of the medicine cabinet mirror."

"Holy moly! If you couldn't get our money back, what the cheese whiz am I supposed to do?"

"Make up some cockamamy story, I did."

"Yeah, but unlike you, I'm a terrible liar."

"And how do you expect to get any better if you don't at least try?"

Cherie did have a point. Still, I had very little confidence in my genetic gift for lying. After all, I'd pretended to be sick every school day since kindergarten and still ended up with a college education.

Cherie said the secret to lying was to think of it as *acting*. "Pretend you're in a movie," she said, pulling on her pumps. "Except you're the only one that *knows* it's a movie. Plus, you gotta give details. Lots of specifics. Talk fast and give lots of particulars."

And so, armed with this CliffsNotes tutorial and a handkerchief full of onion slices, I dropped Cherie off at One Shell Square and drove over to the Claiborne Tower Apartments.

At 9 a.m., the lobby was already crammed with dozens of Black mamas, their limbs being tugged at by squalling toddlers, their breasts suckled by tiny infants.

The only white person, aside from me, was the lady in the barred cage.

Aha! Stealing from the federal government was one thing. But this was a clear-cut case of Whitey keeping the Black man down.

I tugged a ticket from the machine, went over and sat on a metal chair. This should be a quick in-and-out, I figured. I'd present my case, get a perfunctory, "Fat chance, little lady," and be out the door before Meal-A-Minit ran out of scrapple.

"Ninety-seven!"

I slunk over to the cage, dabbed my eyes with my onion-filled handkerchief, teared up and whimpered, "I need to break my lease."

"Okay, sit down."

What the frog?

How come I had to see somebody? Why couldn't they just have turned me away at the window? Sure, I promised Cherie I'd go on this fool's errand, but now I had to actually *talk* to somebody? Oh, why wasn't she here! The girl was a world-class liar, I had to give her that. Ten times better than I ever aspired to be. We were pretty competitive but she was the clear winner on this one.

Then it hit me. If I was getting to talk to a supervisor, I actually had a shot of getting our money back.

MR. AUGUSTINE'S walnut-paneled office was ten times nicer than the waiting room, and easily a hundred times nicer than our Calliope apartment. Behind the giant desk sat a coffee-colored man with eyes a fetching shade of sparkling amber. He smiled at me through large, commercial-worthy, blindingly white teeth and my heart did a cartwheel and landed in the splits.

Mr. Augustine was easily the most stunning man I had ever seen up close. That perhaps anyone, aside from Mrs. Robert Redford, has ever seen up close.

"So, *cher*," he said, offering me the chair across the desk from him. "They tell me y'all be needin' to break your lease?"

"Yes, sir," I sniffled, pressing the onion-filled hankie into my eyes and having it come back stained with gobs of black mascara. "You see, my girlfriend, Cherie, ran off with her boyfriend, uh, Walt. He's a lawyer. Downtown. One Shell Square. Fifty-one stories? Tallest building in New Orleans? Ya heard of it?"

Mr. Augustine smiled and gave me a little chuckle.

"The problem is, I have no, as Miss Sally would call it, 'Viable source of income.'" And then, I dabbed at my eyes, and the tears flowed like, well, like someone with onions in her handkerchief.

"This Walt-fellah? He a Chalmation?"

"A, uh, what?"

"He staying with his mama'n em, down *rivah* in Chalmette? *Catlick* fellah? St. Aug High?"

"Uhhh, I'm pretty sure he went to college. Him being a lawyer and all."

"*Elleshyew?*"

"I don't know what that is."

"L.S.U.," he spelled it out.

Journey of a Teetotaling Virgin

"*Ohhhh*, I donno. The point is, we – I mean 'I' – really need our – I mean 'my' – money back because we – meaning 'I' – can't afford the apartment on our – I mean 'my'- own. So, how about it, Mr. A.? Give a girl a break?"

I peeked through my wet fluttering lashes to see that, inexplicably, the room had not exploded from all my lies.

Mr. Augustine gave me a soft look, full of not only empathy but enough electricity to light all 1,036 units at the Claiborne Tower Apartments. He pulled out a giant checkbook, plucked the fountain pen off his desk and gazed up at me.

"So, $130, is it? Or you got the one bedroom for $150? Or the 2-bedroom for $195?"

"Eighty-five," I admitted, without thinking.

Criminy! I could've made money off this deal.

Mr. Augustine looked confused.

"I didn't think we had any—*Ohhhhh*— Y'all get a lease?"

"Nope. Miss Sally promised, but—"

"Ya pay in cash?"

"Yeah."

"And your apartment's here or—"

"Off campus," I said, using Miss Sally's expression. I was tempted to call it the Calliope Housing Project, but I didn't know if I should push it.

Mr. Augustine gave me a little knowing smile. I felt like I was in a poker game. One where I hadn't seen my own hand. He smiled again, this time, more of a wary grin. He put away his checkbook, swiveled around, and began twisting the dial on a small cast iron safe on the floor behind his desk.

I rose a little bit in my chair. Just enough to see there was enough money in there to buy the Claiborne Tower Apartments outright and have enough left over for a big ole Grand Opening.

Mr. Augustine swiveled back around and held out $85 in bills. "Sorry it didn't work out, li'l lady. But maybe we'll see ya back here someday. On the main campus, I hope."

Wow! That was easy.

Then, it hit me. He'd been talking about, "rent." I thought I might get our security deposit back, but not rent. We *had* lived there, after all.

And then, I had this crazy thought.

I think I can get it all back.

"Why, thank you, sir," I said, rising.

And then I swooned, just like I'd seen ladies do in too many movies to mention. Mr. Augustine practically leapt over the desk to catch me. I looked up into his dreamy bedroom eyes and my heart skipped a beat.

"Oh, my," I gulped. "I guess I'm a bit wobbly, what with all the wall-washing, and cockroach-stomping, and leaving the apartment in better shape than I found it, and all."

"Crush?" asked Mr. Augustine.

"Kinda. You?"

Mr. Augustine went over to a pint-sized refrigerator and returned with a bottle of Orange Crush.

"Well," he said, smiling his 1,000-watt smile. "I guess you do deserve a little *lagniappe* for all that scrubbin'."

And then, he opened the safe and counted out $100 in $20 bills. Our entire security deposit.

I was this close to making a getaway when Mr. Augustine asked where I would go? What would I do? Or as he so eloquently put it, "We can't be havin' you wanderin' 'round Schwegmann's inna house coat 'n curlahs like some kinda maw-maw."

I gulped my soda pop in silence, planning my exit strategy. Clearly, I'd not written this B-movie beyond the happy ending. And now, Mr. Augustine wanted a sequel? And then, I said the only truthful words I'd uttered in the entire ten minutes we'd known each other.

"I wanna go home to my mother!"

And that's when I learned the hairy eyeball isn't just a white thing.

It's a human thing.

Chapter 6
Jobs Even I Won't Take

September 15 - 30, 1972

Vietnam: Peace talks continue in Paris *Watergate:* Seven burglars indicted by Grand Jury *In Other News:* San Francisco's BART begins passenger service *On TV:* The Bob Newhart Show; M*A*S*H* *On the Radio:* Mac Davis' "Baby, Don't Get Hooked On Me" *Bands Behaving Badly:* Paul & Linda McCartney get caught growing weed

New Orleans, Louisiana

SETTLING INTO our new apartment *"ovah da rivah"* didn't take long given the only things Cherie and I owned were two 10-speed bikes, a sewing machine, typewriter, and beanbag chair. After just a few nights on our white plush carpet, we voted to use our refund money to buy a waterbed. Okay, not an *entire* waterbed, no way we could afford that. But the big plastic bag, so that was a start.

It soon became apparent why waterbeds needed frames. And heaters. Without them, a lone sleeper sinks directly onto the floor and is enveloped in a big bag of fluid, the temperature of Lake Superior. The solution is for two people to be in bed simultaneously, which is why waterbeds were so popular back in the 1970s. This created a problem, however, since I went to bed at 9 and got up at 5, whereas Cherie went to bed at midnight and didn't get up at all if she didn't have to. And even when we were both in bed, we had to turn over in unison or somebody would have to get up and break out the Dramamine.

To say Cherie and I were minimalists was an understatement. We could either sit on the bean bag chair or on the floor. We could either sleep on the floor or the equivalent of a large flabby seal the temperature of a 7-Eleven Slushie. Our laundry dried on the handlebars of our 10-speed bikes, and our meals were consumed standing over the sink watching the neighbors watch us through our curtain-less windows.

Still, we made do. Cherie learned to sew with her sewing machine tucked between her splayed legs, regulating the push pedal with her thigh, while I perfected the skill of typing while lying on my stomach.

Still, like most apartment-dwellers, we longed for a table and chairs. And so, we snuck out to the swimming pool in the dead of night, liberated the white, wrought iron patio furniture and relocated it to our living room.

Finally, it felt like home.

"YOU THE CHICK needs a phone?"

A hunky shadow fell across my bikini'd body, blocking the blistering sun reflecting off the pool. I peered into a halo of gossamer hair falling around a face I could not yet see.

"Apartment 110? You left the note?"

BellSouth Bobby was cute. Of course, he was, or I wouldn't be telling you this. I could go on waxing poetic or you could just Google Jon Voight, in the film, *Midnight Cowboy*.

The next morning, Bobby dropped by with a half dozen honey-dipped donuts. And the next morning. And the next. And just like that, Cherie and I had another boyfriend.

Now to be fair, this time, it wasn't our fault. We were traveling together, new in town, knew no one, we were each other's best friends, and always together. Whenever we met a girl we liked, she became our friend. And when we met a guy we liked, he became our boy-friend. Anyway, we liked Bobby and he must have liked us back because once again, Cherie and I were flummoxed as to whose arteries he yearned to clog the most.

As for Perfect, his letters still arrived weekly, albeit never with a nod as to our future coupledom. With summer done, he'd ceased pouring pilings for a stairway up the rocks, vacated the remote island off British Colombia, and headed east for parts unknown.

Journey of a Teetotaling Virgin

He picked up my letter, forwarded by his mother to Pittsfield, New Hampshire, a town he described as, "so small it doesn't even exist on a lot of maps." From there, he met up with a high school chum in Vermont, then traveled through New Hampshire into Maine, where he rambled around for a few days.

Then came this.

> *Fayzo,*
>
> *I've been frantically looking for a place to live & work to replenish my bank account & so far, I've been failing.*
>
> *Yesterday I realized why. Every time I get to a town, the next one looks better. I want to live in the country, but I have to work in a city. Anyway, I can't handle the isolation right now. It's all very weird.*
>
> *Your letter was excellent to receive and sounded very different from anything previous. You actually sound like you know your own mind & have a little confidence in its workings. Dig it!*
>
> *Now I'm off to try some new places, maybe Massachusetts.*
>
> *There's a place for me, somewhere, a place for me. Dot, dot, dot.*

A place for him? How about New Orleans.

NOW THAT we had a decent place to live, Cherie quit Manpower and got a real job at a German restaurant in the French Quarter. Best of all, she got to wear a dirndl and consume unlimited amounts of wiener schnitzel for her employee meals. I was pretty jealous, but we had a pact never to work at the same place, so it was back to the classifieds for me.

Most of the listings were for things I was completely unqualified for. *Negro* butcher. *Colored* cleaning lady. *Dependable colored* woman—wrong on both counts. There were lots of "boy jobs." Handyman. Roughneck. Roustabout. Derrickman. Tugboat captain. All nestled between no less than six pleas for delivery boys for the *Times-Picayune*.

Fay Faron

As for girl-jobs, I soon learned, "attractive barmaids" at the Hummingbird Lounge earned $102 a week, while "white barmaids" on Sophie Wright Place, got just $90. The going rate for "white go-go girls" on Bourbon was $3 an hour, although it was unclear how long one could prance atop a grimy bar before some caveman clawed you off and ravished you in front of God and everyone.

"Freelance Writers to do Research on a Variety of Topics," turned out to be a job writing term papers for college students. *Pah-leese.* I didn't write my own term papers, why would I write somebody else's?

I applied at the Spaghetti Factory at Jackson Square, but I didn't get the job because the manager said he wasn't allowed to date the help.

Huh?

The next day I got an actual job offer.

The Court of Two Sisters was an upscale French Quarter eatery located in a pre-Civil War townhouse on Royal Street. Its entrance was a carriageway, its dining room had floor-to-ceiling windows, there was a tropical courtyard, and an all-you-can-eat buffet offering delicacies ranging from crawfish to bread pudding.

Mr. Fein hired me on the spot and told me to call him the next day about training. And when I did, he told me to call him the next day about training. This went on for a week, until one day I forgot to call Mr. Fein about training and then when I called the next day, he fired me because I hadn't called the day before about training.

THE AD READ:

WOMEN INVESTIGATORS
New concept in undercover work. Do you qualify?
Interviews from 10 a.m. - 2 p.m. weekdays. 2200 Tulane

I drove over to Tulane and South Galvez, parked, and zigzagged through the drug dealers and hookers to what looked like a vacant building. The door was propped open, and there was a cardboard sign that read, "Private Investigator" Scotch-taped to the glass. I followed the arrows to an empty office where a skinny middle-aged Black man sat behind a desk piled high with papers.

"Well, look-a-chu!" bellowed Mr. English, circling me like I was a racehorse. "Ain't you da spittin' image ah Miss Nikki!" The man smiled and his right incisor twinkled. Actually twinkled. Like Tony Curtis' had in *The Great Race.*

Miss Nikki turned out to be James Franciscus' blonde, curly-haired assistant on the TV show, *Longstreet,* set in New Orleans and featuring a blind insurance agent solving all kinds of crimes.

Mr. English tossed me a half dozen issues of *True Detective* magazine, told me to go home and read them, and I could start the next day. I was about to ask what my duties might be when an even skinnier Black man popped in to thank Mr. English for bribing the judge so he could get out of "da OPP," as he put it, which I later learned was shorthand for the Orleans Parish Prison.

"I'm not sure this is a good fit," I said, rising.

"Aw no, boo. I do all da judge-shit. But I needs meself a foxy lady like yo-self if'n I be wantin' to be expandin' my Domestic Shit Department."

"You have a Domestic Shit Department?"

"Yes, indeedy!"

"So, what would my duties be?"

"Well, right now we been springin' da bros what's got's demselves in-car-sar-ated fer slappin' around der old ladies. But I can see now, dat don't seem rite."

"I should think not."

"'Cause bitches got rights too!"

"That's very enlightened, Mr. English. You are indeed a man ahead of your time."

"Yeah, you right! So, I figure we can do dese gals a favor by catchin' dere cheatin' baby-daddies in da act."

"Are you saying you want me to flirt with married men?"

"Gawd, no!" laughed Mr. English. "I needs me some pic-tures! We gotta catch dese caps in da act!"

"Da act?"
"Da sack!"
"You want me to go to bed with them?"
"How else we gonna prove it?"

BACK IN COLLEGE, when Mr. Todd encouraged me to consider a career in Creative Writing, I don't recall him mentioning anything about the treasure trove of opportunities writing for the classifieds. In fact, I was still under the impression that the Help Wanted section was actually non-fiction. Which is my official excuse for answering the following ad.

> *USHERETTES*
> *ADF Entertainment Services is accepting*
> *applications for usherettes and hostesses.*
> *Applicants must be at least 16 years of age,*
> *attractive with a pleasant personality. Apply in*
> *person with two recent photographs.*

ADF were my father's initials! God must want me to have this job!

My interview was at 10 p.m. in an old Victorian in the Lower Garden District. At the top of the stairs was a parlor which now served as a waiting room. There was one other applicant, a young woman in a short skirt and white go-go boots. As for me, I was deep into my *Ryan's Daughter* phase.

The movie, set in 1916 Ireland, was about the town adulteress, played by Sarah Miles, who spent most of the film in a long-sleeved, high collared, white starch shirt and long black skirt that covered her entire body except for her face and hands. My modern-day version was a navy-blue turtleneck tunic that snapped between my legs, and a dark skirt that extended well past my black boots.

Go-Go Gal and I chatted for probably twenty minutes waiting for the previous interview to end. When the girl finally emerged, she gave us a long, lingering version of the hairy eyeball, then exited. Go-Go Gal was in and out in an instant. Then it was my turn.

"Come in," said Mr. LeBlanc, a distinguished gentleman in his mid-forties, brown hair graying at the temples, and a Cuban cigar dangling off his lip. "Sit, please."

"Thanks. I didn't fill out an application or anything."

"Let's just chat first. See if you might be interested."

"Oh, I'm interested all right. I *looove* movies!"

"Movies?"

"The usherette job?"

"Oh, right," said Mr. LeBlanc. "Actually, that job's taken, but we still have some hostessing and modeling positions available."

"Far out! If you think I'm pretty enough to be a model. If not, hostessing is groovy too."

"All right, then. Now, our company caters to clients, men mostly, who come to New Orleans looking for a good time. Your job would be to make sure they have one. You might go to parties or just stay in. Whatever the man wants."

"Bitchin'."

"You do massage?"

"Uh, no."

"No matter. That part doesn't last long anyway. The thing to remember is that ADF has a reputation for guaranteeing our clients have fun. *A lot of fun.* More fun than anyone else in town can show them. Know what I mean?"

"Absolutely! Fun's why I came to New Orleans. But it'd sure be awesome to get paid for it. Wink-wink."

"I like your attitude," he smiled.

"So, tell me more about your customers," I said, thinking this was going rather well. "Would I be showing their wives and kids around as well? I used to be a camp counselor so I'm really good with kids."

"Okay, first, we call them 'clients,' not 'customers.' And while you might be asked to entertain two at once, it'd be rare for them to be married, at least to each other. As for kids, well, that's just gross."

Huh?

"Uh—Have you done this type of work before?"

"Ushering? Sure as shootin'. I worked at the Phoenix Metro when I was sixteen. They hired me on Christmas Day, probably because somebody didn't show up, but I got fired by New Years, when I told the manager he was disgusting when he put a half-eaten box of Jujubes back in the case after some lady said they were stale. Meanwhile, I saw *Alfie* something like fifty times."

"Well, this, uh, there's no ushering job, so let's move on. Have you done any escort work?"

"I was a school crossing-guard. Does that count?"

"Not at all. Modeling?"

"Not really. I graduated from Charm School, but I lost the certificate. I hope that's not a deal-breaker. Oh, and I came in 19th in Arizona's Miss Maid of Cotton contest, my freshman year in college. But we only had that one picture taken. I'm not sure you'd call that modeling."

"Okay, I'm thinking you might not be right for this," said Mr. LeBlanc, standing.

"Oh, no! I really want this job!"

"Unless, of course, you're willing to learn."

"Absolutely, I wanna learn! Consider me an empty vessel waiting to be filled."

"Hmm. That sounds just like what I'm looking for."

"Great! When do I start?"

"Well, first, I need your assurance you'll do whatever it takes to satisfy a client?"

"Duh!"

"Every time?"

"Yes sir. *Every single time.*"

"Unless you're on your period, of course."

I was about to tell Mr. LeBlanc that I could work right through my ladies' day, because I didn't get bad cramps or nuthin.' But then I started thinking there was something really odd about this interview. Where was the talk of salary? Health coverage? Profit sharing? All the things the Jim Dandy Fast Food Company offered in their ad?

Mr. LeBlanc pulled out an advertisement torn from a magazine. On it was a girl reclined behind a giant bottle of Scotch. Her bare shoulders and legs were sticking out either end, the rest of her discretely hidden behind the big bottle of booze.

"You find this offensive?" he asked.

"*Nooo.*" I was starting to dread the direction this was going.

"Would you have a problem posing for such a photo?"

"Uh— *nooo.*"

Just as long as I could disrobe behind the giant bottle of Scotch.

Mr. LeBlanc sucked on his cigar, stretched his head back and gave me a long lingering head-to-toe once-over. I pulled my sleeves down further down onto my wrists, wishing I'd worn gloves. And possibly a ski mask.

"Okay," he said. "Take off your clothes."

I froze. Unbelievably, all I could think of was that if I took off my clothes, Mr. LeBlanc would see the indents my white tube socks made on my calves.

Just then the phone rang. Mr. LeBlanc answered and engaged in what promised to be a lengthy conversation. He waved me to begin undressing. When I didn't, he waved me goodbye.

And so ended my career as a medium-priced call girl.

Fay Faron

Chapter 7
Rollin' on the River

October - November 1972

>*Vietnam:* Kissinger declares "Peace is at hand" *Watergate:* Nixon re-elected in landslide *In Other News:* American Indians occupy federal offices; Rugby players resort to cannibalism to survive Andes air crash *On TV:* "Maude" gets an abortion *At the Movies:* Last Tango in Paris *On the Radio:* Johnny Nash's "I Can See Clearly Now"

New Orleans, Louisiana

I EVENTUALLY found work at a sidewalk café at the corner of Chartres and Toulouse, in the French Quarter. Café Banquette was a place where sweethearts lingered all afternoon over carafes of strong red wine, and mule-drawn carriages clip-clopped past our French doors while "Knights in White Satin" ricocheted between the century-old brick walls.

Café Banquette was popular not only with the tourists, but the artists who worked the fence around Jackson Square. It was also the end spot for day-drinkers on their pilgrimage down Chartres as they refueled at local joints like the Chart Room, Maspero's, Napoleon House, and the Gallery House, just cattycorner to us.

It was at Café Banquette where everyone split into groups. Some stayed for our Dagwood-sized sandwiches and cheap mixed drinks, others trotted off for the Early Bird special at the Alpine Café. Still others stumbled over to Krystal's for their 15 cent, onion-infused square hamburgers.

With October, came the dryer, cooler weather September had denied us. Gone were the days when you had to dab Off behind your ears like fine perfume. Cherie and I both had jobs we loved. We got to bike to work, take a free ferry across the Mississippi, consume plentiful and delicious employee meals, and pay our rent in $1 bills.

Life just doesn't get any better than this.

And although, technically we were "Westbankers," the French Quarter was where we lived our lives, hanging out at local haunts and shunning both the drunks on Bourbon and the uppity tourists shopping for overpriced antiques on Royal.

Our favorite hangout was Buster Holmes, a soul food restaurant deep in the scary end of the Quarter. This charmingly seedy cafe with its chipped black walls and community tables, was as New Orleans as it gets.

At Buster's, you could find businessmen dining alongside roustabouts and Tulane medical students chatting with Black mamas about the meaning of life. And while nothing on the menu cost over $2, for those in need, Buster charged nothing at all. And the only way you could tell the paying customers from the charity cases, was the latter had more food on their plates.

One evening, Cherie and I had just settled into Buster's sweltering back room and ordered up a couple of Monday's Special: red beans and rice; 35¢, or a dollar if you wanted an Andouille sausage on top.

We were watching in sweaty awe as the Black Buddha-faced cooks stirred steaming pots of possum, alligator, crawfish, and nutria, when a young man plopped down beside us.

Like us, Marc was new in town, but unlike us, he had a real job working as an engineer for an oil company in the CBD. And although Marc had only been in town a few months, he had already immersed himself in the culture, simply by going out every night, joining up with whoever he happened to meet and tagging along wherever they happened to be going. Marc was the kind of guy who would have not only moved into the Calliope Housing Project, but would have stuck around to sing the blues with the mamas on the fire escapes.

When the handsome hunk suggested Cherie and I meet him at a nightclub called, Club My-O-My, we eagerly agreed, anxious not to let the other one get a leg up our next community boyfriend.

Journey of a Teetotaling Virgin

BY THE TIME we arrived at the warehouse on the 900 block of Conti, Cherie and I were feeling mighty good about our beautification efforts. That is until we got a good look at the babes slinging drinks inside the cavernous space.

Talk about dolled up.

No wig was too big for these dames. No hair too black. None too platinum. No gown too low. No slit too high. No laugh too bawdy. No foundation too thick. No eyelashes too long. No stilettos too tall.

Plus, they all looked like movie stars. And I don't mean Jane Fonda, Goldie Hawn, and Faye Dunaway. I mean really old movie stars like Jayne Mansfield, Mae West, and Carmen Miranda. As for the patrons, if they weren't actual mafioso, they could've certainly played them on TV.

We found Marc sharing a small table with a Scarlett O'Hara-lookalike cooing in the ear of a Jimmy Hoffa-wannabe. At the table next to him, Ida Lupino was bouncing on the lap of Pretty Boyd Floyd while up on stage, Veronica Lake was warbling, "Girls Who Drink Beer at the Beach Always Get Sand in their Schlitz."

"Here ya' go, sugar," said Lucille Ball, dipping her embarrassingly scant cleavage down to Marc's eye-level. She gracefully glided his Jax beer onto the table and proceeded to plop down my Baily's Irish Cream and Cherie's grasshopper, covering us both in frothy suds the color of coffee brown and minty green.

Marc tucked a $10 bill in her bustier, Lucille blew him a kiss and sashayed off.

"That chick's hitting on my date," I seethed.

"Our date," Cherie corrected me. She took a discrete look around and nudged me to lean in. "Check this place out," she whispered, trying to talk without moving her lips.

"Yeah, I know. We're *waaaay* underdressed."

"No, you dope. Look again."

Nonchalantly, I scanned the room. What these chicks lacked in wholesome good looks, they made up for in wigs and—*what?*—Adam's apples?

"You shore are beautiful," Al Capone cooed to Joan Crawford at the next table. "If you'se a woman, I'd marry ya."

"That girl's a guy!" I gasped.

"They all are, you putz."

Up on stage, Hedy Lamarr was singing, "Everyone in the Circus Gets Wet When the Man on the Flying Trap Pees."

"I don't get it. They're lesbians?"

"No, you stupid idiot. They're *guys.*"

"They can't be both?"

"Donno. This is way outta my wheelhouse."

"Doesn't make any sense. Why would anybody wear high heels when they didn't have to?"

"Beats me."

We stayed for all three shows, and I never could figure out if they were (a) girls who liked guys, (b) girls who liked girls, (c) boys who liked boys, or (d) boys who liked girls. Actually, I'm still a bit unclear on how the whole thing works

ONE DAY, a movie company was filming the new James Bond flick, *Live and Let Die* right outside Café Banquette. During my break, the lighting guy let me climb up his 18' ladder to check out Roger Moore, the latest 007 in the super spy franchise.

I might have gone up that ladder a waitress, but I came down a star. At least as far as Table No. 4 was concerned.

"You done any modeling?" asked the man-half of the corporate-looking couple.

"No, have you?" I cooed, sliding down his Bourbon and water.

Now to be fair, guys were always asking chicks if they were models. It usually happened right before or right after they said they worked for the CIA, but if they told you anymore, they'd have to kill you.

As it turns out, Corporate Man was legit. In fact, he and Gray-Suited Business-Lady were in town for a cosmetology convention and were looking for "local gals," willing to give up their weekend in lieu of a free head-to-toe makeover. One look at my curly blonde locks frolicking unrestrained from brown roots to split ends, and I was declared a perfect, "Before."

And so, I spent the weekend at the Fairmont Roosevelt Hotel—the very same place Elvis stayed while filming *King Creole*—and by Sunday evening, my $87 valued cut-and-color had transformed me into an exquisitely coifed, "After." I was also wined and dined. Admired and flattered. Propositioned and proposed to.

Plus, I got 50% off on all the clothes I modeled (which I still couldn't afford) and went home with $55 worth of Redken products designed to maintain my fleeting state of perfection.

And, oh yeah, they threw in a boyfriend for free.

Hey-Bear was a cutie-pie, Redken salesman with ink-black hair, ivory skin, a lilting Cajun accent, and a propensity to use local expressions like "making groceries," and "I been havin' it awhile."

Hey-Bear's surname was spelled H-E-R-B-E-R-T, which he pronounced, "A-bear," hence my nickname for him. Hey-Bear was young, ambitious, good-looking, and on a quest to sample every fine restaurant in New Orleans.

On our first date, he took me to Chris Steak House, the first in a chain of restaurants that would someday be known as "Ruth's Chris Steak House," the name change necessary after a fire forced the eatery to relocate, while the purchase agreement tied the original name to the first location. The night we went, Fats Domino was in a back booth playing cards with friends and gobbling down a $13 Porterhouse steak-for-two.

On our second date, Hey-Bear took me to Marti's on Rampart, where Tennessee Williams was chowing down in the blood-red dining room at a table next to us. Our third date, alas, turned out to be our last.

Here's how that happened.

After a romantic dinner on a wrought iron balcony overlooking Bourbon Street, Hey-Bear and I went back to my place. We were barely through the door when I kicked off my shoes and began pulling off my earrings—which were, by the way, killing me. When

I turned around, I was floored to see Hey-Bear had shed his tie, had his shirt unbuttoned, and was in the process of unbuckling his alligator belt.

"Whoa, fellah! What'cha doing there!"

"Same as you, *cher.* Slippin' into nothing less comfortable."

"I'm taking off my earrings. Which are, by the way, killing me."

"And your shoes?"

"Also killing me."

"Well, that dress looks a little tight."

I'll spare you the details. Suffice to say, Hey-Bear perceived the shedding of these very painful accessories as a signal that we were going to have—pardon my French—Real Live S-E-X. And in case you missed the title of this book, at this juncture of my life, I didn't have Real Live S-E-X.

Which I innocently admitted, thinking it was no big deal since, (a) If I was a virgin, everyone else of my age and marital status must be too, and (b) that having certain parts of your bodily apparatus untouched by human hands was a valuable—dare I say, essential—quality to look for in a mate.

And yet, with that simple announcement, Hey-Bear's clothes sucked back onto his body as if his chest had suddenly turned into a Hoover vacuum cleaner. After which, he made a hasty, and I might add, inelegant, exit.

Whoa! What just happened here?

Could it be that Hey-Bear was no longer a—*gasp*—virgin.

Nah. What were the chances of that?

All through high school and college, all my boyfriends had been good Christian guys who knew how far they could go and on which date they could go there. Along with the mandate that they *never, ever* venture south of the border. At least not until wedding cake and sparkling cider were involved.

But, by the way Hey-Bear scooted out of there, it was like *I was* the one with the Major Flaw!

Harrumph, as Cherie would say.

LOSING HEY-BEAR caused barely a blimp on my heart monitor. And that's because Café Banquette was turning out to be quite the Single Guy Central. And so, when one of my regulars asked me out, of course, I said yes. Especially when I heard there'd be food involved.

At age 33, Ray was a decade older and already showing a smidge of flab around his middle. Thankfully, what the man lacked in sex appeal, he made up for in his career of selling 2-for-1 coupon books, where the second entrée was free.

So yes, it cost Ray literally nothing to date me.

And although his magic coupon book was suspiciously devoid of fine dining—apparently, I wasn't his first girlfriend—I reveled in discovering new delicacies like the giant juicy burgers at a dingy tavern on Esplanade called Buffa's, roast beef debris po'boys at Johnny's on St. Louis Street, and cheese grits at the Hummingbird Grill, a 24-hour diner on St. Charles whose sign, "No Talking to Imaginary People," went largely ignored.

One night after stuffing ourselves at Poncho's Mexican Buffet on Gravier—"All-you-can-eat for $1.49"—we strolled down Bourbon Street.

Bourbon wasn't always this sleazy, Two-for-One-Ray informed me. In the 1940s and 1950s, it was a like one long block party with plenty of parking for locals, happy to pay the one-drink minimum for the tame but tantalizing entertainment.

In fact, one such regular was Governor "Uncle Earl" Long, who practically lived at the Sho-Bar, where his flame-haired stripper girlfriend, Blaze Starr, strutted her stuff.

But all that changed in the 1960s when three corporate hotels were built within stumbling distance of the increasingly lurid, live entertainment. The club owners were only too happy to trade their thrifty, well-behaved clientele for these new drink-until-you-fall-down drunk, out-of-towners.

They painted their windows with half-naked ladies, invented scary new cocktails and paid strippers to lounge in their doorways enticing passersby. And in the most outrageous come-on of all, a joint called Big Daddy's had a live girl swinging out their second-floor window over the street.

By the early 1970s, Bourbon Street had become a deafening around-the-clock assault on all five senses. The only places locals still went were the dueling piano bar at Pat O'Brien's; the 809 Club where buxom, brunette torch singer, Chris Owens, headlined for her husband, Sol; and Johnny Gordon's piano bar in the gaslit back room of Lafitte's Blacksmith Shop Bar.

But we were headed to another local joint, the Gateway Lounge, on the 200 block of Bourbon Street. That's night's entertainment was to be 33-year-old teen-throb has-been, Frankie Ford, famous for his two American Bandstand appearances and his hit song, "Sea Cruise."

We were sipping our rum and Cokes at a couple of window seats when the Frankie Avalon lookalike did a doubletake at something just behind us on the street. Suddenly, he rushed out of the cozy bistro and was soon back, dragging with him a disheveled old Black man cradling a trumpet in one hand and a Big Ass beer in the other.

Frankie introduced the gentleman as "needing no introduction;" which judging from the applause seemed to be true.

And then to an awed and reverent audience, the old guy proceeded to blow his horn like Louis Armstrong come back to life. I have no idea who this fellow was, but it was my first inkling of how New Orleans could gobble you up and spit you out, and then go about her business as if you were nothing more than gum on her grimy sidewalk.

It was past ten, when Two-for-One-Ray led me up the grassy embankment, and over the railroad tracks that ran along the levee behind the Cafe du Monde. We sat on the grass overlooking the Mississippi, and there beneath a full moon, as a tiny tug pushed a giant barge around the extreme bend in the river, in a lovely baritone, Two-for-One serenaded me with, "Ol' Man River." A cappella, no less.

This was by far the most romantic thing that'd ever happened to me. It was the kind of evening I'd dreamt about with Perfect but had never even come close to. But, hey, if I couldn't turn a Perfect into a Ray, maybe I could turn a Ray into a Perfect. Worst case scenario, I'd never go hungry.

Hand in hand, we strolled back to Ray's loft just off Decatur Street. And although I hadn't been all that attracted to the guy, his song had melted my heart. What I needed now, was to find out if Ray was a good kisser. Ten minutes of making out, perhaps a little light petting above the waist, and I could make an informed decision as to his boyfriend potential.

Ray's airy loft was sectioned off, not with walls but with furniture. The corner kitchen had copper pots hanging from a 14' ceiling. The Persian rug sat atop the rough, plank, cypress floor. The furnishings were sparce, but expensive. It was like an actual grownup lived there.

When I returned from the little girl's room, the loft was aglow with the flickering flames of cookie-scented candles shooting shadows of the potted palms onto the walls.

But where was Ray?

Then I saw him. In bed. The sheet was pulled down to his waist, his pasty white chest covered in wiry black hairs that extended onto his shoulders.

Jumpin' Jehoshaphat! Two non-virgins in a row? What were the odds of that?

"Well," I said, carefully, trying to save my much-appreciated meal ticket. "I can see you're tired, so I'll just go."

"You're leaving?" Ray asked incredulously. "What are ya, on your period or something."

"No," I said, defensively. As if my period was any of his business. "I wanna make the last ferry is all."

I thought for sure I was going to get away with it, maybe save the relationship, at least long enough to sample the Buck Forty Nine Steakhouse coupon I'd been eyeing in his little book.

"You saying I bought you dinner *three times* and now, for no good reason, you're not gonna sleep with me?"

I was about to point out the obvious. That I should have a reason *to* sleep with him, rather than to have to come up with one *why not to*. But then, he sat upright in bed and practically growled, "Don't tell me you're a—"

"Go ahead," I challenged him. "Say it."

"A virgin?"

"I prefer 'Unclaimed Treasure.' But yes. And proud of it, I might add."

And with that, Two-for-one Ray rose out of bed like the eruption of Vesuvius over Pompeii. He wrapped the sheet around him and came at me looking like the only reason he wasn't going to throttle me was that he'd have to drop the sheet to do so.

"Are you saying I wasted my coupons on a fuckin' *virgin?*"

"Oh, please. You had to eat anyway."

"Get the fuck outta my house!"

"Well, that's not very nice. And just for record, I wouldn't make out with you now if you were the last Sherpa on Everest!"

"Get outta here, you, you, you—"

"Go ahead. Let it rip."

"You fuckin' virgin!"

Ray opened the door, pushed me out and slammed it so hard the wind knocked me backwards.

Furious, I rang his buzzer.

"Get the hell outta my building or I'll call the goddam cops!"

I pounded harder. Kept ringing the buzzer until he finally opened the door.

"Yeah?" snarled Ray, standing there in a blue velour bathrobe, his initials monogrammed right where his heart should've been.

"Just so you know," I said, staring him down. "There's no such thing as a *FUCKING* virgin!"

And with that, I turned and ran for the last ferry.

Chapter 8
To Les-be or Not to Les-be

December 1, 1972 - January 15, 1973

Vietnam: *"Christmas Bombings"* ***Watergate****: Four plead guilty to spying* ***On TV:*** *First "Dick Clark's New Year's Rockin Eve"* ***At the Movies:*** *Man of La Mancha; The Poseidon Adventure* ***On the Radio:*** *The Temptations' "Papa Was A Rollin' Stone;" Helen Redding's "I Am Woman;" Billy Paul's "Me and Mrs. Jones;" Carly Simon's "You're So Vain"*

New Orleans, Louisiana

AS A COLD and rainy winter descended upon the city, Cherie proclaimed it was time to move on. I wasn't so sure. I found New Orleans to be fun and exciting, with surprises around every corner. Exactly what I was going for in life.

What I loved most were the people. In California, everyone was so respectful of each other's privacy that nobody talked to each other. In New Orleans, folks thought nothing of asking if you were married, how much money you made, and what you paid in rent. They asked, you answered, and you connected. Buster Holmes said it best. "My mama'd be mad if I didn't say 'hello' to everybody I met on the street."

And yet, go figure, Cherie wanted to leave. She said she wanted to accomplish something in life, even though she couldn't say exactly what.

"We've been here two months already," she complained. "We've had two apartments, two jobs and two boyfriends each."

"I know!" I sang out in agreement.

Cherie argued that Florida might very well offer better jobs, better apartments, better boyfriends, but most certainly better weather. And so, I reluctantly agreed to move on.

We gave notice—using our security deposit as our last month's rent, and on November 30th, moved our stuff to Belle's, our new best friend from the St. Charles Baptist Church, Uptown. And then in the dead of night, we snuck the patio furniture back to the pool area from whence it had come.

Our intent was to go home for Christmas, meet back up at Belle's, collect Chum and continue on to Florida. Cherie scored a student fare by showing up at the airport in pigtails and smoking—her impersonation of a petulant teen—while I caught a ride with a guy looking to share gas to Phoenix, where I'd send the holidays, and then drive back in my parents' old Rambler station wagon.

As for Belle, it was a fluke Cherie and I'd met the schoolteacher at all since we'd only attended church a couple of times, quitting once our parents were satisfied we'd found a good one. There was no point in going any longer anyway since all the cute guys were already married. We ran across Belle after the service, half-hidden behind a bush, smoking a cigarette. Sensing a kindred rebel spirit, we struck up a conversation.

I was immediately intrigued by the mild-mannered teacher at a hoity-toity all-girls' school on Prytania Street, since one of my fictional heroes was the romantically delusional Edinburgh schoolteacher in the 1969 film, *The Prime of Miss Jean Brodie*. The title character, played by Maggie Smith, filled her pre-World War II students' heads with notions of art, free love and fascism when they should have been studying math and chemistry.

We soon learned Belle was no Miss Jean Brodie. Shy and timid as a turtle, aside from smoking, Belle didn't have a rebellious bone in her somewhat chunky body. Whereas Miss Brodie was bursting with self-confidence, Belle could better be compared to the meekest of Miss Brodie's students, Mary McGregor.

> Jean Brodie: *What about you, Mary McGregor. What are your interests?*
>
> Mary McGregor: *I haven't got any.*

> **Jean Brodie**: *That is what I'm here for, Mary McGregor. To provide you with interests.*

So eager was our very own Mary McGregor to please, we had to be careful what we asked of Belle, lest she give us everything she owned and then take out a second mortgage so she could buy us a pony. Belle said yes to piling our valuables in her living room for the weeks we'd be gone. Yes to taking care of Chum, including twice-daily walks. Yes to leaving Cherie's Z in one of the few parking spots outside her house. She even said yes when we suggested she quit her job and join us on Our Grand Adventure, now on the fast track to Florida.

Phoenix, Arizona

I HAD HIGH hopes Perfect might make it home for Christmas, but *nooo*. And that's because he had a job. A *real* job. In New York City, of all places.

In November, he'd written from Vermont.

> *Faybo,*
> *I can't remember when I've been so lost for something to do. Why don't you write when you decide where you're going to be? You can't just run around forever, you know."*

Then, in December, came this.

> *Ten minutes before I got to NYC, I didn't even intend to stop. Now, I've been here an amazing 22 days, during which about six months of my life have transpired.*
> *The last 7 days have been mind-bending. Incredibly, I have a job, apartment, friends, my shit together & a rejuvenated God-concept.*
> *I don't really have time to explain, let alone soak it in myself. Now I'm running for weeks on end & I'm finally getting into something bigger than myself.*
> *Now I'll be here probably two years.*

The job turned out to be an outdoor activities counselor for a Black-designed, Black-run, Black-staffed program for youthful offenders in Harlem. Perfect had always had a bent for social issues, but now it seems he was going full throttle into social work. The ultimate mountain-climbing, tree-hugging nature boy settling down in New York City?

Never saw that one coming.

I ARRIVED in Phoenix only to find my parents' old Rambler station wagon, Bessie, had died and gone to Old Car Heaven. Luckily, my brother had a vast collection of clunkers, one of which he sold me for $40. This I considered a real steal until it came to a grinding halt at Stuckey's in Chandler. That's when I realized who the real thief had been. At a lifespan of 40 miles for $40, the Buick might have made the *Guinness Book of World Records* for the costliest car ever sold.

The next day, my father took me downtown where I picked out a brand-spanking-new cherry-red Toyota Corona with a hatchback suitable for sleeping. Pops paid $1,900 cash, our agreement being I'd pay him back at the same 3.3% interest his savings account paid rather than the 6% the dealership charged. At $60 per month, the car would be paid off in three years.

I named my new best car-friend "Mrs. Turner," after the lady whose cow started the Great Chicago Fire of 1871. Years later, I discovered the lady's name was actually Mrs. O'Leary, but by then, the red hatchback had blown a rod thirty miles north of Las Vegas and was sold for $40 scrap, so it hardly mattered.

El Paso, Texas

I HUNKERED DOWN for my first night in Mrs. Turner, right there, safe and sound in El Paso's Motel 6 parking lot. What I hadn't anticipated was the laborious climb over the seats to flip on the ignition whenever the temperature dropped below freezing.

At 3 a.m., I decided to drive on, lest Mrs. Turner turn into an igloo in what turned out to be the worst snowstorm to hit Texas in modern history. And so, I started driving east on I-10, through an 888-mile-long snow globe.

By dawn, conditions had deteriorated to near white-out. What few a.m. radio stations braved the frozen airwaves screeched out warnings to abort any imminent travel plans and hunker down for the duration. But still I drove on, keeping pace with my only visual reference, a big rig's taillights up ahead.

It was late afternoon when Mrs. Turner let out a mighty shudder, the sound I would imagine a jet plane might make if it exploded mid-air. I switched off the ignition and the noise gurgled into a scary silence.

Soundlessly, I glided to the shoulder of the road. Or what I hoped was the shoulder since I couldn't see past the hood. I tried the ignition. It scraped a few times and then ignored me altogether.

Everything was deadly still. I watched as Mrs. Turner's windshield fill with snow, erasing my little red existence from Planet Earth.

"Hey, God, remember me? I know I've been shining you on as of late." I prayed, leaned back, and prepared to die. "But if you could just send—"

"Hey, there!"

Wow! That was quick.

A thick blue mitten smeared away a spot on the frosted glass, revealing a trucker's face as red and puffy as his checkered hunting cap. Rescued from certain death, the trucker dropped me off in the small town of Kerrville and the Toyota dealer dispatched a tow truck to go retrieve Mrs. Turner.

"Sounds like a bum engine," said the dealer. "I'll write Japan first thing Monday. We should have a new one in about six weeks."

"But the salesman said the parts were available nationwide," I informed him. "It's the only reason my dad agreed to buy a car from the country that tried to kill him in World War II."

"Sorry, toots. Salesmen will say anything. You're old enough to know that."

Clearly, it was time to call SuperMom. Ten minutes later, the dealer had agreed not only to swap out my engine with one from the showroom floor, but to pay for my room at the local Motel 6. My mother was just that good.

When I talked to Mom again, she filled me in on what everyone else in America with a television already knew. There was a man on top of the Howard Johnson Hotel in New Orleans shooting people.

It all began that very Sunday morning when 22-year-old Mark Essex carjacked a Chevy Chevelle and drove it into the hotel's parking lot. Climbing the fire escape, he found three Black employees taking a smoke break. Assuring them he was "only there to kill honkies," he pushed past them into the hotel. The workers ran to alert management even as Essex encountered a Virginia couple, a doctor and his wife, on their belated honeymoon. He shot the doctor in the chest and his wife in the back of the head. He then stepped over their lifeless bodies into Room 1829, soaked a telephone book in lighter fluid and set the curtains on fire.

By the time police arrived, the ex-Navy man had already shot two firemen off their ladder as they scaled the building trying to rescue victims trapped in the fires, he himself had started. He was also shooting bystanders in Duncan Plaza, the park outside City Hall.

Seeing the coverage on live TV, a Marine Corps pilot commandeered a military helicopter, loaded it with police sharpshooters and flew to the scene. By then, cops were stationed on the rooftops of the surrounding high rises, their bullets falling short of reaching the concrete bunker where Essex was hiding.

It was after dark when the shooter stepped out. He took aim at the chopper, hitting its transmission and sending it into a tailspin. Still, showing himself proved his undoing since it allowed sharpshooters from nearby rooftops to fell him with over 200 bullets.

By the time the 11-hour siege was over, Mark Essex had wounded thirteen people and killed nine, including five police officers. It was the bloodiest day in New Orleans history to date.

When I called Cherie at Belle's, she told me some even more shocking news. It seems she hadn't seen our hostess in days. Cherie said Belle showed up occasionally, but just to grab some clothes and leave again.

It was impossible to imagine our quiet, conservative friend was shacking up with somebody. A far more reasonable explanation was that we were imposing, and Belle was too polite to say so. I told Cherie to go stay with one of our other (few) friends and I'd find her when I got back. Which was how Cherie ended up moving in with our honey-dipped boyfriend, BellSouth Bobby.

New Orleans, Louisiana

TERRIFYING DOESN'T begin to describe BellSouth Bobby's apartment. The walls were black. The windows covered in tin foil. There was a motorcycle parked on a tarp in the living room, his not-quite-clean socks drying on its handlebars. The only thing the least bit reassuring was there was no dead-body scent wafting through the floorboards.

"Come outside," Cherie whispered, before I could even drop my backpack. We went out and sat in Mrs. Turner, and Chum dozed off to the scent of new car smell.

As Cherie told the story, Bobby had been more than agreeable when she asked if we might stay a few days. The first night they *slept together* (!) on his *framed* (!!) waterbed *with heater* (!!!)— although Cherie assured me there was no hanky-panky going on.

At least not with her.

Cherie said it was after midnight when there came a banging on BellSouth Bobby's front door. Bobby just shrugged, rolled over and went back to sleep. The pounding continued on around each of the tinfoil covered windows. By the time it reached the bedroom, Cherie was cowering in the corner, her toes tucked beneath her flannel nightgown, her eyes wide with fright.

Finally, Bobby got up and let the girl in. From the other room, Cherie said, there came lots of shouting. The sound of glassware being flung about. Motorcycle parts being drop-kicked onto the wall. The girl sobbing. And then, her body being tossed—*thud!*—against a wall. All went quiet for a few minutes, and then came an even more disturbing noise. "Pigs grunting in the woods," was how Cherie described it. At dawn, Bobby returned to bed as if nothing had happened.

We agreed that since our host was ignoring the incident, as good guests, we should as well.

I CAUGHT UP with Belle at her Uptown apartment. "We didn't mean to run you outta your pad," I apologized.

"Well," said Belle, "I sorta-kinda met someone."

"Hey, that's great! What's his name?"

Belle stammered something I couldn't quite hear. When I asked her to repeat, she peeked up through her light brown, mascara-less lashes and mumbled, "Mary Jo."

"Oh, okay."

Ohhhh!!!!!

Yes, indeed. As it turned out, while Cherie and I were off celebrating the birth of our Savior, Belle was out discovering she was a lesbian.

Here's how that happened.

Belle said she'd never really been into boys, not even back in high school. She figured she just hadn't met a guy who knocked her socks off. Then, she met Mary Jo. And it was this Mary Jo-person who informed Belle that the reason she'd never felt funny downstairs with a guy, was that she was—*gasp*—gay.

I quizzed Belle, trying to gently prod her out of accepting her layman-diagnosed condition. Had she any inkling she was gay before this Mary Jo-Person declared her so?

Nope?

Aha! Well, wasn't it just possible, this Mary Jo just wanted to get in her pants?

Belle assured me that Mary Jo knew about such things. She'd been a lesbian all her life, after all. She knew another one when she saw one.

Still, I felt it my Christian duty to inform my friend that (a) it was illegal, (b) a certifiable mental illness, according to psychiatrists, (c) she could lose her *job,* and her *apartment* and (d) *nobody* liked lesbians, not even the Women's Movement.

"So, you think I'm going to Hell?" asked Belle.

As kindly as I could, I reminded her that the Bible very clearly stated that homosexuality was an abomination before God. Still, I assured her if I got to Heaven first, I'd have a personal word with The Big Guy on her behalf.

"It's up to Him to judge," I said, piously. "Not me."

"Good," said Belle, "because I want you to meet Mary Jo."

Holy guacamole.

"**THIS ISN'T** a double-date, right?" asked Cherie, peering across Esplanade at Ruby Red's Roadhouse where a dozen hand-in-hand females were entering and exiting. "Tell me this ain't no double-date."

"Oh, please, we do stuff together all the time. We *live* together. We *travel* together. We *sleep* together. Okay, not *sleep*-sleep together, but share the same water-blob. You never felt like we were on a date before."

"We were never having dinner with two lesbians before."

"They're *not* two lesbians. They're one lesbian and a confused, malleable young woman in the evil clutches of Devil Spawn."

"Okay," said Cherie. "Except what if this all-powerful Mary Jo-person turns *us* into lesbians as well?"

"God will protect us," I said, hopefully.

"He didn't protect Belle."

I thought about it a second. "I don't wanna be a lesbian!" I wailed.

"I don't wanna be a lesbian either!"

"Does this mean we can't kiss boys anymore? I *looove* kissing boys."

"I'm not giving up kissing boys! Even if Mary Jo turns me into a lesbian, I'm still going to go on kissing boys!"

"Well, just so you know, I'm not smacking you on the lips, even if I am a lesbian. Not now, not ever! No way! Not even on the cheek. Yuck!"

"Oh, yeah? Well, I'm not kissing you either!"

We really were competitive.

RUBY RED'S was softly lit by Tiffany lamps hanging from its rough ceiling, spreading a golden glow over ladies of all ages staring dewy-eyed at each other across wooden spool tables. On a raised platform in the corner, a robust lady cook was flipping burgers, catching them with her spatula and sliding them onto a sizzling grill.

"There they are," I said, finger-waving to Belle, who looked happier than I'd ever seen her. She had on a yellow sundress, was nestled into the shoulder of a much older, far more angular woman, both of them swaying dreamily to, "Puff the Magic Dragon," playing on the juke box.

"Don't make eye contact," Cherie warned as we crunched our way over the peanut shell-littered plank floor. "Mary Jo can't turn you into a lesbian if you don't make eye contact."

"Where'd you read that?"

"Leviticus."

"Hello there, beauties!" said Mary Jo, as we slid onto our beer-barrel stools across from the happy couple. Mary Jo leaned over as if to shake my hand, holding it a bit too long, just as she did her steely gray gaze.

"Uh-oh," whispered Cherie. "You're a gonner."

Mary Jo ordered for us because that's just the kind of gal she was. Jax beers and steak-burgers all around, the latter an easy choice since that was the only thing Ruby Red's served. They turned out to be the same quarter pound, 100% sirloin steak-burgers served at Chris Steak House, except Ruth's were $6, and at Ruby Red's, they were just a buck.

"Bitchin' good," I gulped, locked in Mary Jo's light gray pupilless gaze. I could feel her essence boring into my soul, yanking it out through my eye sockets and stomping on it like the peanuts beneath our feet.

Mary Jo said everything at Ruby Red's was local, from the Jackson Brewery beers served in ice cream goblets, to the peanuts from the Southern Seed Company on Decatur to the Tiffany lamps purchased on Royal Street.

Bitchin'," I kept saying over and over. Like it was the only word I knew.

"Relax," said Mary Jo. "It's not like the fuzz are gonna raid the joint."

"Well, it *is* illegal to be homosexual," Cherie informed her.

"No, it's not. It's only illegal to do something about it."

"Well, it's still an abomination before God," Cherie insisted.

"Where'd you get that?"

"Leviticus?"

"Lucky guess," said Mary Jo. "Leviticus 20:13, to be exact." The older woman took on a scholarly tone, reciting a verse she'd obviously memorized. "'If a man practices homosexuality, having sex with another man as with a woman, both men have committed a detestable act.'"

"See!" said Cherie, clearly vindicated.

"Still, it says nothing about a woman having sex with a woman."

"It's implied," said Cherie, weakly.

"I thought you took the Bible literally."

"I do."

"Okay, so the second half of that verse reads, 'They must both be put to death, for they are guilty of a capital offense.'"

"That does seem a bit harsh," Cherie conceded.

It wasn't until we were back in Mrs. Turner, locks pounded down, that I exhaled.

"That Mary Jo chick gives me the willies," I shuddered. "I could just feel her staring at me. Couldn't you just feel her staring at you?"

"That's because she *was* staring at you," said my always supportive friend.

Chapter 9
When Teetotaling Goes Awry, Can Virginity Be Far Behind?

January 16 - 31, 1973

Vietnam: *Nixon predicts "peace with honor"* ***Watergate:*** *John Mitchell found to have financed burglar breakin* ***In Other News:*** *Airports begin passenger screening; Roe v Wade legalizes abortion* ***At the Movies:*** *Last Tango in Paris* ***On the Radio:*** *Stevie Wonder's "Superstition"*

New Orleans, Louisiana

CHERIE AND I slept at the foot of Mount Motorcycle for the remainder of January while BellSouth Bobby slumbered in his black bedroom with the tinfoil shades. Thankfully, the girlfriend did not return.

When I went back to Café Banquette, I learned I'd been fired in my absence, given a new manager was hired while I was away, and he fired everyone the old manager had hired. But since Cherie—who always did the right thing—until she didn't—was *once again* committed to working out her two weeks' notice, I decided to go looking for another job.

Not to worry, said BellSouth Bobby. He knew of a bar in need of white go-go dancers. We drove to a disheveled wooden structure on South Causeway, still showing damage from 1969's Hurricane Camille. One lone drunk was laying halfway across the bar while a tiny Asian girl in a bikini and white go-go boots strutted atop it, deftly plucking dollar bills from his upstretched hand.

"No," I said.

"No, what?"

"I'm not doing this."

"You wanna make money, don't cha?"

I just looked at him. Clearly, Cherie and I needed a better system for vetting our next boyfriend.

THE NEXT DAY, BellSouth Bobby and I rode our bikes out to Audubon Park. Our route to the ferry confirmed what Cherie and I had suspected all along. There was no idyllic Californiaesque bike path to be found west of the Rockies. Instead, we found just a limited choice of bumpy jaunts through iffy neighborhoods populated with potholes the size of washing machines.

The free ferry connecting New Orleans' two oldest neighborhoods, the French Quarter and Old Algiers, was located at the most extreme bend in the river. Both neighborhoods were roughly seven blocks by fourteen, their width running alongside the Mississippi, given that riverfront property was a valuable commodity back in the olden days when waterways were the most expedient way to move goods across long distances.

But the nearly identical footprints of the neighborhoods was where the similarities ended.

The east bank had always been the commercial side of New Orleans, settled there because of its visibility to see enemies approaching from both upriver and downriver. The "Eastbank" was the domain of the opera houses, the ballrooms, the fine restaurants, high-class taverns and the very best brothels.

The "Westbank" was where the slaves were processed. Where the stockyards had been. Where the trains were reassembled after being ferried across the Mississippi on their journey west. It was also the home of many of New Orleans best Black musicians, their modest houses just blocks away from stately plantations, like that of New Orleans' long serving mayor, Martin Behrman, who held court on his Pelican Ave. front porch during his reign in the early 1900s.

But now, Old Algiers was clearly past its prime. The fine bones of its turn-of-the-century Creole cottages, shotguns, camelbacks,

Arts & Crafts, and antebellum townhouses, a virtual poster child for, "The City that Care Forgot."

Bobby and I boarded the same wooden ferry landing shown in the 1965 film, *The Cincinnati Kid,* pedaled three blocks up Canal Street, then followed the St. Charles streetcar line to Audubon Park, where we settled into the damp grass across from Loyola University. Bobby pulled out a camel-skinned bota bag, threw back his head and with perfect aim, shot a shimmering stream of henna-hued burgundy between his Jon Voight-y lips.

I was shocked, scared, and a little bit thrilled.

Daytime drinking? Unprecedented!

Ever since Cherie and I began consuming alcohol—i.e., arrived in New Orleans—we'd been searching for a cocktail that could be tolerated all the way down the gullet. We'd tried Whiskey Sours, Mai Tai's and Hurricanes, but none were as tasty as the fruit juice they polluted. I had high hopes for Baileys Irish Cream, but it just made me feel bloated and gassy. And although Cherie favored the Grasshopper, to me the minty, frothy mess tasted like chalky green, Pepto Bismol.

Still, I had to admit, this red stuff wasn't half bad. Plus, inexplicably, it improved my judgment, my sense of humor, even my vision—but alas, not my hearing. The more I drank, the bluer the sky became. The greener the grass got. The more Jon Voight-y, BellSouth Bobby became.

And then, *sob,* Bobby's bota bag was oddly drained. And so, we pedaled back down Magazine Street, dodging mean old men with honky horns who got annoyed every time one of our 10-speed bikes toppled over. But that was okay because BellSouth Bobby was cute and funny. And I was cute and funny. And even falling off our bikes was cute and funny. Okay, maybe not to mean old honky-horn men, but cute and funny, nonetheless.

And then, he took me to Pearl's Oyster House where I scarfed down my first-ever half-dozen raw oysters, along with a half-dozen more, the latter grilled and gurgling with butter, garlic, and Parmesan cheese. Bobby paid the bill in quarters, dimes, and nickels, all gathered from his job of emptying pay phones for a living, a confession he'd never have made without a few belts under his belt.

After that, we pedaled down Canal Street toward the ferry. And then, who should we run into, quite literally, but Two-for-One Ray. And I swear to pieces, I'd have screamed, "He paid full price!" had I not been too busy picking myself up out of the gutter to do so.

EVERY DAY, I went down to Café Banquette to collect my four days of back pay, a total of $16. And every day, the manager gave me some cockamamie excuse as to why he didn't have it. Since the café not only didn't take credit cards but paid their employees in cash, this made no sense at all. But I kept going just the same.

By 4 o'clock, boredom and low blood sugar would've teamed up to lure me into a nap. Day after day, I bedded down on Bobby's lumpy, dirty carpet, trying to get comfortable. One day, the temptation to crawl into his bed proved far too tempting. Knowing Bobby didn't get off work until five, I found no reason not to take my nap in his cozy, comfy waterbed. Not beneath the covers or anything, mind you, just on top. I had plenty of time to get myself up, out, and freshened up before he got back home. What he didn't know couldn't hurt me.

I was awakened by a heaviness pushing me down into a vortex of squishiness, as a rising tide swelled up around me. By the time I was half awake, my panties were down, and Bobby was thrusting himself between my legs.

Pearly Gates, Heaven

"*I need to talk to God,*" *I said to Javier, a distinguished angel who looked a lot like Desi Arnaz.* "*Something really bad's happening to me RIGHT NOW!*"

"*Sorry, Charlie. Busy God-day. Foreman's fighting Frazier for heavyweight champ. And then you got your Supreme Court vote on Roe v Wade. Whole lotta praying going on Down There. My suggestion, take a number and pray for a cancellation.*"

"But this is an emergency! I'm having sex and I don't wanna!"
"You got insurance?"
"Insurance?"
"As in—have you asked Jesus to be your Lord and Savior?"
"Yes! Yes, I have!"
"Did you FEEL anything when you got 'so-called' saved?"
"Like what, exactly?"
"Euphoria? Sense of peace? Exhilaration? Glee? Joy? Jubilation?"
"Just a little wet from all the dunking."
"Sorry, chickadoodle. Doesn't sound like it took. Happens sometimes. Glitch in the system. Might wanna try again later."
"But I need saving RIGHT NOW!"
"Well, you should have thought of that before taking a nap in the dude's bed."

New Orleans, Louisiana

IN HE WENT.

Again. In and out. In and out.

Scraping me raw. Thrusting over and over. Jabbing away as I struggled to get free. I screamed for him to stop, but it only seemed to rev him up even more. Finally, BellSouth Bobby let out a mighty shudder and rolled off onto his black slimy, satin sheets.

"Whew!" he said. "Like, wow." He slid around on his back like a dog scratching its backside.

I slipped onto the floor, gasping for air as the gray tunnel of fog retreated back into the corners of the room. I was tugging my jeans up over my sticky thighs, stuffing my feet into my boots, when Bobby peered down at me.

"Where ya' goin'?" he asked.

"New York," I said, simply.

New Orleans to New York

NOT REALLY TRUSTING Mrs. Turner not to have another cross-country conniption fit, I took the "Leave the Driving to Us" Greyhound option.

Montgomery. Atlanta. Charlotte. Richmond. Washington. Baltimore. Philadelphia. The 30-hour bus trip paused at each city just long enough for passengers to grab a bite to eat, and for me to jot a postcard off to Jack Easley, telling him everything was fine.

Except everything wasn't fine. Far from it. Because everything had changed. Simply put, I wasn't a teetotaling virgin anymore. And if I wasn't going to be a teetotaling virgin, then I didn't know what I was supposed to be.

The decision to run to Perfect was visceral. What Bobby had done couldn't be undone. But maybe it could be replaced. If I could just get to Perfect ASAP, and do it again, this time with the man I loved, then maybe, just maybe, I could replace the *bad* thing with a *good* thing in my mind.

By the time we rolled into Virginia, I was angry. But not at BellSouth Bobby. At myself.

Back in college, I'd scoffed at the notion that foreplay was the gateway to Real Live S-E-X. That all my necking would lead to no good end. That someday I'd tease a boy so unmercifully, he'd literally lose control over his body. And what happened next wouldn't be *his* fault—it'd be *mine*.

And that's exactly what had happened. Turns out, my Sunday school teacher had been right, all along. I'd spent five years playing Russian Roulette with my virginity, and now Bobby's bullet had blasted right out of his penis and into my vagina.

It was like Javier had said, I should *Never, NEVER, NEVER* have taken a nap in the dude's bed.

New York, New York

PERFECT'S 5-STORY apartment complex was the last stop on the A Train, his building right out of *West Side Story*, with fire escapes zigzagging down both sides of the brick structure. I was about to punch in his apartment number when a young man came hurrying out, and I slid in behind.

"Lordy," said Perfect when he saw me standing in his doorway. "Well, well, well. C'mon in."

We talked far into the night. Of course, we did. Talk was all we ever did. About how airlines were going to start screening people's luggage because of all the skyjackings. About how everyone was referring to the burglary of the DNC headquarters as "Watergate," after the office complex where it happened. About the plane crash in the Andes, where the soccer-playing survivors had resorted to cannibalism in order to stay alive. We talked about everything—except *us*. If I didn't know better, I'd think there wasn't even an "us."

"So, what'cha think about Roe v. Wade?" he asked.

I didn't want to say "What?" because I was always saying, "What?" which made me look like a stupid idiot. And that's because Perfect always knew everything about everything, whereas I invariably knew nothing about anything.

"Abortion made legal in all fifty States? Catch the news, Cronkite?"

Criminy. Could I possibly be—gasp—pregnant?

No way, no how. It just wasn't possible. Not the very first time you *Did It*. The odds were, what, like a zillion to one?

"Well," said Perfect. "I think it's great. About time chicks got a say over their own friggin' bodies. Enough of these shitty old white guys telling 'em what to do. Am I right?"

I couldn't believe the irony. Abortion had become legal in the very same month and year I'd first had Real Live S-E-X. Talk about your cosmic kwinky-dink. Yet, even I, with my "Sign from God" mentality, couldn't imagine this was a signal from God that I should go forth and fornicate. I might be ignorant, but I wasn't delusional.

For three days, we tiptoed around the ex-virgin in the room. I tried to pretend nothing had changed, but my cheerful, charming self somehow seemed forced. Now that we were finally alone at last, I kept waiting for Perfect to make a move. But nope.

Apparently, it never occurred to him. It was like every time I saw the guy, we were back in the getting-to-know-you stage. But I didn't need no stinkin' getting-to-know you, I needed *knowing*. Like in the Biblical sense.

By the end of three days, I was so riddled with lust and longing, I was physically uncomfortable. And so at the end of Day 3, in the middle of one of his monologues about "What Was Wrong with the World," I slid onto the floor and began pulling on my boots.

"Where ya going?" asked Perfect.

"New Orleans," I said simply.

PERFECT DROVE ME to the Port Authority bus station, yelling at Micah to get off my lap pretty much the whole way. It was as if the 120-pound pooch knew more than he did about the power of touch.

Given I hadn't picked up a bus schedule on my way in, we were flying blind as to when a bus would be leaving in the direction of New Orleans. Finding ourselves with hours to kill, Perfect took me on a driving tour of Manhattan.

Our first stop was the brand, spanking new World Trade Center, the Twin Towers filling up with tenants even before the official ribbon cutting. At "Slime Square," as he called the grimy, crime-ridden center of the city, we parked and watched a group of Good Samaritans trying to revive a man outside the *"xxxtasy"* theater. A cop stopped, called someone on his walkie-talkie and raced off. All around us, druggies threw up in litter-strewn gutters, sidewalk preachers bellowed scary Old Testament warnings through bullhorns, and drug dealers loitered outside sex shops while foul-mouthed family disputes spilled over into the street and big-busted streetwalkers in mini-skirts cat-called to drivers in slow-moving cars.

Back at Port Authority, I climbed into the back of the van and started shoving all my bits and pieces into my backpack.

"So, you gonna fess up?" asked Perfect

"I have no idea what you're talking about," I said, pushing Micah's nose out of the way.

"So how come a month ago, you were all loop-de-loop about New Orleans and now you're walking around like some kinda zombie."

I ignored him, just kept nudging Micha's nose out of my backpack.

"C'mon, *wazzup,* chickie-wah-wah?" Perfect moved closer, dislodging Micah, along with my backpack. He took my chin and looked deep into my eyes

Now? Really? Now? You had three days, and NOW you make a move?

The Atlanta bus's headlights swept through the van.

"I did it," I said. Instinctively. Organically. Totally without thinking.

"Did what?" Perfect murmured, pushing my hair back behind my ear.

Gulp. Take a breath. Say it.

"I had sex."

One thousand one. One thousand two. One thousand—

"Sex?"

"Yup."

"Real live S-E-X?" Perfect asked, sitting back on his haunches.

"Third base and beyond," I said, softly

"Lordy." Perfect just stared vacantly out the window as the Atlanta bus filled up fast. I couldn't tell if he was impressed or appalled.

"You know the worst part? I wasn't even in love. He wasn't even *The One*. Not even close. Sex should be a big deal. It should mean something. Know what I mean?"

"Yeah," said Perfect. "Yeah, I do."

Port Authority's loudspeaker blasted out last call for the bus to Atlanta. Perfect scrunched up his mouth like he was either genuinely sorry to see me go, or he was mimicking what he thought sorry might look like. With him, you never really knew.

I reached for the door handle.

"Okay. Bye, then," I said, hoping for an opening, rather than an ending.

Even then, he could have stopped me. Damn the bus, he could've said. Damn New Orleans. Damn the guy that got there first. Stay here and let's make it a second first-time to remember.

"See ya," was what he said instead.

Chapter 10
And So, We Drove On

February 1 - 15, 1973

>*Vietnam:* POWs released from Hanoi Hilton **Watergate:* Senate forms investigative committee **In Other News:* U.S. & Cuba sign pact to combat hijacking **On the Radio:* Elton John's "Crocodile Rock" **Bands Behaving Badly:* Paul McCartney fined for growing weed

New Orleans, Louisiana

BY THE TIME I returned from New York City, Cherie had both cars packed and was itching to go. I said an awkward goodbye to BellSouth Bobby as I was careening out the door.

And I do mean awkward.

"Cherie says you're a virgin?"

"Well, not no more."

Thanks to you.

"Don't worry, I didn't tell her. But I gotta say I'm flattered you chose me. Guess this means we're meant to be."

Chose you?

I just stood there gobsmacked while he blathered on about how "they" say when you save a man's life, you are then responsible for him for the rest of his life. It was like now that he'd shtupped me, it was his duty to keep shtupping me on into infinity.

"Look, I gotta go. Cherie's already in the car, honking."

Which she was but wasn't.

"Okay, but you'll write? Lemme know where you are?"

"Ah, yeah, sure. Chum! C'mere, girl! C'mon!"

Bobby reached into his jean pocket, pulled out a wad of crumpled bills and thrust them at me. It must have been $30. I looked up at his sweet smile, peeked around to make sure Cherie wasn't watching, and then in my first slide down a slippery slope, tucked the money into my purse and ran for Mrs. Turner.

Buccaneer Bay, Florida

ACCORDING TO the brochures, Weeki Wachee Springs was a virtual dreamland where the sky was always blue, flowers blossomed all year long, paddleboats floated on still lakes and flamingos stood around on one leg contemplating their navels. It was a land of ducks and peacocks, of natural springs, and families in tire tubes floating down lazy rivers populated by manatees.

For me, Weeki Wachee Springs was a place where professional mermaids frolicked in a giant aquarium in bikini tops and scale-tails while playing on piano keys, applying lipstick, riding mechanical seahorses, and sipping tea at bistro tables while tiny fishes hovered above their plates.

Cherie was her usual grumpy self when I informed her I was born to be a mermaid.

"Really?" she said, staring me down over our shared Grand Slam breakfast at Denny's. She peered out at the cold morning, the air as thick and gray as a moldy milkshake. "I came from fog," she said. "I'm done with fog."

"But it's my destiny!"

"Yeah, really? I mean, *is it really?*"

"*Absolutely!* I've got the long blonde hair, the lithe—"

"Albeit busty—"

"—swimmer's body. Plus, I took synchronized swimming in high school. And don't forget I was a lifeguard, so if any of the hunky mermen—"

"No such thing—"

"Well, technically, there's no such thing as mermaids, so—"

"You know, you gotta keep your eyes open."

"I can keep my eyes open. I do it all the time. I'm doing it right now."

"Underwater. And you gotta smile. Underwater. Big toothy grin. While little fishies poo all around you."

I argued I could do that. Just not too persuasively. I couldn't even convince myself.

And so, we drove on.

The Everglades, Florida

SINCE CAR-SLEEPING is a skill most guidebooks do not even begin to address, just a little more bang for your buck, I will do so now.

The Golden Rule of Car Sleeping is to hide in plain sight so you go unnoticed by both cops and mashers. Obviously, rest stops are out, given they're frequented by both. The motor inn parking lot is an excellent option since it's already filled with out-of-state vehicles piled high with luggage. In fact, the only difference between you and the paying customer is (a) they're paying and you're not, and (b) they're sleeping inside, and you're not. Plus, there's the added bonus of being able to dash into one of the recently vacated rooms for a quick shower before the maid comes around.

Alternatively, the ordinary middle-class neighborhood can provide some of the best car-sleeping in America. A lot of people don't know that. The trick is to park on the property line so each homeowner thinks the other has an overnight guest. On the downside, if they happen to have an overly vigilant Neighborhood Watch, you might be looking at a night of musical chairs on a variety of property lines.

We caravanned down Florida's west coast, skirting a Gulf of Mexico we'd not yet seen. At Naples, we turned onto "Alligator Alley," Florida's 80-mile-long straight shot to Miami.

The Everglades were still showing the scorched earth of the previous summer's wildfire, the flames of which came within twelve miles of downtown Miami. Lightning fires had always been nature's way of clearing out old growth to make way for the new. The difference now was the city's expansion into the marshland had so compromised the fragile ecosystem that the recent two-year drought had caused 500 wildfires, many burning simultaneously.

Our plan had been to stop at the edge of The Glades and drift off to sleep to the soft chirping of cicadas. Of course, that was before we'd actually heard cicadas. Still, we'd no more than pulled over when a cop car skidded up like we'd just robbed The First National Bank of Swamp & Trust. After a stern lecture on crocodiles and panthers and pythons—*oh my!*—we were given a police escort to the home of a hot little Fort Lauderdale divorcee who not only put us up for the night, but made us waffles the next morning.

And then, we drove on.

Miami, Florida

IT WAS CLEAR from our first glimpse of Miami that God could not possibly want us to live in this messy metropolis of leather-skinned retirees cremating in whatever sliver of sun managed to filter through the plethora of high rises.

We drove beneath the thundering din of incoming snowbirds to the neighborhood of Little Havana. But where were the Cuban exiles rolling their own cigars in sunny sidewalk cafes pulsing with Latin rhythms? The spicy Carmen Miranda types downing tiny cups of searing coffee? The children slurping ice cream in flavors of mango and pineapple? Instead, we found two commercial arteries, far too wide to pop across every time we saw a random, "English Spoken Here" sign.

And so, we drove on.

Florida Keys

RESUMING OUR SEARCH for our perfect winter home, Cherie and I headed down Overseas Highway, through a string of small, sparsely populated islands tumbling off the mainland.

Finding Key Largo nothing like the 1948 Humphrey Bogart/Lauren Bacall movie of the same name, we drove on. Yet, every key proved to be little more than a smattering of ramshackle bait shops and trailer parks. It was like driving the same stretch of

Journey of a Teetotaling Virgin

the half-road/half-bridge in an endless loop. The only change was that the further south you went, the longer the bridges and the smaller the islands.

It was dusk when we came across a hippie camp set up on a narrow strip of land with beach visible on both sides of the road. We parked amid a cluster of vans painted with sunflowers and peace symbols. There were dented cars littered with trash, including one with a "Honk if You Love Jesus" bumper sticker.

The dozen or so longhairs in tie-dye tee-shirts were happy to share their campfire offering of dumpster-rescued vegetables, even including us in their passing of a stubby, hand-rolled cigarette that smelled nothing like tobacco. It might not be exactly our Florida fantasy, but at least it was one we could afford.

That night, Cherie and I retired, her to her Z and me to Mrs. Turner. Then at midnight came the rain. The lightning. The thunder. It was like trying to sleep in an exploding carwash.

At first light, came the sound of engines sputtering to life. I peeked out and watched our new best friends drive off through the drizzle without so much as a "See ya."

"Breakfast?" Cherie called, rolling down her window just enough to get her mouth out sideways.

"You got it!"

And then, I drove north instead of south. And Cherie followed, because she's just how directionally-challenged she is.

By the time we found a diner, I had my speech all worked out. We'd come a quarter of the way to Key West, said to be the jewel in this crown of keys. But what if it wasn't? What if we drove all the way there just for a different collection of hippies, and bait shops? Plus, with gas a whopping 35¢ per gallon, now with us in two vehicles, could we really afford to explore the entire 1,350 miles of Florida's coastline? I voted we head on back and check out the west coast of the Sunshine State.

I expected a fight. "God wants us to live in Key West," Cherie would probably say. Although how she'd come up with this conclusion was anyone's guess, except that it was her latest brain-fart.

Amazingly, Cherie agreed with me.

And so, we drove on.

Chapter 11
Sunshine & Showers

<u>February 16 - April 15, 1973</u>
**Vietnam:* Last POWs released, including John McCain *Watergate:* WH Counsel John Dean flips *In Other News:* "Black September" terrorists occupy Saudi Embassy; Marlon Brando refuses the Oscar in protest of treatment of American Indians; World Trade Center opens *On TV:* Laugh-In ends; Premiere of The Young & the Restless *On the Radio:* Roberta Flack's "Killing Me Softly with His Song;" Vicki Lawrence's "The Night The Lights Went Out In Georgia" *Bands Behaving Badly:* John Lennon & Yoko Ono form a new country without laws & boundaries, national anthem is silence*

Sarasota, Florida

EVERYTHING ABOUT Sarasota was idyllic. The compact little downtown had a lazy, spacious feel to it, as if taking nourishment from the farms and orange groves surrounding it. Turn-of-the-century Mediterranean and Spanish villas were everywhere, many incorporating the art deco theme of the 1930s. John Ringling's Venetian palace sat proudly on Sarasota Bay, a boat-shaped cottage peeked out of a downtown orange grove, and the terra cotta-glazed high school could've passed for an English prep school. Most impressive of all, the First Baptist Church's blindingly white steeple made almost you want to worship.

"*Perfecta-mundo!*" Cherie and I yelped in unison, out our respective windows.

We parked downtown, shoved a few nickels in the meters, and settled into a booth in a spaciously airy diner called Fatstuff's.

The eatery with the long glass window overlooking Main Street was named, or at least should've been, for its owner, John, who looked like he personally tasted every hoagie just to make sure it wasn't poisoned. The robust Italian took our order, stopped by a back booth to play his hand in a game of bridge, tussled the heads of four kids playing Jacks on the linoleum floor, greeted a couple of Sarasota Players dropping off theater tickets, and was back in the kitchen in time to flip our sliced sirloin on the grill.

By the time our shared $2 cheesesteak—drizzling with grilled peppers, mushrooms, and sweet Spanish onions—arrived, Cherie and I were deep into the classifieds.

"You gals looking for a job?" asked John. I was up and grabbing a smock off the rack before Cherie had even laid down her pen.

"One-bedroom condo," she read as I bounded by with a tray full of red plastic baskets. "Bay view. Boat docking. Heated pool."

"Awesome!"

"Seventy-five bucks."

"Outta sight!"

"Per week."

"Bummer!"

"Order!" John called from the kitchen.

"Check this one out," said Cherie on my next pass. She twirled the paper around and there was one lone item circled in black magic marker, arrows pointing at it from all directions.

Store or office
2 rooms paneled
$70 per month

"I think God wants us to live in an office," said Cherie.

"Doesn't God want us to take showers?"

"God wants us to live indoors first, think about showers later."

AT 5 O'CLOCK, we exited Fatstuff's, tore up our respective parking tickets, and drove over to 6th Street and Mango. The six-unit strip mall was a combination of offices and workshops, half with aluminum roll-down doors, and half with ordinary office doors. All looked vacant.

"What'cha think?" asked Cherie, studying the single-story structure.

"I think God's got some 'splainin' to do."

A 1956 Ford pickup pulled into the parking lot across the street. An old man got out, patted the black lab in the truck bed, pulled out a wad of keys and started shoving them, one by one, into the lock of Unit #3.

Figuring it was unlikely anyone would rent to two random hippie chicks, Cherie and I decided on a semi-plausible ruse. The story was that she was a hotshot literary agent, looking for a place for her equally hotshot best-selling author/client, aka me. Since this involved a whole lot of lying, it fell into the category of things Cherie was so good at that I never bothered to compete.

Cherie greeted the old man and followed him inside. Ten minutes later, she was back, pressing $140 in $1 bills into the old man's hand.

Cherie had no more than climbed into Mrs. Turner than the story came tumbling out. How she'd strolled around the dingy 20 by 20 square foot space with the intensity of Smokey the Bear checking for forest fires. How she'd regarded the grimy floor like she was Mr. Clean, ran her finger over the dusty countertop like she was the White Glove Lady in the Endust commercial, peered into the toilet bowl like a wary Ty-D-Bol Man, then flushed it with the disgusted intensity of Josephine the Plumber. Then Cherie turned to our future landlord and declared, "Perfect!"

"So, we got the place?"

"Darn tootin'. The guy would've rented to a crocodile if it'd shown up with first-and-last clenched between its teeth."

Moving in didn't take long. We tossed in our beanbag chair, filled our water-blob from the outside hose, salvaged a wooden cable spool to use for a table, and snagged a couple of plastic lawn chairs from someone's trash. As for a shower, the outside hose would do in a pinch, and for a more thorough scrub-down—hair-washing, leg-shaving, etc.—there was always the free cold-water showers at the beach.

MY JOB AT Fatstuff's lasted only as long as it took to get my first paycheck. Sixteen dollars for a 20-hour week just didn't cut it. Not when I was racking up $1.20 per day in parking tickets. Not that I intended on paying my parking tickets, but still.

The problem was, although 1966's Minimum Wage Act guaranteed an hourly rate of $1.60, waitstaff got just half that, the remainder expected to be ponied up by grateful customers too lazy to go to the kitchen to pick up their own danged meals. And so, I waved a sad goodbye to John, his four Jacks-playing kids, the bridge game in the back booth, and the special appearances by the Sarasota Players.

And then, I went looking for another job.

Thankfully, there were plenty of employment opportunities in a town where 90 percent of the population was over 65. I was hired at Martine's, one of several elegant restaurants competing for the senior dollar along Tamiami Trail, the 275-mile roadway running between Tampa and Miami.

With its dark-paneled dining room and mahogany tables, Martine's offered complete dinners of prime rib, steak, seafood, roast, casseroles and lamb, along with unlimited trips to the salad bar—all for the low, low price of $2.95. And although the Early Bird Special was just $1.95—the same as a Fatstuff's cheesesteak—as it turns out, customers felt far more compelled to tip when their meals didn't arrive in red plastic baskets.

The thing I liked least about Martine's was the uniform, undoubtedly designed to trick patrons into thinking their waitress was actually a waiter. The ensemble consisted of a white shirt, black jumper, black bow tie, nurse's shoes, and black hairnet, with not even a wisp of curl encircling the ear.

As for Cherie, once again, she won the employment sweepstakes by scoring a gig as a cocktail waitress at the most happening place in town, Holiday Inn's Roof Garden Supper Club on Lido Key. Not only was this lively piano bar a magnet for well-heeled, young regulars—any one of which could've danced professionally—but Cherie got to wear crop tops and mini-skirts, the mini-er, the better. She had only to sashay up to a table, flip her long pale locks and purr, "Who's got the drink in the funny glass with the olive?" to get a tip and often a date.

I WAS HEADED to Martine's for another day of finagling quarters out of the pockets of frugal geriatrics, when a blonde Adonis dodged traffic as he bounded across Tamiami, seemingly oblivious to the fact that I was dressed in Martine's penguin-inspired uniform at the time.

"I'm young! You're young! Let's date!" was Hal's heartfelt pickup line. It was the kind of come-on that could only work in Sarasota. But work in Sarasota, it did.

Like most Floridians, Hal had come out golden-brown at birth. His naturally blonde hair was enhanced by a popular product called Sun In, which was pretty much lemon juice in a spray bottle. Hal had one of those post-high school football bodies that looked like it'd probably go to seed by the time he was thirty. But I didn't care because I'd be long gone by the time he was 25.

When I told Cherie about Hal, she got wildly excited. Far more thrilled than when I normally announced another float in The Boyfriend Parade.

"I wanna meet the guy," she announced.

"Not sharing another boyfriend, pal."

"You're so cynical. I just wanna make sure he's good enough for my bestie."

The next time I went to Hal's, Cherie came along. She was barely through the door when she asked to use the "little girls' room." Hal pointed and she disappeared down the hallway.

Cherie was gone an awfully long time. Thinking she must have fallen in or was in dire need of a Tampon, I was about to go looking when she emerged in one giant fluffy towel, her wet hair wrapped in another.

"You dirty dog!" I seethed.

"Not no more," she shot back.

MY DISCOVERY OF Hal the Heartthrob's Major Flaw came during our first and only make-out session. We were going at it pretty hot and heavy when I heard a distinct click-click-clicking, clearly audible over "Saturday in the Park," blasting from the hi-fi.

At first, I thought it was the soundtrack. But *nooo*. As it turned out, when the record stopped, the click-click-clicking continued on. And then, when he went to flip over the album, the clicking went with him. And then, when Hal returned, so did the clicking; albeit at a far slower pace than when he left.

We got going again and then I noticed the clicking had picked up to a high-speed rat-a-tat-tat.

"It's you, you son of a biscuit! You're the gol-dern clicker!"

Yes, indeed. As it turned out, Hal the Heartthrob had an artificial heart valve, the result of a motorcycle accident when he was sixteen. Hal assured me he wasn't going to die, at least not anytime soon. Which was completely unnecessary since I didn't need a stethoscope to check the state of his ticker. Still, I'm not pretending it wasn't weird to be fooling around with a guy that sounded like a toy helicopter might explode from his chest and go flapping around the room.

Bottom line, Hal's artificial heart valve put the kibosh on the whole romantic vibe. That's the thing about Major Flaws. You never see them coming.

THE FIRST OF February, I invested in a small box of cards. And on each, I painstakingly typed out the following alert.

This is to announce
the 24th consecutive annual
BIRTHDAY of Fay Cheryl Faron
on February 27th, 1973, in Sarasota, Florida

P.S. Your presents would be appreciated even

if your presence cannot be.

I sent this notice to everyone I thought might be good for a couple of gifts. Mom and Dad. Gram. Even my brother and his wife, although that was a long shot since they were traditionally too busy buying stuff for themselves to think of anyone else.

Perfect wrote back...

> *"Fayette,*
> *"I am in receipt of your gracious invitation. And while your appreciation of my presence is appreciated, you are no doubt also appreciative of the appreciable distance & difficulties involved in my arrival, given the erratic nature of my vehicle. In closing, may I say, I'd be delighted to attend, however, if I do not arrive in time, go ahead without me.*
> *I remain appreciatively yours.*
> *You Know Who"*

I even sent an invitation to BellSouth Bobby, figuring any guy who'd thrust thirty bucks in my direction might be good for a couple more. He wrote back, his letter penned in red ink, written on a sheet torn from a spiral notebook and stuffed into an envelope, the kind with the 11¢ stamp already printed on it.

> *Hello Baby,*
> *I don't know where to start. So much has happened. I'm not sure what I said yesterday in in the letter I wrote because I was drunk. I almost didn't mail it but decided I should. So I did, even without reading it.*
> *It's hard for me to write. I have to be able to see your face and know that when I say, 'I love you,' it's what you want to hear. If it isn't, it becomes a burden. Or a weapon. I know it would never be a weapon with you, but it might be a burden.*

The truth was Bobby's love *was* a burden. I realized now I should never have written him when we first got settled. He answered almost immediately, sending me money and instructing me to call. Which I did, not when he told me to, but a few days later in hopes of not connecting. When I didn't try again, I got this.

> *Legs,*
> *You really did a good job of making me mad when you didn't call Friday. You still have my love. If you want it. If not, screw you.*
> *Call me. You've got the number.*

My plan was to write less and less, call when I was pretty sure he wouldn't be there, in an effort to ease out of the default relationship without hurting his feelings.

Actually, I thought our uncoupling was going rather well until he showed up. I was getting ready for work when I heard a vehicle skid to a stop just outside. I peeked out and there was BellSouth Bobby, smiling at Mrs. Turner like they were old friends.

My first thought was to flee. Except how? The only door was the one at which he was knocking. The only other exit was through the bathroom window, far too small to squeeze through. And even if I did, Bobby was parked beside Mrs. Turner, so there was no way I could slip past him.

Slowly, I pushed open the door. On the step was a pink bakery box, inside my favorite snack, Hostess Twinkies. Twenty-four of them, one for every year I'd been alive.

Awwww.

"Hubba hubba!" called Bobby, popping out from behind his van. In an instant, he was swinging me around like he was Fred Astaire and I was Ginger Rogers, made all the more pathetic given I was dressed more like Fred than Ginger at the time.

No way was BellSouth Bobby coming to live with us. On that Cherie and I agreed. He slept on our beanbag chair the first night, and the next day, went out and rented a yellow and orange dome tent in someone's back yard for, you guessed it, $25 a week.

Bobby seemed to have plenty of money; much of it in quarters, nickels and dimes, as happens when you rob payphones for a living.

Instead of looking for a job, he hung out with Cherie while I was at work and with me while she was at work. Which meant Cherie and I were spending more time with our boyfriend than with each other. Which is not how the whole best friend thing is supposed to work. Still, there was no denying the guy came in handy when it came to fixing our showerless abode. Even rigging up a garden hose over the toilet, which seemed like a good idea until Cherie fell off and sprained her ankle.

I tried to love him. I really did. "Love the One You're With," played the reluctant soundtrack of my brain. But I just wasn't feeling the vibe. There was no denying it. Perfect made my heart go pitty-pat and Bobby didn't. It was just that simple.

Meanwhile, we continued to *Do It* because as it turns out, once you've had sex with a guy, you have to keep *Doing It,* or he gets his feelings hurt. *Doing It* becomes the default. And if you don't want to *Do It*, you have to come up with an excuse like, "I've got a headache," or "I'm having my period." And there's only so many mitigating circumstances one can spew forth before the inevitable "relationship talk."

And nobody wants that.

"METHINKS Bobby's got the hots for your bod," said Cherie. We were on our knees at the time, painting the cement floor jungle red, curtesy of a can of paint we found in the closet. Well, most of the floor anyway. With the water-blob and spool table too heavy to lift, we simply painted around them.

You know, he's not a virgin," she said.

"I'm aware."

We were at opposite walls, painting our way inward when our butts met back at the water-blob. We'd just bumped each other out of the way when Cherie suddenly sat back on her haunches.

"Oh, snap!"

"What?"

"You two've done the deed, haven't you?"

Crap on a stick! I couldn't lie even when I kept my mouth shut.

"It was an accident," I stammered.

"What? It fell in?"

We squiggled out the door butt-first, literally painting ourselves out of the room.

"Real Live S-E-X?" asked Cherie, sitting on the stoop, her legs splayed out to catch the morning sun. "Just to be clear."

"Turns out, there's no other kind," I informed her.

Was I the only one who knew this?

Cherie was silent for a minute, her face turned upwards, drinking in the sunshine. Then, she laughed.

"What?"

"Nothin'."

"C'mon, spill it."

"Well, you know how everybody looks back on their first time. 'Oh, yes,'" she trilled, "'my dear husband and I did it on our honeymoon. We were on the Left Bank of Paris at the time.'"

"Yeah?"

"So, get this. Your first time was—wait for it—Unincorporated Jefferson Parish."

Criminy. This just gets worse and worse.

It wasn't a week later that Cherie decided to go home. She gave all kinds of reasons. Florida was getting hot. She didn't like serving booze at the Roof Garden Supper Club. She wanted a hot shower. But I knew the real reason. She didn't want to end up like me. Of course, I'd already ended up like me, so I had a lot less to lose.

"You and Bobby gonna be shacking up?" asked Cherie, as she packed up her Honda.

"No way, Jose. I've already gone back to being a virgin."

"Oh, please. Sex is the potato chip of life. Nobody can do it just once."

"Not me. I have scruples."

"Spoken like a true teenage mother."

"I'm not a teenager."

"Well, if you don't get some protection, in thirteen years, you're gonna be the mother of one."

AS MARCH marched on, I knew I had to tell Bellsouth Bobby we were breaking up. In fact, my next Grand Adventure was already in my sights, leading a bicycle trip through New England that summer for the American Youth Hostels.

I'd discovered hosteling on my first trip to Europe in 1969, staying in castles and cathedrals at rock bottom prices. As it turned out, New England had a network of equally eclectic and inexpensive digs, plus they offered bike tours for any teen with the stamina to pedal 25 or so miles between them.

Talk about your dream job. I had merely to take a week-long leadership course in Connecticut to be considered for this new career path. The problem was, the program didn't start until June, and although Florida was already blazing hot, New England was still blanketed in snow. And so, I decided to "Spring down" in Appalachia for a couple of months.

Now, I just had to get rid of BellSouth Bobby. I mean, what would be the point of going to all the trouble of finding a new job and apartment, if you arrived with the same old boyfriend?

My opportunity arrived when Bobby asked me to give him a haircut. Where he thought I'd picked up this skill, I do not know. Still, I'm a big believer that you never know until you try. And now I know. I definitely do *not* know how to give haircuts.

So, there he was. Simple, trusting BellSouth Bobby, lounging naively in his aluminum lawn chair in his yellow and orange, light-infused nylon gazebo, waiting for his makeover. I circled him, trimming his golden, shoulder-length locks while I worked up the courage to break his heart.

"I'm thinking of going to Appalachia," I said, nonchalantly. Bobby twisted his head around to look at me. I twisted it back and continued snipping.

"You didn't see *Deliverance?*"

"Nope, I read *Christy.*"

In case you missed either of these, *Deliverance* is a 1972 movie where some guys go on a rafting trip, and one of them ends up getting brutally raped by a bunch of inbred mountaineers. *Christy,* on the other hand, is a 1967 novel in which a good Christian girl, much like myself, ventures off to teach sweet little children who live in the pretty mountains.

"And then, I've got that bike-thingie," I continued.

"What bike-thingie?"

"I told you about that," I said, casually filling him in, trying to make it sound like a month-long bicycle trip through New England would be boring.

"So, when do we leave?"

Uh oh!

Distracted, I snipped a hunk of Bobby's golden locks that didn't need snipping. Thankfully, I was behind him so I could even things up before he caught on. Quickly, I clipped the other side to match.

"Don't you have to get back to New Orleans?" I asked. "Sell your Bug? Pick up your paycheck? Clean out your apartment?"

I continued snipping, buying time. The more I hacked, the worse things got. I chopped a chunk off the top, thinking this might improve the look. It didn't. That's the thing about haircutting. Practice doesn't necessarily make perfect. What it makes, is shorter.

Maybe I'm too uptight, I thought. My art teacher was always telling me to loosen up and let the creative juices flow. Following that advice, I made a series of random chops. Apparently, what works for art does not necessarily translate into cosmetology. Finally, I moved around to survey my handiwork.

"Hahahahahaha!!!!!!!" I shrieked, dissolving in laughter.

Trust me, it's never good when your hairdresser does this. Bobby grabbed a mirror, clutched his heart, and let out a little gasp. Which only made the whole thing even funnier.

Bobby hid out in his gazebo for several days and then went out to buy a baseball cap and never came back.

Well, that went well, I thought.

Chapter 12
Comeuppance of a Teetotaling Virgin

<u>April 16 - May 15, 1973</u>

***Vietnam**: 250 military & 8,500 U.S. civilians remain in Saigon ***Watergate**: Four senior WH officials resign; John Dean fired: Washington Post wins Pulitzer Prize **In Other News**: American Indian standoff ends at Wounded Knee **At the Movies**: Serpico; Paper Moon **On the Radio**: Tony Orlando's "Tie A Yellow Ribbon Round The Ole Oak Tree **Bands Behaving Badly**: Jerry Garcia caught with LSD*

Atlanta, Georgia

BY THE TIME I reached Atlanta, I was already finding Spring wasn't keeping up her end of the deal. Rather than backtrack into warmer weather, I opted to settle down in *Gone With the Wind* Land for the duration.

But where was Tara? Aunt Pittypat's white picket fence? The graceful old plantations? The ladies in white dresses playing croquet on spacious lawns?

Rhett Butler, for pity sake!!!?????

Instead, I found Atlanta to be a city of workmen pouring concrete into rib cages of high-rise steel skeletons. Of kerosene lanterns flickering over gaping excavation sites and street-corner evangelists shrieking Apocalyptic warnings. In this city that'd raised up both segregationist governor, Lester Maddox, as well as civil rights leader, Dr. Martin Luther King, Jr.—now under the governorship of Jimmy Carter—citizens were still protesting the 1971 federal mandate regarding school bussing. It was like the city was in the early stages of transitioning, and they weren't sure to what.

Always drawn to the most historic part of the city, I found my way to the site of the first Union Station, the one Confederates blew up to keep it out of Union hands, the scene recreated as a backdrop for Rhett and Scarlett's fiery kiss in *Gone With the Wind*.

After the Civil War, Atlanta became a transportation hub connecting the sugar and cotton plantations of the South with the markets in the North and East. Shopkeepers set up beside the railroad tracks, loading goods through their back doors even as customers came through the front. By the turn of the century, over a hundred trains a day were rumbling through Atlanta, virtually cutting the city in half.

To facilitate traffic, iron bridges were built over the tracks, and the shopkeepers moved their operations to their second stories, leaving the cobblestone streets, gas lamps, wooden posts, marble archways and turn-of-the-century storefronts to languish in a dim netherworld until Prohibition when speakeasies and juke joints moved in.

With the end of Prohibition, this city beneath the city, lay vacant until 1969 when two Georgia Tech graduates refurbished the abandoned candy shops, feed stores, fixture, furniture, and shoe emporiums into a retail and entertainment center they called Underground Atlanta.

Initially, the subterranean mall was a hit, in no small part because Fulton was the only wet county in a sea of dry ones. But then when neighboring DeKalb relaxed its liquor laws, Underground Atlanta dropped its strict dress code in order to compete. Thugs and transients moved in. Legitimate customers stayed away in droves.

The seediness of Underground Atlanta was a mere reflection of the inner city pulsing just above its ceiling of railway ties. Up top, hoodlums shook down bystanders at bus stops while shoplifters peddled their ill-gotten gains outside the very places they'd just vandalized and vagrants rifled the pockets of drunks passed out in the doorways.

And even though Underground Atlanta was now three parts Skid Row and one part Disneyland, the corner of Lower Pryor and Lower Alabama streets seemed like a fine place to peddle hotdogs from a wooden cart while my faithful, weenie-infused watchdog, Chum, lay comatose at my feet.

Job.

Check.

DIVING INTO the classifieds, I found no listings for apartments under $125 per month. Even with Cherie, that would've been a stretch. Without her, it was impossible. Then under, "Rooms for Rent," I found this:

> *Rooms for attractive, clean, quiet & refined bsnsladies. Lovely old Victorian. $12.50 a week. No pets.*

I soon learned "attractive" was a euphemism for "white." My lack of references didn't concern Mrs. Mollie, nor did Chum, since the poor pooch was banished to Mrs. Turner. I felt guilty, but she could either sleep there alone or toss and turn with me together, such was the housing situation in Atlanta.

Place to live. Check.

TO SAY I didn't like Atlanta would be like saying Scarlett O'Hara didn't care for carpetbaggers. I had no co-workers, no customers I wasn't afraid of, and even though my room at Mrs. Mollies' gabled Queen Ann had lace curtains and a pink chenille bedspread, I had nothing in common with my fellow *bsnsladies* aside from us all being white.

Mornings, I could be found in Grant Park writing faux-cheery letters to my folks, chatty postcards to Jack Easley, yearning tomes to Perfect, and scribbled notes to BellSouth Bobby, complaining how one could not work nickel-and-dime jobs, and live alone in America.

Hint-hint.

Fay Faron

Every day, I'd go down to the post office to see if Mom's birthday cookies had arrived. The Sarasota postmaster had *promised* to forward them as soon as I wrote with a good address. And although the cookies never came, I did get this from Perfect.

> *Dear Birth-Fay,*
> *I was on my way down to the FTD flower shop to arrange delivery of your present. Somewhere between the roses & the chrysanthemums, it occurred to me that my own birthday was not yet one month past & I didn't receive so much as a fucking card from you. Hence, I proceeded downtown & returned all the gifts to Tiffany's.*
> *Otherwise, everything is simply wonderful & all other hippy shit.*

SUNDAY NIGHTS, I always called home, a condition of My Grand Adventure Travel Agreement. Knowing if I admitted that Cherie had defected would result in an immediate recall to Phoenix, I claimed she was staying a few more days in Florida "to get her act together." My parents actually bought this, given the payphone didn't have visual capabilities so they couldn't see my nose twitch, as it did whenever I lied. Mom speculated Cherie was probably in love and I played along. But I wasn't "waiting, and waiting and waiting," as I claimed, because clearly, my friend was gone for good.

Meanwhile, the financial hole I'd dug for myself was only getting deeper. My $4 per day paycheck barely covered my rent at Mrs. Mollie's, let alone enough for me to move on. And then, just when I thought I couldn't be any more depressed, Chum ran away.

For three days I searched, by foot or by bike, in case she came back to find Mrs. Turner—the only Atlanta home she'd ever known—gone. The morning I awoke to find her scratching at Mrs. Mollie's window was the day I decided I had to find a way to leave Atlanta. With my only options returning to Phoenix or calling BellSouth Bobby, I phoned my generous benefactor. Collect, of course.

Boyfriend. Reluctantly checked.

BY THE TIME I headed to Appalachia, parts were falling off Mrs. Turner faster than kamikaze pilots over Okinawa. The first to go was the rearview mirror back in Sarasota. I salvaged it off Tamiami Trail, duct-taped it in place and drove to the Toyota dealer. When the mechanic had no screws to reattach it, my only option was to (a) wait for them to arrive from Japan, or (b) move to a city with a bigger dealership.

I was barely out of Atlanta before the heater knob fell off. By the time I crossed the Virginia border, the screws from the stick shift had disappeared into Mrs. Turner's littered floorboard.

It seems Dad was right. Japan was still out to get us.

Marion, Virginia

THE MINUTE I drove down Main Street, I knew I'd found my Appalachian home. In Marion, every 19th century brick building was an architectural wonder. The Beaux-Arts style Smyth County Courthouse. The Lincoln Theater with its golden fresco interior, patterned after an ancient Mayan temple. Even the Norfolk & Western Railway Depot with its detailed porches, hipped roof and dormer windows.

Then, there were the churches. In fact, this metropolis of 8,000 must've had more places to worship, per capita, than anywhere else in the world.

There was the First Methodist Church, the United Methodist Church, the First United Methodist Church and the Mount Pleasant United Methodist Church.

For outlanders, there was the Methodist Episcopal Church, the Mount Pleasant Methodist Episcopal Church, the Christ Episcopal Church and the Ebenezer Lutheran Church.

Conspicuously absent was any place resembling a cathedral or temple.

As for employment opportunities, there was nothing. Not at True Value Hardware, the Overall Factory, nor Parks-Belk

Department Store. The only place I just couldn't make myself go was the sprawling and creepy Southwestern State Hospital, which old-timers still called the "Southwestern Lunatic Asylum."

Bobby wired $30 to the local Western Union, which allowed me to respond to an index card posted at Piggly Wiggly offering a $12 per week rental on a Silver Streak trailer in a cow pasture south of Marion.

I settled in and watched the Smoky Mountains come alive in the Springtime. I spent my days hanging out on the steps of the trailer, reading and renewing my tan while Chum played keep-away with a dog and two puppies, stealing their ball and racing through the apple trees as they barked endlessly.

Every day I vowed to take photos, deterred only by the price of film. And every day, I'd be glad I hadn't because each day was more glorious than the one before. In the end, I took no photos at all.

But alas, my life as a trailer trash trophy wife was coming to an end since back in New Orleans, Bobby selling everything he owned in preparation for joining me.

I went down to the post office to check for my birthday cookies and found this.

> Legs,
>
> It looks like I sold my Bug. It's 10 a.m. now and they're coming for it at 12:30. I started with a price of $1,950 but I'm letting it go for $1,675.
>
> With any luck I'll have my van put back together & hit the road by Saturday.

AS THE SECOND week wore on, Chum seemed less her usual peppy puppy-dog self. And she was getting so fat. And her little teats were growing. It wasn't long before I could no longer ignore the obvious.

Chum was preggers.
Knocked up.
With pup.

Journey of a Teetotaling Virgin

I went to the library and learned the gestation period in dogs was nine weeks. Assuming Chum had Real Live Puppy-Dog Sex during her three missing days in Atlanta, she'd be giving birth in June, hopefully *after* the AYH Leadership Training course rather than during it on the dining room floor of the director's wife who'd so graciously offered to keep her.

Chum's condition got me to thinking. When had I last had *my* period? God forbid I should write these things down.

Back when I was an actual teetotaling virgin—instead of just playing one for my folks—there was no need to keep track of such non-events. When it happened, it happened. However, if I were going to continue my wicked, wicked ways—*key word, "if"*—then I really should get myself a calendar. Maybe even birth control.

Nah.

That would be like admitting I was going to have sex again. Which clearly, I wasn't.

Besides, if there *was* a baby inside of me, wouldn't I feel it? Have some connection to it? Would I not have some inkling as to when this momentous thing happened to me? Felt something different that time? For an event so life-changing, it seemed impossible I wouldn't know the minute it happened.

With lots of time on my hands, I began obsessing over my lack of spontaneous bleeding. I examined my breasts and thought, yes, they did seem a tad larger. But then, I'd never squeezed them before, so maybe not. They seemed a bit tender as well. But then, kneading the life out of them might do that. Without a full-length mirror, nor even a scale, it was hard to tell if I'd gained weight. But even if I had, I'd never consumed hushpuppies on a daily basis, so there was that.

Well, heck, it hardly mattered. A few more days and I'd get my period and all this worrying would be for nothing.

A FEW DAYS later, I found myself huddled in a sunny corner in the children's section of the Smyth County Library, sneak-reading a book with the mean-spirited title, *So, You Got Your Period!*

Although written for pre-teens, it was far less embarrassing than asking the librarian where I might find a copy of, *So, You Think You've Been Knocked Up!*

I turned to the section listing the various methods of birth control and the chances one could get pregnant with "normal usage" of each.

> *The Pill: .09 %.*
> *IUD: .08 %.*
> *Sterilization: .05 %.*

Quickly, I scanned to the methods Bobby and I'd been using.

> *No birth control: 85 %.*
> *Condom: 18 %.*
> *Fertility awareness—my so-called "rhythm method"—24 %.*

Okay, so there was a 127% chance I was pregnant. Still, I couldn't be. "It wasn't right! It wasn't fittin'!" as Grandma would say. Right before she dropped dead of shame. Still, an innocent rabbit didn't have to die for me to know God was never going to let me get away with having premarital sex.

"Penises go in, babies come out," sayeth the Lord.

As the days progressed, I started doing everything I could to jumpstart my period. Like actually jumping up and down. Taking scorching hot baths. Sleeping with the trailer door open, figuring the cold mountain air would freeze any living thing—quite possibly, including me. When all else failed, I took to drink.

Every couple of days, I'd slither into the ABC Store for a bottle of Thunderbird. Except Sunday, because Smyth County was dry on Sundays, so I drove 44 miles to Bristol, Tennessee, only to discover I couldn't purchase more than two bottles, so it was hardly worth the trip.

Still, by not planning ahead—and by this, I mean both stocking up on booze, as well as having protected sex—I was deep into miserable. I went to Hungry Mother State Park and rolled down a hill, purposely hitting every tree I could find along the way. I jumped up and down so much it felt like I was trying to jostle Ketchup out of a bottle. I stood on my head so long I nearly passed out. Nothing worked. I swear, I could have cut off my left leg and still not bled.

I found myself sleeping all day inside the trailer, too depressed to even go outside and enjoy the glorious Spring weather.

Pearly Gates, Heaven

I stood looking through the iron gate at the sparkling golden street that never needed polishing because nobody ever walked on it. Hitler was playing Three Card Monte with The Disciples, taking them to the cleaners since the game is a total con.

"You again?" snarled Celeste. "You can't just keep showing up without an appointment."

"It's called PRAYING. Isn't that what people are supposed to do in times of need?"

"Sorry, toots. You must've missed the whole, 'When Two Or More Are Gathered in My Name' rule. Come back when you've got a prayer-buddy."

"That's the POINT! I can't TELL anybody!"

"Okay, but make it snappy. These lines don't move themselves."

"Frankly, they don't seem to move at all. Does anybody ever actually GET into Heaven?"

"Watch yourself, little lady."

"I'm pregnant," I blurted out for no reason I can think of.

"Yeah? So, what'cha want me to do about it?"

"Make it not true!"

"You made your bed, missy. Now lie in it."

"Just for the record, I've never made a bed in my life."

"So, marry the putz! It's not like you can support yourself, much less some little ankle-biter."

"But I don't love the guy! Plus, my parents want me to marry some as-yet-unidentified Christian dude, not some jerk who robs payphones for a living."

"So, hide out for nine months, leave the kid at a fire station, then go home like nothing happened."

"I'm not doing that!"

"Okay, so have your mom claim it's hers. Let her raise you and the rug rat both."

"My mother's 52. She'll end up on the cover of Newsweek. *Look, I don't wanna go over your head or anything, but I wanna talk to God."*

"GOD? YOU WANNA TALK TO GOD!!!!????"

"Isn't that what prayer—"

"Okay, keep your tie dye on. Lemme just check the manual."

"There's a MANUAL? NOW you tell me there's a manual?"

Celeste pulled out two tattered mimeographed sheets, stapled together with the title, *"Unwanted Pregnancy: Best Practices."*

"When was that thing written?"

"Lemme see. Five hundred BC. New edition's due out any day."

"What's new about the new edition?"

"Roe v. Wade."

Marion, Virginia

IT WASN'T THAT I didn't want children. In fact, I intended to have a little girl someday. Maybe others, but certainly a little girl. A little girl with strawberry blonde curls and sparkling blue eyes and a sprinkling of freckles splashed across her button nose. And she would always be two, or three, or four or five, because those were the cutest ages for little girls.

But I didn't know her name yet because she wasn't a child yet. She was a future child. A pre-child. And being a considerate, obedient pre-child, my little girl would just have to go back to Heaven and wait until I could find and meet—and marry—her perfect father.

I couldn't believe it. It simply could not be that My Grand Adventure would end in a cow pasture in Appalachia. I felt like I'd gone off to find gold in California and my wagon train had broken down in Death Valley.

I gave myself three more mornings of rolling down hills. Three afternoons of boiling hot baths. Three evenings of too much Thunderbird wine. Three nights of tossing and turning. And then I called Bobby. And when he showed up, I was never so glad to see anybody in my life.

Knoxville, Tennessee

KNOXVILLE turned out to be even more depressing than Atlanta, if that was possible. At least Atlanta was *trying* to reach for the stars, poor dears.

In fact, as far as I could see, not much had changed since the city was named, "Ugliest City in America," in John Gunther's 1947 book, *Inside U.S.A*. Since then, Knoxville continued deteriorating as textile and manufacturing plants were undercut by foreign competitors in the 1950s, and its railway hub usurped by the highway expansion of the 1960s.

Bobby and I rented a room in student housing, just off the University of Tennessee, Knoxville campus. Every day, we'd drive down to Planned Parenthood, trying to wait out the protesters until it was clear they weren't leaving until the doctors did. Only then, would we slink back to our room in the 100-year-old Victorian mansion.

"Today's the day," I told Bobby, one rainy morning as we staked out the coal-smudged brick clinic from across the street.

"You sure you wanna do this? 'Cause you know I'd marry you. And I'm not just saying that 'cause I'm a little drunk from last night."

"Thanks, that's sweet. But let's try this first."

Our plan was to stroll nonchalantly down the sidewalk, then at the last minute, Bobby would distract the protesters while I bounded up the stone steps and into the second-floor entrance.

Everything was going as planned, even as I dodged a mama with dismembered doll parts safety-pinned to her apron. I took the steps like the Allies storming Normandy.

"Don't murder your baby!" screamed one militant mother.

Fay Faron

"Those docs are baby-killers, ripping off baby's limbs and disemboweling their little bodies!" yelled a kid with a crew-cut.

I kept going, even as a lady swatted me with her sign reading, "Thank you Mommy for Letting Me Live!" I could still hear her screaming as the glass door sucked shut behind me.

I tried to calm myself as I waited for the lady in scrubs to look up.

"Yes?"

"I'm here for the, uh, procedure."

"You have an appointment?"

"Can't you just work me in?"

"Sorry, miss. Counselor's gone for the day."

"I don't need counseling, I need a, uh, you know, un-do."

"Sorry, sweetie. You need to be made aware of any trauma you might suffer."

"Look, lady, I don't mean to be rude, but I've suffered all the trauma I intend to just getting in here."

"Still, we'd like to talk to your young man."

"I don't have a young man."

"You don't know who the father is?"

"Oh, I know who the father is. He's just not my young man."

The nurse said I needed to take a test to make sure I was really pregnant. I explained how God was never going to let me get away with having premarital sex, but she just chuckled and said that was hardly scientific proof.

I left, breached the picket line a second time and raced to the van, praying the whole way that I'd fall down and lose the baby.

"We need to find someplace more progressive," I told Bobby, climbing in Mrs. Turner. "Some place more urbane. Less South. Any big northern city's just gotta be more hospitable towards unwed mothers-not-meant-to-be than here in Knoxville."

"Like where?"

"I'm thinking D.C."

"I got $300 for the procedure, but no money for gas."

"So, we hitch."

Journey of a Teetotaling Virgin

BOBBY AND I caught a ride with a long distance trucker driving straight through to D.C. with the help of a bottle of "Black Beauties," the amphetamine of choice for long-distance truckers at the time.

Gus talked nearly as fast as he drove, his stories floating upwards and swirling around so long they seldom came back to earth. His C.B. crackled with talk of "alligators," (trucker talk for cops) "Bambi's," (blown out tires) and "bears in the bushes with a bird dog," (state troopers armed with radar.)

By mid-afternoon, the sky was as dark as my mood. A waterfall of rain poured down the windshield, shimmering in the oncoming headlights, even as thunder exploded around us, and lightning chased us through the long dark afternoon.

"Can't hammer up this hill," grumbled Gus, popping another black pill. I shot Bobby a worried glance. We were going *downhill*.

An hour later, the rain had morphed into a soothing drizzle. I laid my head on Bobby's shoulder, Gus turned up the radio and Janice Joplin joined our pathetic little party.

That's when I finally cried. But not for my pre-child, because she was going back to Heaven where she belonged. No, I was crying for the last nail in my coffin of a romance with Perfect. It was like we were in that Michelangelo painting, the one where the fingers reach for each other but never quite touch. But in the masterpiece, the hands remain forever yearning. In real life, Perfect was all but gone. Yes, he was still writing, but never with a hint that we'd ever see each other again.

I buried my head in Bobby's chest and cried some more. Because BellSouth Bobby wasn't my Bobby McGee, Perfect was. And "Me and Bobby McGee" was *our* song. Except Perfect didn't even know we had a song.

And then I felt the truck sliding. More sideways than forward. I pressed my feet into an imaginary brake pedal, but that didn't work any better than Gus who was doing it with the real thing. The front wheel slid over into a ditch, and the truck tipped—*thud!*—

onto its side. It came to rest with me sandwiched between Gus and Bobby.

For a few sickening seconds, I thought I was going to die. Obviously, God was not okay with babysitting my pre-child until I could find a suitable partner. And Gus and Bobby would have to die too because when The Good Lord's got a mad-on, He's not all that concerned about collateral damage.

We climbed out, all of us shaken and bruised. Gus flagged down a trucker and went off to find a telephone. Bobby and I dashed across the freeway to a grassy median between the highways.

We threw down our sleeping bags onto the soggy grass, and I trudged through the woods lit by flashing headlights as vehicles roared by on either side.

For the first time, I realized why girls called their period their "friend." If only my friend would come to visit *right now*, she'd be the best friend I ever had. I promised God that I'd *never ever* have sex again, if only my friend would show up with a Get Out of Jail Free card.

And then, it happened. For once, God actually answered my prayer. "Flo" did indeed come for a visit.

I never knew if I lost the baby, or I wasn't pregnant at all—and I never wanted to know. Still, I vowed to keep my word to *never, ever* have sex again. And if I did, to *NEVER EVER* enjoy it.

It seemed the least I could do.

Chapter 13
My Big Fat Phony Sewing Machine Giveaway

<u>May 16- 30, 1973</u>

Watergate: *Ongoing televised Senate hearings; Archibald Cox named special prosecutor* ***On TV:*** *All In The Family & Mary Tyler Moore win Emmys* ***At the Movies:*** *Day for Night* ***On the Radio:*** *Stevie Wonder's "You Are The Sunshine Of My Life"*

Knoxville, Tennessee

THE AD in the *Knoxville News Sentinel* read:

> *SALES TRAINEE*
> *$160 per week plus commission.*
> *Excellent opportunity for advancement.*
> *Must be neat in appearance, aggressive, have late model automobile, free to travel within 150-mile radius of Knoxville.*
> *Apply at Bryant Industries*
> *4638 Rutledge Pike.*

I was flying high when I called home to brag about my new career selling sewing machines door-to-door in Appalachia. I told my parents how Mr. Bryant had boasted I was the first girl he'd ever hired, and if I worked out, he'd be hiring plenty more "pretty sales gals." How I'd get $320 for two weeks training, and after that, commissions ranging from $30 to $50, depending upon the price of the machine. Plus, a $40 bonus if I unloaded more than seven in a week. Plus, if I had to stay overnight, the company would pay for my hotel room, meals, even gas.

Fay Faron

"The top sales guy, Cal—he's the guy who's training me—he makes $100 *every single day*. And he's two years younger than me and doesn't even sew so I might make even more!"

"Does Appalachia even have electricity?" asked my ever-practical dad.

I assured him that some people did.

"What about the bike trip?"

"It's not 'til June."

"So, you're going to let Mr. Bryant train you, then just up and quit?"

"Well, if it works out, I'll give up the bike tour. Or ask Mr. B. for time off."

"Still pregnant?"

What???!!!!

"Chum hasn't had her pups yet, has she?"

Whew!

"No. They're due in June."

"You expect her to give birth in the back of a Toyota?"

"Of course not. I'll be in Connecticut by then."

"So, you've told the lady who's keeping her—the director's wife, isn't it?—that Chum'll be having her pups on her dining room floor?"

I swear, my parents could be such bummers.

MONDAY MORNING, I met Cal at the Bryant Industry Headquarters, a single-story brick building with a parking lot built for thousands of customers who never showed up because, why should they, when Bryant Industries came to them?

Cal loaded eight sewing machines into the trunk of his shiny white Cadillac, along with a miniature, black antique looking thingamajig that looked like (a) something your child might use to make doll clothes, or (b) your great-grandma would've used to patch your great-grandpa's Civil War uniform.

"So how does this work?" I asked, flipping through his box of leads, each on a separate index card, all in different handwritings.

"You'se seen that drawin' down at West Town Mall? The one where's you ken win yo-self a sewin' machine jus' by droppin' yer name inna lil' box?"

I explained I already had a sewing machine. Or *did have* until I traded my half for Cherie's half of Chum.

Cal explained that on the day of the drawing, somebody won first prize. Somebody else won second prize. And everybody else won third prize.

"So how does Mr. Bryant make money, if he's giving away sewing machines?"

"That's where the jawin' comes in, sistah! We's off to see ever ignorant hillbilly ain't nevah been past the mouth ah the holler. And we be tellin' 'em that lil' gizmo they won, that ain't worth diddley-squat. Might as well throw 'er in the kindlin' box. But then, I says, 'the ole man back at the store would whup my hide iff'n he knew wha I'm about ta do, but I'd be willin' to knock a hundred bucks off'n one of them right fine machines if'n ya be wantin' ta be upgradin' from the little Black Beauty.'"

"The Black Beauty?"

"That's what we call it."

"But what if they don't want an upgrade? We didn't bring enough Black Beauties for everyone."

"Hells bells, gal! You gotta a war-sher missin' in that head ah yer's? Iff'n youse can't sell the hillbilly on the upgrade, you shorefire better back outta there with the Black Beauty, er Mr. Bryant's gonna dock fifty smackers right outta yer paycheck."

"But they won it!"

"Shore 'nuf did," said Cal, checking his teeth in the rearview mirror.

EACH DAY we drove further into the Smokies as we worked the closest leads first. We passed through Bean Station, Bull's Gap, and Strawberry Plains, along with similar clusters of aluminum-sided shanties, with plastic lawn chairs and Astroturf-lined porches. Every holler was more remote than the last, every house more isolated. Kids swung on truck tires hanging from Sycamore trees, mothers chased chickens around with brooms and muddy children banged through screen doors and old men sat on wooden crates, strumming their banjos.

For the first week, I was entranced. I loved being chauffeured through the remotest parts of Appalachia, and especially being invited into people's homes. Cal bounced his clean white Caddy through the muddy potholes like it was a jeep, all the while yakking about how Charlie Pride had found Alice Cooper's boa constrictor in the local Hyatt Hotel. And how Nixon had showed up at Billy Graham's Knoxville revival just before the 1970 election.

Amused in spite of myself, I watched as Cal shucked and jived his way to sale after sale. Making ten percent of everything he sold, the slick salesman in the pale blue bellbottom suit didn't hesitate to lower the price, even taking a cut in his commission rather than making no sale at all. Even more amusing, Cal never came close to dropping the Black Beauty.

In a slight-of-hand maneuver worthy of David Copperfield, he'd badmouth the little machine, then take it with him when he went to fetch a "real gol-dern sewing machine"—forgetting to bring it back when he returned. Cal invariably made the sale, but even when he didn't, the winner never realized he wasn't in possession of his prize until long after we were gone.

One day, we visited an old Black man in Tallassee who prided himself on having the biggest shack on the ridge. Cal played to his ego, pitching the top-of-the-line sewing machine until the man, with great pride, went to his special hiding place, gleefully returning with five $100 bills, which he proudly slapped, one by one, into Cal's sweaty palm.

I told myself this was a win-win situation. The old guy was obviously proud he could afford the very best sewing machine. And Cal, of course, was equally thrilled to have made the sale. Still, the guy's wife didn't look nearly as excited as she ran around putting buckets under their leaky roof.

By the end of the second week, Cal's charm was wearing thin. I couldn't help but notice he had no qualms about browbeating even the poorest, so-called, contest "winner" into purchasing a "real gol-dern" sewing machine. It was a game to him. A game he'd say or do anything to win.

As we drove deeper into the mountains, the log cabins became smaller, the roads ruttier, the piles of rusty vehicles ever higher. Old men in overalls sat on front porch rockers, sipping moonshine from glass bottles. Young girls hung laundry on ropes strung between trees as toddlers tugged at their skirts. Dirty cherub faces peeked from beneath mops of hair, their clothes too big or too small for their frames, their heads too large for their bodies, their eyes too huge for their heads. Everyone looked old, even the children. And there were so many of them. Five or six at every cabin we passed. It was as if their parents hadn't figured out what caused them, let alone how to stop more from coming.

By my final day of training, Cal's shameless pursuit of a sale had rendered me a companion of sullen silence. As much as I tried to tell myself that having a proper sewing machine would enrich these people's lives, I couldn't imagine how many of them could even afford fabric. Still, I continued to give Cal the benefit of the doubt, thinking if he ever came across someone who clearly couldn't afford one, he'd back off and let them be.

And then, we came to the poorest house we'd visited so far. The shanty's walls were papered with newspaper to keep out the cold. There was no running water, only a well. No indoor plumbing, just an outhouse. No heat aside from what wafted off the iron stove. I'd never seen poverty like this in my life, and by then I'd seen a lot of poverty—most of it in the last week.

In this cabin lived Mr. Gentry, his wife and their nine children. Mr. Gentry wore a layer of black coal dust which had permanently changed his skin tone to gray. Mrs. Gentry looked like she was sixty, which she couldn't have been, given the infant she carried in a sack across her midriff. Their oldest child was a shy and pretty 16-year-old, who could've played the Debbie Reynolds part in

Tammy Tell Me True. In a chair by the fire, Gramps sat coughing, bundled up in a blanket, his legs kept warm by the coal-smudged knee pads he once wore as he crawled through the mines. There seemed no future, nor even hope for this sorry little family.

I turned to Cal, giving him the hairy eyeball, silently imploring him to just let this one go. Where before, I'd given him a pass, there was no doubt pushing this man to buy a sewing machine would be beyond the pale.

"Mr. Gentry, sir! Seems like you'se done won yo-self a dadgum sewing machine!" Cal proudly held out the Black Beauty. When Mr. Gentry didn't reach for it, he set it down on the kitchen table.

"There's some mistake been made," said the gentleman. "I fear I didn't enter no sewing machine contest. I can attest to it."

"Lemme see," said Cal, pulling an index card from his box of leads. "Cassie Gentry?"

"That's my shining joy," said the proud papa, aiming his soft smile at the girl standing shyly in the corner. Her eyes fell to the Black Beauty and widened in delight. Mr. Gentry shook his head. "Never won nuthin' afore in my life," he muttered. "Reckoned I never would."

"Well, you shore as thunder done won somethin' now! Now, sister Cassie here, can sew her hind-end off iff'n she wants ta."

Cal kept at it, unmercifully badgering Mr. Gentry into swapping out the Black Beauty for a "real gol-dern sewing machine." Mr. Gentry continued to decline even as Cassie stood over it, petting the little gizmo like it was a kitten.

Cal didn't even bother getting the $500 machine out of his trunk. Disappearing with the Black Beauty, he returned with a $400 sewing machine. When he couldn't sell Mr. Gentry on that, he swapped it out for the $300 model. Then the $200 model. And finally, the $100 model. When Mr. Gentry still didn't bite, Cal started discounting the no-frills option even further. Lowering it to $75, his commission would be just $7.50. The polite and deferential Mr. Gentry still wouldn't bite. Nor would Cal budge.

Journey of a Teetotaling Virgin

"Why, Mr. Gentry, sir, Sister Cassie's way too purty to be goin' to school in them rags she's got on. With a right proper sewing machine, that lil gal could snag a feller right quick. Meanwhile, she'd be making britches an' bloomers for yer whole danged-gum family!"

By then, I was shooting daggers. Mr. Gentry could barely afford to feed his children. He had an outhouse. Newsprint for wallpaper. He couldn't afford fabric, let alone a friggin' sewing machine. Cal's shameless greed could no longer be rationalized. He had to stop. And yet he would not.

As we entered our second hour in Mr. Gentry's home, Cal was sweating so profusely I thought he might have a stroke. I knew there were just two ways this could end. Either Mr. Gentry would have to buy a sewing machine or he'd have to throw us out. And he was too polite to do the latter.

In the end, Cal wrangled $10 out of Mr. Gentry, with the promise to pay the remainder in monthly installments. The poor man figured if he didn't, he'd have two more mouths to feed. And he was probably right.

That night, I collected my second week's training pay, another $160. But it didn't feel nearly as good as it had the week before. By then, I could no longer rationalize that Mr. Bryant would make his money back on me. There was simply no way I could peddle sewing machines under false pretenses.

And yet, I had to at least pretend. Spend a couple of weeks knocking on doors, trying to make a sale in a forthright and honest manner. And since I'd now be paid totally on a commission basis, this would be a giant waste of time, not just for me, but my would-be customers as well. But what choice did I have? I'd taken Mr. Bryant's money and now I had to earn it. Or at least, pretend to.

MONDAY MORNING, I loaded six sewing machines into Mrs. Turner, along with one Black Beauty. I was driving away when I saw Mr. Gentry parking his old truck with the bumper sticker reading, "I'm a Proud Coal Mining Man." He got out, tucked the sewing machine Cal had sold him under his arm and entered the office.

I was so mad, I could spit. What a giant waste of everybody's time and dignity. And yet, here I was with a hatchback full of sewing machines, off to annoy the fine folks of Appalachia.

I drove to the first address, a Craftsman style house in a Knoxville neighborhood called Lindbergh Forest. I knocked lightly, and when nobody answered, turned and fled. I found the second house and knocked. Again, no answer. Well, this is going great, I thought. Eight more no-shows and I can go home.

Then, drat, at the third house, a woman answered. I'd tried to knock softly and run away quickly, but she was faster than I was.

"You don't wanna buy a sewing machine, do you?" I asked.

She assured me she did not.

"Okay. Thanks. Bye."

It was only 1 p.m., and I still had seven more "winners" to visit. But why bother? They probably wouldn't be home anyway. I'd just be wasting my time. And my gas, which was worth a whole lot more. Instead, I decided to go hang out at Shoney's, maybe grab a Big Boy hamburger, and then go back and explain to Mr. Bryant that I was obviously a lousy saleslady—*who knew?*—but I'd be happy to try again tomorrow.

And then, I'd do the same thing the next day. And Wednesday. And Thursday. And then on Friday, I'd explain to Mr. Bryant that it was official. I was a terrible, completely un-trainable salesperson—so sorry I let you down, but I just can't take any more of this rejection. I quit! That done, I could finally retire on my $320 golden parachute.

Then on my way to Shoney's, I started thinking about what a scuzbag Cal was for badgering poor Mr. Gentry. And what a scoundrel Mr. Bryant was for thinking up this phony scheme in the first place. But I had to admit, I'd been a jerk as well. I knew I was never going to stick around to sell sewing machines, so shame on me too.

And that's when I hit upon a plan to redeem myself. Or perhaps take my scumminess to a whole new level. I checked my watch. I could just make it there and back before the warehouse closed.

CASSIE WAS peeking out the screen door, watching as Mrs. Turner bumped along the rutty road, Chum with her head out the window, biting at bugs.

I found Mr. Gentry beneath his old truck, banging away at some broken thing. His boy of twelve was in the driver's seat, turning over the ignition as it screeched in protest.

Mr. Gentry slid out and eyed me warily. Acting braver than I felt, I walked toward him, the Black Beauty tucked under my arm.

"Here," I said, holding it out. "Cassie won this fair and square." He wouldn't take it, so I just shoved it through the truck window and set it on the boy's lap.

And then, I got in Mrs. Turner and drove away.

Fay Faron

Journey of a Teetotaling Virgin

Chapter 14
How I Spent My Summer Vacation

Summer 1973

Vietnam: Kent State Massacre case reopened **Watergate:** WH tapes discovered **In Other News:** John Paul Getty's grandson kidnapped in Rome; VP Agnew nailed for tax evasion **At the Movies:** American Graffiti **On the Radio:** Jim Croce's "Bad, Bad Leroy Brown;" Maureen McGovern's "The Morning After;" Diana Ross' "Touch Me In The Morning"

Bantam Lake, Connecticut

THERE WAS A man following me. A quarter mile behind, but his bike was keeping pace with mine and I was practically killing myself trying to outdistance him on the winding, Connecticut country road.

Because I couldn't be caught.

Well, okay, I could be. And this mystery rider, whoever he was, was certainly proving that. It's just that I mustn't be. Because if I were, I'd be tossed out of the American Youth Hostel Leadership Training Course and everything I'd been longing for would be lost.

I felt like I was in that 1969 movie, *Butch Cassidy and the Sundance Kid,* where the duo spent much of the film trying to outdistance an expert posse.

Butch to Sundance: "These guys are beginning to get on my nerves. Who ARE these guys?"

IN JUST a few days, I'd swapped the crumbling cities of Atlanta and Knoxville for Connecticut's winding country roads, white wooden fences and brown grazing horses.

Gone was the terrible burden of my pre-child threatening to arrive years ahead of schedule, along with the engineer of that particular train wreck, BellSouth Bobby. And thanks to my AYH leader's wife, Ruth, Chum had her very own cardboard box in the corner of her lovely dining room, just in case the pups arrived while I was in training.

Truthfully, life since college had been far more jarring than I'd anticipated. Back then, the world consisted solely of kids my own age, all dancing to the same tune. We all knew how far you could go on a first date and how much further you could go on the third. The girls all knew what sleeping on brush rollers felt like, and the boys knew the best way to avoid the draft was to stay in school and get a good education. Everyone knew where they were when JFK was shot, and how to hide under their desks during a Cuban missile strike.

And then—*poof*—I was out of college, and everyone was decades older. Or a different race. Or some other religion. In this new world, mamas sang to their babies on fire escapes beneath signs warning of falling bullets. Leather-skinned Floridians beach-baked by day, and under-tipped their waitresses by night. Mountain folk lived in papier-mâché houses and "never saw nothin' beyond the holler."

And even when I met kids my own age, they were selling drugs on an Atlanta street corner, skinny-dipping in a Santa Cruz Mountain pond, or cooking up roadkill on a Florida beach. All I had in common with them was our long hair and bellbottoms. If indeed, they were wearing anything at all.

At Bantam Lake, once again, my world consisted of kids my own age. Clean-living kids, just like me. Enthusiastic bike-riders, just like me. Travelers, who like me, were determined to see all of this world before going on to the next.

These were my peeps!

WHO WAS THIS GUY?

Perry? Nah, it couldn't be Perry. Perry hated me. Why would Perry be following me?

Whoever he was, he was too far back to identify me, just as I was him. But if he caught up, then he'd surely tattle to our intrepid leader, Bill Nelson, who'd made it perfectly clear that nobody was ever to ever ride alone. And yet, here I was, left behind by stronger bikers on the winding Connecticut country road.

And hilly.

Did I mention hilly?

Sure was hilly.

THE AYH COURSE was designed to teach the basics of leading a two-to-four-week long bicycle trip, mimicking as much as possible an actual tour, so that none of the kids would sneak off and call their parents, begging to come home.

Every morning, we'd do chores, a staple of youth hosteling. After a vigorous ten minutes of sweeping, mopping, washing dishes, etc., someone would be assigned to pack that day's lunch, someone else to plan dinner, and another someone to come up with a shopping list for the next day's meals. By noon, we'd all be biking around Bantam Lake, shopping for dinner on the way back, then cooking it up in the big hostel kitchen.

For classes, our leader, Bill Nelson, would spin tales of past leaders' challenges, solutions, successes and failures. We learned how to fix flats, manage our $10 per-day-per-kid budget, divide up the workload, apply first aid, pack saddlebags so the weight would be distributed equally between the wheels, even how to put up a tent blindfolded, just in case we ever had to do that in the dark. Evenings would find us roasting marshmallows around a campfire, Bill regaling us with tales of the early days of hosteling.

It was just after World War I when German schoolteacher, Richard Schirrmann, began taking his students on weekend outings to rebuild their sickly bodies. One afternoon, they got caught in a rainstorm, taking refuge in a farmer's barn for the night. The farmer fed them a dinner of eggs and milk, and a local baker provided fresh bread.

That night, Schirrmann lay awake envisioning a string of rough accommodations, close enough together enough that students could bike, hike, even ride a horse between them, all within a day. His hope was that by exposing young people to different countries and cultures, it would promote world peace.

In 1912, Schirrmann took a job as a curator at Altena Castle in Casslemont, Germany. Setting aside one room as a dormitory for girls, and another for boys, he created the world's first youth hostel. Other European nations followed, and in 1932, the International Youth Hostel Federation was born. It had one simple pledge. Everyone was welcome regardless of race, creed, or color.

That same year, Massachusetts schoolteachers, Monroe and Isabel Smith, escorted a Boy Scout troop to Europe, joining up with one of Richard Schirrmann's bike tours. They'd just crossed over from France into Germany when a group of Nazis took exception to the Black boy in their group. Quick-thinking Schirrmann sent the Smith's and the kid back into France while he and the others continued on through Germany. In the group that stayed were three Jewish cyclists the Nazis had overlooked—along with 17-year-old Bill Nelson.

It was Isabel and Monroe Smith who set up the first American youth hostel in a crumbling 99-room mansion just outside their hometown of Northfield, Massachusetts. "The Chateau," as it was called, was built by a wealthy New Yorker in 1909, for $2 million. The hostel lasted just a few years, the last guests sprinting for safety, even as concrete chunks fell from the walls onto their bunks.

The Smith's moved the fledgling AYH headquarters to a Victorian house on Northfield's Main Street. They were soon joined by 19-year-old Bill Nelson, who decided to quit medical school and devote his life to hosteling.

Bill searched out Depression-era farmers willing to turn their barns into dormitories and earn extra money by acting as house parents. Within a decade, he'd set up more than forty hostels, mostly in farm cottages and schools, but some in exotic locations like a historic railway hotel, a lighthouse, a donated boat, a turkey farm, a century-old church, and even a retooled boxcar graciously hauled across Canada, courtesy of the Canadian National Railway.

And, of course, the 40-bed Bantam Lake Youth Hostel that I was desperately trying to pedal back to.

ROADKILL!

Okay, I'm pretty sure Bill Nelson would never recommend closing your eyes while speeding downhill on a wobbly bicycle, but Bill Nelson wasn't here, now was he? Nobody was here, in fact. Just me and a country road and my cycling-stalker, never gaining, never falling behind. Still, keeping my eyes shut to avoid seeing roadkill while barreling down a hill at 100 m.p.h., I'd be lucky if I didn't end my days as one of Bill's cautionary tales.

I took a quick glance over my shoulder. Yup. Still there. Up on the crest of the hill, his long legs straddled over his ten-speed bike, black cowboy hat shading his face, peering at me through binoculars.

Binoculars? Seriously?

I used my downhill speed to get halfway up the next hill, just like Bill taught us to do. Rest at the top, he said, never at the bottom. Along with the "never ride alone" rule, of course. But I didn't rest at the top. Or at all. I couldn't because I had to outrun my own personal Energizer Bunny.

THE FIRST NIGHT in Leadership Training, introductions were made around the campfire. My Grand Adventure captured everyone's imagination, but it was Jack Easley who stole the show.

Time and again, the conversation would return to the pen pal I'd never met. There was endless speculation as to what Jack did for a living. If he was married. And if he was *still* married after getting a year's worth of postcards from a girl he'd never met. I assured them Jack was probably some old dirt farmer whose dreary life was made fleetingly more interesting by getting postcards from all over the U.S.

Before the week was out, many of my fellow trainees had pledged to send Jack postcards from their own trips as well. And that was how Jack Easley went viral before viral was ever even invented.

I liked everyone, but there was one guy who didn't like me. Perry. Perry was a 34-year-old swim coach at De Anza College, just 25 miles from where Cherie and I had lived in Los Gatos. Perry had driven cross-country with a leggy blonde who wore blindingly white Keds that never seemed to need washing. Perry's smile quickly dissolved when I asked if he knew my friend's mom, who also worked at De Anza College.

Turns out Perry was married. Just not to the blonde.

Oops!

I mean, what are the chances of hauling your new love thang all the way across country, only to run into somebody who knows somebody who probably knows your wife?

Okay, sure Perry hated me. But enough to stalk me? To do me—*gulp*—bodily harm? Still, somebody was following me. Never gaining. Never losing. Okay, sure I wanted to stay in the AYH Leadership Course; but what I wanted even more was to live! And, now with an empty canteen—another Bill Nelson no-no—this option might soon be off the table.

I took refuge atop the next hill and waited for Perry to catch up. I figured the least that could happen was that he'd rat me out, effectively ending my career as a seasonally employed bicycle tour guide. I just hoped he'd call an ambulance first.

It wasn't five minutes before "Perry" caught up. Except it wasn't Perry at all. The black cowboy hat belonged to 56-year-old Bill Nelson, not a bead of sweat glistening off his unlined brow. But rather than get angry, Bill gently chastised me for riding alone and then suggested we pedal on in together. Which turned out to be the best thing ever, because I got one-on-one time with a great man who was already a legend in the world of hosteling.

Journey of a Teetotaling Virgin

On our last day of training, Bill handed out our trip assignments. Happily, I got my dream itinerary. Four weeks peddling through Vermont, New Hampshire, Cape Cod, Martha's Vineyard and Nantucket. Thirty days. Six hundred miles. Ten kids. Room and board for the entire month of August, *plus* $300.

Praise Jesus! I died and went to heaven!

Salem, Massachusetts

HOME BASE for the month of July was my AYH dorm mom's 330-year-old cottage in Salem, thirty miles north of Boston, in the shadow of The House of the Seven Gables.

Jodie was a 40-something graphic artist with a wardrobe of baggy jeans, and hiking boots as sensible as her prematurely gray bob haircut. Jodie was the kindly aunt I never had. If the world were a hurricane, Jodie would be its eye. Her only house rule was to never scrub the centuries-old sink with Ajax, but I could live with that. After all, I'd never scrubbed a sink in my life, why would I start now?

My other best friend was my bunkmate, Babs, a striking 23-year-old teaching assistant who lived in a studio apartment in the North End of Boston. With her dark curly hair, porcelain skin, and bright blue eyes, she was the Veronica to my Betty. Eager to save on rent, we made plans to share an apartment in the North End, come September.

On weekends, the three of us would bike out to blustery Marblehead for clam chowder, chow down on baked beans at Boston's Faneuil Hall, even drive to Ipswich to consume one, two, three, even four-pound lobsters on a weather-beaten picnic table at a roadside shack. So enchanted was I with this never-before affordable delicacy, that I kept track of how many lobsters I ate that year, vowing to break my record each year of my life. Alas, I never came close to besting the seventeen I consumed in 1973.

It was in Babs' North End apartment that Chum finally gave birth to eight adorable Collie /who-knows-what-else pups. Having been conceived in Atlanta, I named them after characters in *Gone With the Wind*.

There was Scarlett, Rhett, Ashley, Melanie, Prissy, and Mammy. And because I couldn't recall Scarlett's sisters' names, the last two were named for the actresses who played them, Evelyn Keyes and Ann Rutherford.

The North End was Boston's oldest neighborhood, and a virtual time capsule of Old-World Italy. Anise wafted from Bova's Bakery on Prince Street. Homemade winemakers tossed their Zinfandel grape skins in the gutters on Salem. Old men sipped espresso in the mornings and red wine in the afternoons at Caffe Vittoria on Hanover. And lovers strolled the streets at midnight, confident the mob permitted no crime other than their own.

Then, just as I was packing for my trip, BellSouth Bobby showed up. When he suggested we bike together to Springfield—a two-day, 100-mile trip—for whatever reason, I thought this was a good idea.

The next day, we pedaled through the local roundabouts alongside thousands of commuters headed for Boston. We reached our halfway point at Sutton Falls, just before dusk. Too tired to pedal the extra mile to the campground, we pulled our bikes into the woods and collapsed, too spent to even put up our tent.

The next morning, we continued on through a pelting rainstorm that soaked us through our rubber ponchos and chilled us to the bone.

Finally, I just fell over in exhaustion. Bobby jostled me back onto the bike and we rode on into Palmer where we took refuge in a bright yellow bakery, wolfing down hot chocolate and warm bread without butter, pulling it apart and stuffing it in our mouths. And then, when the bakery closed at three, we pedaled through the rain the remaining 23 miles to Springfield.

Springfield, Massachusetts

SPRINGFIELD COLLEGE Camp Youth Hostel was nestled in a woodsy enclave on campus, just steps from Lake Massasoit and Forest Park. Conveniently located near the restored colonial village of Storrowton, the hostel's forty bunk beds were always in demand.

The next morning, Bobby pedaled off to the train station in Springfield while I nursed my hinny in a hammock, then rode over to the Jumbo Market to shop for supper. By 4:30, I was greeting my teens and their parents.

It was a motley crew. There was 15-year-old Mary, who spoke nothing but baby-talk. Her 16-year-old best friend, Susie, a girl so short she had to slap the pedals down and grab them with her toes on the way back up. Seventeen-year-old Mikey, who must have flunked anatomy because, clearly, he thought I kept my ears in my boobs. Fourteen-year-old Jimmy, who preferred the company of girls. And 18-year-old Lex, who was legally blind, but not to worry, said his dad, he could see shapes and shadows, so as long as he followed the white line, he'd be fine.

Uh, okay.

That night, we cooked up SpaghettiOs in the hostel kitchen. (The Jumbo Mart was not nearly as jumbo as its name suggested.)

The next morning, we checked the pressure in our tires, distributed our 40 pound+ saddlebags equally between our front and back wheels, filled our handlebar bags with canteens, snacks, cameras and suntan lotion, and pedaled north through the Connecticut River Valley beneath a tapestry of eagles coasting down to pluck fish from the river. All this against a backdrop of beavers vanishing behind dams as quickly as they appeared, and horses grazing behind white picket fences.

Thirty-two miles and a 430-foot climb later, we reached the Little Meadow Hostel in Sunderland, Mass. The next day would take us another 31 miles uphill to Guilford, Vermont. Thankfully, our next day sent us *wheeeing!!!* 13 miles downhill past white steepled churches, farmers in bib overalls waving their white handkerchiefs, and the magical Santa's Land in all its candy cane glory.

The next two days had us climbing 63 miles to our highest accommodations yet, the Gray Ledges Youth Hostel, on the ski slopes above Grantham, New Hampshire.

Now with our bodies strong, we had the energy to do something other than fall exhausted into our bunks each night. We explored the ice-cold creeks, the remote trails, and the quaint New England towns. And then, as a reward for all our hard work, we had a 28-mile-long gentle downhill slope to the Ragged Edge Youth Hostel in Danbury, New Hampshire. This was followed by a 3-day descent into Alton and Durham, settling at 49 feet above sea level, at the hostel at Ipswich, Mass.

It was on the last day of this long drop to sea level that the blind boy, Lex, followed the white line right into a pothole that sent him sprawling.

That night, I called Bill Nelson, expecting some folksy tale about how to lead a blind child downhill at speeds in excess of 100 m.p.h. Instead, my mentor declared the boy should go home.

By the time Lex's parents arrived at the LaSalette Youth Hostel, their son was regaling us with everything the rest of us had missed while we were so busy *seeing*. How he could tell when we were close to water by the slapping of the waves against the riverbank. How the apples smelled as they ripened in the orchard. How his upper lip tasted of salt when he sweat. How a slight shadow flickered across his face when a bird flew by.

And when Lex's parents took him away, it was as if we'd lost the heart and soul of our little group.

Boston, Massachusetts

BY THE TIME we arrived in Boston, we'd come an impressive 330 miles in eleven days. Pedaling past lakes and streams, over mountains and covered bridges, alongside churches and lighthouses, right through the heart of American history.

We spent the next two days in Boston hiking the Freedom Trail, paddling swan boats through Boston Common's Frog Pond, shopping along Newbury Street, and chowing down on Philadelphia steak hoagies in the shadow of the 62-story John Hancock Tower, waiting for its mirrored windows to pop out and shatter to earth, as they'd been doing ever since construction began.

Hyannis, Massachusetts

FROM BOSTON, we took the train 72 miles to Hyannis, the kids popping out at every stop to send postcards to Jack Easley. They sent pictures of sand dunes and salt marshes, of cranberry bogs and nesting osprey, of virtually every pond and marsh that lined the railroad tracks.

The "city" of Hyannis turned out to be little more than a circus of shopping centers, motels and billboards, part resort, part suburban sprawl. We settled into the hostel two miles north of town, then pedaled back to have a lobster roll picnic outside Hyannis' biggest attraction, the Kennedy Compound.

We easily found the six acres of prime waterfront real estate where Joe and Rose's nine rambunctious children once played football on the spacious lawn and sailed their yacht off a private dock into Nantucket Sound.

This first generation of the Kennedy dynasty had produced one President, one Attorney General, one Senator—and a whole lot of drama. So much, in fact, there was said to be a "Kennedy Curse."

It all began in November of 1941, when Joe Sr. ordered a lobotomy for his oldest daughter, 23-year-old "intellectually disabled" Rosemary, in an operation would leave her institutionalized her for the rest of her life.

Then in 1944, 29-year-old Joe Jr.—Joe Sr.'s first pick for President—was killed in a wartime plane crash. In 1948, the patriarch's second daughter, 28-year-old Kathleen (aka, "Kit") Kennedy, perished in a plane crash in the south of France. In

Fay Faron

December of 1961, Joe Sr. suffered a stroke that left him unable to walk or speak. In August of 1963, President John F. Kennedy, and his wife Jacqueline, lost their 2-day-old son, Patrick. Three months later, JFK was assassinated.

And yet, the curse continued.

In June of 1964, Ted, now a Senator, suffered a broken back and a punctured lung in a plane crash that left two others dead. In June of 1968, his brother, Attorney General Robert Kennedy, was assassinated while campaigning for president. In July of 1969, Ted Kennedy drove his car off a small bridge on Chappaquiddick Island, an accident which caused the drowning of 28-year-old Mary Jo Kopechne.

And then on the very day we stood peeping through the dense hedges of the Kennedy Compound, fate took yet another swipe at the family when Bobby and Ethel's 21-year-old son, Joseph P. Kennedy II, crashed his Jeep on Nantucket Island, leaving his teenage passenger paralyzed.

Martha's Vineyard, Massachusetts

THE NEXT DAY, we took the ferry 40 miles across the Sound to Martha's Vineyard. Twenty miles long and nine miles wide with a population of 6,000, the island's sparsely populated interior of hedgerow-covered stone fences, forests of oak and pine, and colonies of rabbits and quail could've passed for the Scottish Highlands.

The coastline of Martha's Vineyard was rimmed by sun-dappled sand dunes and scalloped by lagoons. The island's narrow roads connected Oak Bluff's gingerbread houses with the elm-arched streets of Edgartown and the old whaling village of Vineyard Haven. At its most remote point, the clay bluffs of Gay Head sat shrouded in fog like a gray hermit hunched over, his back to the world.

Naturally, we headed off to Chappaquiddick to check out the site of the infamous incident that had torpedoed Ted Kennedy's presidential aspirations.

Until then, the kids—all good little Kennedy-worshipers—had never questioned the Senator's claim that he'd simply taken a wrong turn to the ferry. Seeing how the dirt road veered off the paved one, it made it nearly impossible to buy Ted's explanation. The lively discussion continued long past when the last s'mores were consumed around our beach campfire.

Nantucket, Massachusetts

AFTER A MERE 2-hour ferry ride from Martha's Vineyard, we found ourselves on Nantucket Island, a 6 by 12-mile stretch of sand so remote its 4,000 residents referred to the mainland as "America."

We settled into our most impressive accommodations yet, the Star of the Sea Youth Hostel, an old Coast Guard station built in 1833. We spent our mornings playing beach volleyball, and our afternoons exploring cobblestone streets lined with weather-beaten dove-gray mansions built by long-dead sea captains.

Finally, it was time to make our way home.

Cape Cod, Massachusetts

IT TOOK US three easy days to pedal 47 miles up the spine of Cape Cod, following the Great Beach with its humpback whales rocketing out of the surf and sinking back beneath the waves under a sky of screeching terns.

Embracing Lex's lessons of evoking the full of our five senses, we *saw* old men with Geiger counters searching for coins hidden in the sand, and dunes littered with beach buggy encampments. We *breathed* in the saltwater mixed with the sunbathers' coconut and turtle oils. We *tasted* the striped bass, bought fresh off the boat and cooked up over a beach bonfire. We *listened* to the wind whistling through the tough meadow grass, a sound mingled with the tinkling giggles of children sliding down the dunes. And we *felt* the cool breeze on our skin and the shimmering eels swishing about our ankles in the bone-chilling Atlantic.

We barely had time to explore Provincetown's lively harbor, its specialty shops, colorful houses, white steeple churches and cartwheeling children in the park before boarding the ferry to Boston.

Giddily awaiting the sight of the city's sole skyscraper, the 52-story Prudential Building, we shared our hopes and dreams around cups of hot cocoa. To a teen, each was a different kid than had pedaled out of Springfield one month prior. Each having gained a confidence born from traversing 600 miles under their own steam.

Short little Susie announced she was going to try out for the girls' basketball team. Mary, our resident baby-talker, had her heart set on joining the debate team. Mikey decided to write up our trip for his school paper—I just hoped he'd keep my boobs out of it. But it was Jimmy who was up for the biggest challenge of all. After trying out his speech out on us, he decided it was time to tell his parents he was gay.

Chapter 15
Frozen in Place

September 1973 - April 4, 1974

> *Watergate:* "Saturday Night Massacre; Nixon named un-indicted co-conspirator in coverup ***In Other News:*** Psychiatrists declare homosexuality not a mental illness; Patty Hearst kidnapped ***On TV:*** Secret Storm ends 20-year run ***At the Movies:*** The Paper Chase; The Way We Were; The Sting; The Exorcist; Blazing Saddles; Mame; The Great Gatsby ***On the Radio:*** Marvin Gaye's "Let's Get It On;" Helen Reddy's "Delta Dawn;" Gladys Knight & the Pips' "Midnight Train To Georgia;" Barbara Streisand's "The Way We Were"

Boston, Massachusetts

FOR ME, FALL had always been the start of the New Year. It was when school began, each year arriving with an inherent hopefulness it would be better than the year before.

And it usually was.

As an eighth grader, I was less geeky than I'd been in the 7th grade. Achieving sophomore status meant I was no longer freshman fodder. And in college, each year I was closer to graduation day.

Or not.

Autumn was, by its very nature, a game-changer. And just because a person graduated—or didn't—didn't change that. For me, Fall would forever be the beginning of the Real New Year.

And this Fall, I was entering a whole new chapter of my life. The previous September, I'd arrived in New Orleans, naive and full of funds, only to be de-funded and de-flowered. Now, I was clear across the country, one in a city of 650,000 souls—two and a half million if you counted the surrounding towns—and just like the Pilgrims of old, Boston was my Whole New World. The only holdover was my boomerang boyfriend, BellSouth Bobby, who'd taken a job pilfering New England's payphones for a living.

Boyfriend. Still checked.

BABS AND I came by our North End apartment via the usual "Fifth Floor Walk-Up Scam." In case you are unfamiliar, the con goes like this:

1. The agent shows you a unit on the "second" floor of a 5-story building. (Which is actually the third floor because street level is considered, "0.") The apartment is nice and affordable and comes with a view of the skinned lambs and headless chickens dangling in the window of Paesanti's Meat Market across the street.

2. The agent escorts you up an additional two flights to a bigger, nicer, cheaper apartment which is *waaaay* better—in no small part because you can no longer see the skinned lambs and headless chickens dangling in the window of Paesanti's Meat Market across the street.

3. Delighted, you sign the lease, perhaps failing to mention your nine puppy dog best friends.

4. You descend behind the agent, high fiving your new roommate, gleeful you've outsmarted the landlord.

5. A few days later, you carry in—or rather *up*—your stuff, for the first time realizing that climbing five flights at a whack is entirely different than stopping for a look-see on the second floor.

6. You curse your rental agent upon realizing the "outsmarted" has, in fact, been the "out-smarter."

The only other person to fall for this con was our neighbor, Lynn, a busty student nurse who worked all week and slept all weekend and who we saw as little of as the non-residents in the rest of the empty apartments on our floor.

Apartment. Check.

ESTABLISHED IN 1646, the North End was initially an eclectic community where the wealthy lived alongside artisans, journeymen, laborers, servants and slaves. By the early 1800s, the commercial wharf had nudged the wealthy over to fancier digs in Beacon Hill, leaving the neighborhood to newly-arrived Irish immigrants fleeing the Potato Famine.

In 1849, cholera swept through Boston, causing one health inspector to describe the 23,000 North End Irish residents as, "a hive of human beings, without comforts, and mostly without common necessities; in many cases, huddled together like brutes, without regard to age, or sex, or sense of decency."

By the 1870s, Eastern European Jewish immigrants were pushing the Irish out to neighborhoods like the South End. Unlike their predecessors, the Jews had needle skills widely appreciated in Boston's burgeoning clothing industry. They established synagogues, schools, and social programs, replacing the run-down tenements with the four and five-story brick buildings still standing today.

By 1922, the Jewish community was moving on to new homes in Roxbury, Dorchester, Brookline, and Newton, leaving the North End to the Italian immigrants driven from their country by poverty, disease, natural disasters and political oppression.

The North End reached its peak population in 1930, 44,000 residents packed into less than one square mile—roughly the density of Calcutta.

Back then, the two commercial streets, Salem and Hanover, were ablaze with ma and pa groceries, open-air markets, butcher shops, bakeries, dressmakers, cobblers and shoe stores, many of which were still in business when Babs and I moved into the neighborhood. And although the population had dropped to a manageable 12,000, many of our old Italian neighbors still lived in cold-water flats, frequenting the public baths for their daily hygiene.

It was shortly after sneaking Chum and her 10-week-old pups into our 5th floor walkup, that Babs and I decided to sneak them out again. Truthfully, I'd have liked to have kept them, but what I wanted even more was shoes that hadn't been chewed.

Fay Faron

The puppies sold for $5 each out of a cardboard box at Haymarket. I know I should have used the bread to get Chum fixed, but I didn't. What I really should have done was to use the bread to get myself fixed, but since I was never having sex again, I didn't do that either.

Heartsick with empty-pup syndrome, I fell sucker to the following ad in the *Boston Globe*.

EXPERIENCED PROFESSIONAL
looking for a future with New England's largest purebred puppy specialist
Puppy Paradise
Apply in person, Rt. 9, Natick, Mass

I walked into the showroom, its walls lined with cages of pint-sized St. Bernard's, Basenjis, Malamutes, Chows, Siberian Huskies, Cocker Spaniels and Afghans. It was like a Disney movie called, *Lady and the Tramp Meets 101 Un-Dalmatians*.

"Experience?" I sang out to Mr. Rosenberg, the Groucho Marx lookalike who managed the store. "You want experience? I just raised eight pooches, and most of the time I wasn't even there."

Unbelievably, that line of reasoning actually got me a job as a "veterinarian" in what turned out to be a puppy mill.

(Of course, I didn't know that at the time.)

Job: Definitely!

Checked, checked, and more checked!

And so, every morning I'd (a) take Chum up to the roof to poop, (b) descend five flights, (c) climb back up to change my clothes, since the hermetically sealed windows gave no hint as to the temperature outside, (d) search around for whatever sidewalk I'd found to park Mrs. Turner, (e) check for slashed tires, and then, (f) drive the Massachusetts Turnpike 24 miles to Natick.

And even though my first two hour's pay went for gas and tolls, I was living out my dream as an animal husbandry version of TV's career gal, "Mary Richards." And just like Mary Tyler Moore,

I got to dress up in cute clothes—albeit mine were hidden under a white lab coat—and work with people—or in my case, critters—who I loved and who loved me back.

And so, I proceeded to spend my days feeding pooches, grooming pooches, sticking thermometers up adorable little puppy-dog butts, feeling cold noses, getting my fingers licked, and cuddling miniature samples of all forty-three AKC breeds God had created.

And although nobody ever visited my puppy-permeated storeroom, I still took great pride in my appearance, painting my nails a perky coral, and even wearing mascara and sometimes even lipstick. And for ten days, I was *happy, happy, happy.*

And then, one morning, I arrived to find my favorite pup, an old English sheepdog, dead in his cage. My screeching brought Mr. Rosenberg—not to join me in mourning poor dead Murray, whose increasingly frail body might have meant something to a *real* vet—but to hush me up so customers wouldn't know dogs died in our care.

Put him in a trash bag, said Mr. Rosenberg. Keep him in the freezer until garbage day. It's your job, get used to it.

Averting my eyes from Poor Dead Murray, I gave one last look to my loving Lab, my springy Spaniel, my dashing Dachshund, my glorious Golden Retriever, my impish Irish Setter, and my beautiful Basset Hound. And then, I dropped my lab coat on the cement floor, and walked out without notice and without even collecting my pay.

Perfect Job: Unchecked.

THE AD READ:

ASSISTANT TO THE BUYER
Excellent opportunity for individual with retail experience.
Position available in our ready-to-wear department.
Enjoy liberal store discount & Blue Cross/Blue Shield insurance
Apply in person to Gilchrist's Employment Office,
4th Floor, 417 Washington St., Boston

Gilchrist's Department Store was one of the "Big Three" retail giants whose curved entrances met at the corner of Washington and Winter Streets. But comparing Gilchrist's to Jordon Marsh and Filenes, would be like comparing JC Penney's to Saks Fifth Avenue.

Founded in 1841, Jordon Marsh was not only the oldest of the brownstone edifices, but at fourteen stories, also the largest department store in all of New England. It was Jordon's that invented credit accounts, the "customer is always right" policy, and money-back guarantees. Jordon's was the first store in Massachusetts to install electric lights, glass showcases, elevators, vacuum tubes, automatic doorways, block-long show windows, and radiant heated sidewalks. Jordon's held fashion shows, art exhibitions and afternoon concerts, even luring customers in with the scent of blueberry muffins, the aroma of which their bakery fanned out into the street.

But the best thing about Jordon's was Christmas when they turned an entire floor into a Victorian Wonderland, where 250 animated figures moved in time to music, and children raced from escalator to escalator, asking their parents at every turn, "Are we there yet?"

Once they reached the "Enchanted Village," the kids all lined up beneath the sign reading, "Good Little Boys & Girls," and were threaded through twenty-eight animated holiday scenes.

A schoolroom of twirling children. A church full of choir singers. A shoemaker pounding a boot. And a cowboy in a pay phone outside a barnyard of horses, goats, cows, and chickens. There was a snowman bowing deeply to reindeer marching sprightly in place, and eight Lionel trains running through it all.

And at the end of all this, jolly old St. Nick waited beneath a 20-foot-tall Christmas tree, eager to hear the children's wishes. That done, parents and kids would be escorted through the door marked, "Entrance to Toyland," to repay Jordon's for their self-serving holiday benevolence.

Journey of a Teetotaling Virgin

Catty-corner to Jordon's was Filene's. Opened in 1881, Filene's ten floors catered to Jordon's same high-end customer, but with a unique marketing gimmick.

In 1908, the company adopted an automatic markdown system for merchandise not sold within the first thirty days. These items—not defective, nor of inferior quality, simply timed-out—were sent to its basement. This cluttered, no-frills cavern lacked proper dressing rooms, leaving ladies to strip down in the aisles in full view of the subway stop that opened right into the store. What didn't sell at Filene's Basement was sent to their even more chaotic sub-basement. And after thirty days there, the unsold items were given to charity.

Like Filene's, Gilchrist's had a bargain basement, albeit smaller, and nestled between the appliances, TVs, and stereos. Like Jordon's, it had a bake shop, the Marble Spa and Bakery, famous for its two for 25¢ almond macaroons, which included a Coke, coffee, or tea. And like both Jordon's and Filenes, Gilchrist's sold everything from apparel, to cosmetics, to home decor, to snowblowers.

But Gilchrist's had one thing Jordon Marsh's and Filene's did not.

Me.

And while, "Assistant to the Coat Buyer" might have sounded impressive, my new job might more accurately have been called, "Company-Keeper to the Coat Buyer." Or even, "Coffee-Fetcher for the Coat Buyer." Still, I was *happy, happy, happy,* in no small part because of the 30% employee discount on everything in the store.

My boss, Mr. B., was a natty Jewish gent of sixty, with a wife so similar in size and style, they might've been mistaken for kitschy salt and pepper shakers at a bar mitzvah. Our conversations were cordial, somewhat formal and thoroughly professional. In fact, we hardly spoke at all, because we had absolutely nothing in common. Truthfully, my boss seemed so flummoxed by my existence, I often

Fay Faron

found him staring at me like I was a space alien requiring endless speculation.

Our most intense interaction came when he'd try to teach me some retail whatnot like inventory or book-balancing. Sadly, these monthly tasks were largely forgotten by the time I had to do them again.

But did I care? Heck no! I got to dress up in cute outfits, walk to work through Haymarket, and have a career in fashion at the most exciting MBTA stop in Boston, Downtown Crossing.

WITH BOSTON'S warm weather as gone as the Columbus Day Parade, there wasn't much to do in the dark afternoons except shop, eat and sleep—the latter being the only thing I could actually afford. And so, I applied for a hostess job at an Italian bistro at the foot of the Charlestown Bridge, catty-corner from Boston Garden.

The ad read:

HOSTESS WANTED
Two nights a week. Elegant working environment.
Apply in person at Polcari's Restaurant,
283 Causeway St., North End, Boston

Mr. John Polcari hired me to assist Paddy, the dashing Irish maître d', seat customers on the nights the Bruins and Celtics played at nearby Boston Garden.

Twice a week, fans would arrive one hour before the game, all expecting to be fed and out the door by start time. On these nights, Paddy, in his tuxedo, and me in my Gilchrist's employee-discounted hostess gown, would welcome our "guests" into our "home" as if we were some magical couple who lived in a glittering corner bistro.

And while it was Paddy who pocketed all the tips, still, I was *happy, happy, happy,* not only because I had a giant crush on the Gene Kelly-lookalike, but because my employee meals consisted of plentiful helpings of Northern Italian specialties like Mussels, Linguini, Shrimp Scampi and Veal Piccata. Delicacies I'd never have been able to afford on my own.

BY JANUARY, Boston's red and gold foliage had burned itself into twigs, leaving behind a world of gray skies and sloshy streets. By the time I got off work at Gilchrist's at five, I'd find myself trudging to Polcari's in the dark.

Always broke, despite my two minimum-wage jobs, most days, I'd eat lunch at my desk, with a weekly treat of Welsh rarebit at the Harvest House.

Every time it snowed, I'd stomp into work and wail, "I can't believe people live in this stuff! I quit!" And every time, Mr. B. would talk me off the cliff, including the time the wind turned my umbrella inside out and threatened to take me away like a hijacked Mary Poppins.

Eventually, Mr. B. and I settled into a kind of grandfather/granddaughter relationship. Giggling in spite of himself, he'd prod me for tales of how "the other half" lived. He'd chuckle over how I kept my clothes in buckets because I didn't have a dresser, and would quiz me as to the latest version of "The Soup," a stew Babs and I concocted from day-old vegetables from Haymarket, which we kept simmering in a Crock Pot on the counter.

It was February, when Mr. B. began taking me on his weekly trips to the branch stores around the state. He'd drive his big white Impala into work, and after lunch, we'd take off for Quincy, Brockton, Framingham, Medford, Waltham, Stoneham, Cambridge or Dorchester.

Thrilled to be touring Massachusetts on Gilchrist's dime, I looked forward to these afternoon jaunts. Out of the office, Mr. B. became downright twinkly. A couple of times, I could have sworn he was flirting with me, except I doubted that he knew how.

Still, as winter wore on, my life became as dreary as the gray skies over Boston. Was this how other people lived? Day after day, doing the same danged thing? Chopping ice off your windshield every time you wanted to go somewhere? Buying new tires whenever the neighbors slashed yours because your out-of-state car was parked on their sidewalk? Working a second job just so you'd have something to do after sundown? Having one boyfriend who bored you, and another who didn't give a hoot?

Grand Adventure?

Bah, humbug!

MEANWHILE, back at the boyfriend, Bobby was getting increasingly pushy about "defining our relationship."

"Have you even told your parents about me?" he demanded one evening at Regina's Pizzeria, a cozy North End pub tucked into a curved building at the corner of Thatcher and North Margin.

"I can't do that. They'd think we were sleeping together."

"We *are* sleeping together."

"Yeah, but you wouldn't want 'em to hate you, would you?"

"I want 'em to know I exist! And if you don't tell 'em, maybe I will. They're in the book, right?"

"No," I lied. "They're very private people."

I snuck a peek at Bobby to see if he was buying this. Dad was in public office. Chairman of the Corporation Commission for the entire state of Arizona. As such, he was findable. Highly findable. A mere phone call away.

Bobby just shrugged. He'd accepted this.

Holy moly. I'd lied and gotten away with it. It was a whole new day.

Still, in hindsight, I probably should've told Bobby right then and there, I had the hots for somebody else. But I didn't because Bobby was my conduit to the best pizza in all of Boston. And with men being paid 38% more than women, such extravagancies were nearly impossible without a sponsor. A boyfriend was just part of your stuff. Without one, you'd be eating sandwiches at your desk for the rest of your life.

At least, I had Europe to look forward to.

As fun as last summer's bike tour had been, Barb and I had always considered New England a precursor for leading an AYH trip through Europe, our second summer.

Then, one day, Bill Nelson called to say there weren't enough European trips to go around, and the few they had would be going to leaders with more seniority. And then, just when I thought things couldn't get any worse, Mom called, asking me to come home and take care of Dad and Gram while she went to Kansas City to close up my grandmother's house.

"Why can't your dad look after your grandma?" asked Babs.

"'Cause he doesn't know a pot from a pan?"

"Like you do?"

Complaining to my roommate about my humdrum life did no good but boohooing to Jodie was even worse. And that's because she'd just registered for a "life-changing" weekend seminar promising to provide attendees with all the tools they needed to unleash their "extraordinary human potential," through visualization, meditation, self-hypnosis and mind control.

This was so like my old AYH dorm mom. Jodie was always trying to improve herself, even though she was nearly perfect in my book. As for myself, I already considered myself well on my way to fulfillment, prosperity, and creativity—at least right up until those phone calls from Mom and Bill Nelson.

Until then, I'd been living my dream, working my way around the U.S. Making mistakes, sure, but quickly forgiving myself and moving on. And if there was something I didn't like about myself, I'd simply vow to just never do *that* again. What better template for "enlightenment" could there possibly be?

But in the end, Jodie got me, because there's really only one answer to, "Don't you want to improve yourself?"

"Uh, yeah, I guess."

"And if you don't like it, you can leave."

"Uh, yeah, okay."

"And there's pastries and coffee."

For a hundred bucks, I'll buy my own danged pastries and coffee.

"And if you leave in the first hour, you get your money back."

"Free pastries and coffee? Sign me up!"

What the Mind Dynamic brochure failed to mention was that you'd have to suspend your bodily functions for an entire ten hours, lest you pee the enlightenment right out of you before it had a chance to coagulate into your Extraordinary Human Potential.

And so, I sat squirming, half listening to how we were all "assholes," "losers," and "fuck-ups," but not to worry, we'd all be fixed by Sunday night. And then, I got this incredible sense of *déjà vu*.

Church! Mind Dynamics was like church! In church, you prayed to God. In Mind Dynamics, you prayed to yourself. The Bible had Original Sin. Mind Dynamics had Asshole/Loser/Fucked-up Syndrome. In the Born-Again world, only Jesus could save you. In Mind Dynamics, it meant having $100 in your checking account, and being able to survive a bursting bladder.

In the end, I escaped just under the magical get-your-money-back time limit by blasting out of my seat, stumbling over seventeen metal chairs and chasing the money changers through the hotel lobby as they scrambled to fold their card table, even as they ran.

That night, Babs drug in after a hard day of enlightenment, plucked the wine bottle off the counter and disappeared into her room. The next morning, she was up and out the door for another torturous day of chasing fulfillment. And yet, Sunday night, my roommate returned *happy, happy, happy,* having been cured of Asshole/Loser/Fucked-up Syndrome, as promised.

As it turned out, Mind Dynamics didn't last much longer than Babs' euphoria. Even as we sat squirming in our seats, California was investigating the organization for making fraudulent claims and practicing medicine without a license.

Guess I left before the happy pills were handed out.

Journey of a Teetotaling Virgin

IT WAS MARCH when my Polcari's job came to an end. Here's how that happened.

As soon as I arrived at work, Paddy told me Mr. Polcari was waiting for me in his office. I was a bit concerned since the boss rarely showed up, and when he did, all I ever saw of him was a shock of white hair as he glided through the hushed reverence of waiters, worked in his office for a few minutes, then disappeared as surreptitiously as he'd arrived.

"It seems you have an admirer," said Mr. P., busying himself with some papers on his desk. Mr. Polcari never made eye contact, which made him practically impossible to flirt with.

"Secret or otherwise?" I flirted, nonetheless.

"Dangerous," was the category he offered instead.

It seems I'd caught the eye of Lennie the Cat, one of seven brothers making up New England's top crime family.

The North End residents' usual hangout was Francesca's Restaurant, given its upstairs dining room was far less conducive to drive-by shootings. But for whatever reason, on this particular night, they decided to throw caution to the wind and frequent Polacari's glass-fronted, street-level bistro.

Mentally, I ran through the group of swarthy Italians worthy of bit roles in that year's Academy Award winning movie, *The Godfather*. And while none of the brothers were as cute as Al Pacino, James Caan, Robert Duval, or even the hefty, aging Marlon Brando, the family of loan sharks, extortionists, gamblers and murderers did sort of resemble the character actors, John Cazale and Abe Vigoda.

"It's sweet of you to worry," I told Mr. P., "but I'm sure Lenny and I have nothing in common, except maybe tax evasion."

Mr. Polcari just looked at me. Humor was not his forte.

After a bit of prodding, I admitted one of them had indeed asked me out, but I'd sidestepped the invite by telling him I already had a boyfriend.

Fay Faron

"That's what cement shoes are for," said Mr. P.—right before he fired me, for my "own good"—presumably before Lenny the Cat made me an offer I couldn't refuse.

IT WAS LATE MARCH when Babs and I lugged a winter's worth of laundry down five flights and over to the washateria on Prince Street. We were perched on a couple of plastic chairs when I pulled out Perfect's last letter and read it aloud to Babs.

> *Fayzola,*
>   *Well, I am again unemployed. Long story. Maybe I'll tell you sometime. Anyway, now I have an expired lease, an expensive truck & no bread.*
>   *I could dig crashing on a beach & getting my ass burned somewhere, but I could also dig getting in some skiing. What I'd dig even more would be finding myself employed before I'm in a severe bind. Have a little $ saved, so am heading for Durham, N.C., to get my master's degree in sociology.*
>   *Wishing you peace, love, bananas, babies, committees, bureaucracy & remote controls.*
>   *Yours Truly*

"It's got all the warmth of a Christmas newsletter, am I right?" I asked Babs as we loaded our stuff into the dryers.

We had just sat back down when we noticed a group of old Italian men just outside the plate glass window. They were cheering on some activity obscured within the group, when someone stepped aside to reveal Chum locked in the throes of passion with a mangy mutt of questionable ancestry. And when I say, "locked in," what I really mean is, "stuck in."

Babs and I raced to the street.

"Bad dog! No more puppies!" I shouted, grabbing Chum's head and pulling. Always the loyal sidekick, Babs began yanking on the boy-dog's tail.

"You should go see him!" my roommate yelled over all the whooping and hollering in a variety of dialects.

"Who?"

"Perfect!" She kicked the boy-dog's back legs out from under him, but he quickly scrambled up again.

"Yeah, but he's like 700 miles away!"

"And when you're in Arizona, he'll be like 2,000 miles away!"

I fell onto my rump and shoved my heels onto the boy-dog's shoulders, trying to push him out of Chum. By now, both mutts were getting rather snappish. In their defense, I'd be cranky too if I was going for a personal best.

Just then, an old woman arrived with a bucket of water, dousing not just the pooches, but Babs and me as well. We all let go, and the boy-dog ran off toward Hanover Street.

"Just do it," said Babs, hands on hips, water dripping off her nose.

"What?"

"Go get your man."

Fay Faron

Chapter 16
Blaze of Glory

<u>April 5 - 7, 1974</u>

***Watergate:** Nixon aide convicted of lying to Grand Jury ***In Other News:** Patty Hearst joins her S.L.A. captors **At the Movies:** The Conversation ***On the Radio:** Blue Swede's "Hooked on a Feeling"*

Boston, Massachusetts

I FAKED the old, "I think I'm coming down with something," on Thursday, in preparation for staying home on Friday. Actually, this was a specialty of mine, having practiced the maneuver every weekday morning since kindergarten, albeit with little success. Still, Mr. B. was no Mom and Dad, so I did indeed get away with my little lie.

The bigger problem was how to break the news to Default Boyfriend that I was off to see The Boyfriend of My Heart. And so, taking the path of least resistance, I said nothing, instructing Babs not to answer the phone, just in case Bobby called.

I rolled into New York City just in time to join Friday's commute traffic. It was another hundred miles to Philadelphia, so I had the pleasure of participating in that city's morning traffic jam as well. It was another hundred miles to Baltimore, another hundred to Washington, and another hundred to Richmond. All along nearly identical, tree-lined interstates.

It wasn't until the last three hours into Durham that I started getting excited. I was finally going to see Perfect again. This could be the beginning of *everything*. This time, my ultimate crush and I might actually get together for real. Either that or I really needed to let go of this fantasy.

Still, there was no denying there was something magical about the guy. The way his dimples danced when he chuckled at man's foibles, as if anticipating the day when the little guy would finally, "stick it to the man."

He must be loving this Watergate stuff, I thought. Reveling in the hubris of Nixon taping himself for posterity, and then those same tapes becoming the smoking gun that would surely be his demise.

As for me, the daily televised hearings hurt my ears—not because of my fondness for Nixon, but because Gram was missing her soaps. Equally egregious was that Dad had anguished through fourteen years of Democratic presidents, only to have God send him Richard Milhouse Nixon.

But I couldn't think about that now. Nor how my liberal boyfriend could possibly mesh with my fiercely conservative parents. Yet, I was certain it would somehow work out. Because Perfect had Magic. And where there's Magic, no mere Major Flaw can long survive.

Durham, North Carolina

IT WAS LATE afternoon when I found Perfect's address on a map tacked to a gas station wall.

I grabbed a go-to cup of Folger's coffee and followed my hand-drawn map down a woodsy road to a two-story house with a gabled roof. I let Chum out to roam and circled the house, checking for some indication this was indeed Perfect's Durham digs. I heard a burst of barking dog and whipped around to find my old fuzzy friend, Micah, inside a sliding glass door, prancing around like he had to pee. I tugged at the handle and found it locked.

"Sorry, fellah. Gotta wait."

I cupped my hands and peered past the bouncing malamute to the mattress on the floor, piles of laundry everywhere.

Well, la-de-dah, Mr. Neat sure has changed his ways. I scanned the room. There was a hair dryer—the kind with the big plastic shower cap and hose—and what were those? Electric rollers?

Crap on a friggin' stick!!!!!!!

Perfect was living with someone?

Of course, he was. It all made sense. His dwindling correspondence. What letters he did write, devoid of personal detail, no longer trailing off with the scant, sweet afterthoughts I'd savored like Belgium chocolate. Instead ending with a quick, "See ya."

Of course, Perfect had a girlfriend. How could a guy like Perfect *not* have a girlfriend? Well, I'd come for commitment or closure, and it was clear which way this was going. Now, I just had to get out of here before he came home. Or worse yet, the girlfriend.

I heard the van pull into the driveway. I peeked around the corner to see Perfect strolling up in his straight-leg Levi's, black tee-shirt, shaggy hair, and denim jacket thrown over his shoulder. I watched as he circled Mrs. Turner, surveying her every dent. Oh, right, he's never seen this car before. All I had to do was wait until he went inside, grab Chum and make my getaway. Forever after, he'd think he'd thwarted a burglary in progress.

"Chum?"

Oh soap.

My so-called, "best friend" was jumping all over him, her little tongue lapping wet kisses at whatever parts of him she could reach. Damn dog.

"Faybulous?"

Yikes.

So now, he can see through walls? Well, no. As it turns out, he could see heads peeking around walls.

"Hey, you," I said, all casual like, gliding out like I'd just dropped by to water the fig tree out back. Chum ran between us like we were a wagon train, and she was Rowdy Yates. "Down, you traitor," I hissed.

"Just in the 'hood," I smiled, all stupid idiot-like.

"*Soooo*—ya' wanna come inside?"

"Oh, no. No can do. Gotta catch some friends down the roadarito."

Seriously? Could I get any lamer?

"Really?" he said. "I mean, really?"

"Okay then, I'm outta here," I said, pushing past him. Perfect shifted playfully to block my retreat.

"You're leaving? Already?"

I finally agreed to sit on Perfect's back porch swing even though it meant the electric rollers would be burning a hole in the back of my head. Micah and Chum wandered around, trying to out-pee and out-poo each other. It was a crapshoot. Literally.

It was difficult to plan my exit strategy, what with Perfect flapping his lips about how I ought to spend the night, at least. All I could think of was what would happen when his girlfriend came home.

Girlfriend: "Hello, darling. And who is this stupid idiot perched forlornly on our porch swing, pray tell?"

Perfect: "No one special, my little love bucket. Just some besotted fool who's so pathetic she's traveled 700 miles to rekindle something that never quite happened in the first place. What's for dinner, my little kumquat?"

Lemme outta here!

On and on, he went. About how his job in New York had morphed from Camping and Outdoor Specialist to Budget Analyst, which consisted mostly of managing their $285,000 federal grant. How someone on the staff was being fired on a daily basis. How he'd found himself in emotional free fall. "A total meltdown of energy," he called it. Which was why he'd quit and was now in Durham getting his master's degree.

Clearly, I didn't figure into this equation at all. Still, there was something between us, I could tell. We kept looking at each other but only when we thought the other wasn't looking. And when our eyes did meet, it was like we both wanted to say, "I'm sorry," even if we weren't quite sure for what.

Instead, we swung. And every time Perfect pushed the ground away, his leg grazed against mine, sending fireworks off in my brain and exploding glitter out of my ears.

Was this just physical attraction? Did he feel it too? If I were to confess my feelings, would Perfect dump his girlfriend and move to Boston?

Promise to write more often?

Laugh it off?

Or worst of all, change the subject, the way he always did just when our talks took an intimate turn?

"So, how's your sex life?"

What???!!!! Seriously???!!! How's my sex life?

"Well, in New York," said Perfect, "you were all boo-hooey—"

The nerve! I hadn't driven fourteen hours to talk about my sex life. I'd driven 700 mind-numbing miles to talk about my *love* life! Except apparently, there wasn't going to be one, given Ms. Hot Rollers of 1974 was probably headed home, even as we spoke.

Seriously, was I not humiliated enough? Did he have to rub it in?

"Can I use your bathroom?"

"Down the hall," said Perfect, sliding open the patio door. I stepped through the disemboweled beauty parlor and followed his directions, down the hallway to the third door on the left.

Hanging in the shower was a pair of pantyhose.

Okay, I get it.

I studied my forlorn little face in the mirror. I couldn't believe Perfect had the nerve to ask about my sex life. Sure, the last time I saw him, I was indeed boohooing about losing my virginity. But how could I explain that that *very same guy* was now my—boyfriend?

I turned on the shower, stripped down, and stepped in. The blistering waterfall scorched my skin, and it felt so good to hurt. I rubbed my eyes, and my hands came away stained with mascara. When I was sufficiently scalded, I used the chippie's cold cream to wipe the black streaks off my face. I dressed and peeked out the bathroom door. Perfect was there in the kitchen, stirring something on the stove.

Silently, I snuck down the hallway, let myself out the front door, crept to the car, gave a sharp whistle and Chum came running. She hopped in the backseat, I got in the front, and we drove off.

The last I saw of Perfect was him standing on the stoop with a teapot in his hand, and the only confused look I'd ever seen on his face.

Richmond, Virginia

THE TRIP BACK to Boston was as long and boring as it had been when I was driving south. The same identical-looking trees lined the road, no matter what state I was in.

This time, I didn't even stop for postcards for Jack Easley. All I could think of was getting back to my bed, where I could bawl my eyes out until Monday morning when I was due back at Gilchrist's.

I made it halfway back to Boston before pulling over at a rest stop. I locked the doors, curled up with Chum in the back of the hatchback and tried to sleep. Truckers' lights kept sweeping through Mrs. Turner, their horns blasting for hookers to come out of the station and service them.

It was after midnight when I fell into a troubled sleep. Again, came the dream.

Pearly Gates, Heaven

I stood staring at the "Welcome to Heaven" sign. The Long Line was just as long, and the Express Line hadn't moved an inch. And still, not a person on the golden streets inside. Everyone was getting antsy, cursing at anybody who tried to reclaim their spot after taking a bathroom break. Most disturbing of all, Hitler was teaching the Twelve Disciples how to goose-step.

What on earth was Heaven coming to?

"Javier!" I called to the hunky angel working the graveyard shift. He ignored me, continuing to bebop to some music only he could hear.

Javier pulled out his earplugs and left them dangling from what looked like a tiny television set in his shirt pocket. "Sorry, babe. Bose noise-cancelling earbuds. Sweeet! Won't even hit Earth until 2019."

"So that's how you guys are able to ignore us?"

"Oh, don't be so judgy. You don't know the pressure Up Here. God got pissed off the other day and sent 148 tornados across thirteen states."

"Bummer."

"Tell that to the 310 souls at the back of the Express Line. Anyway, I'm guessing this is about Perfect."

"You know about Perfect?"

"Oh, we KNOW everything. We just don't DO anything."

"How come?"

"Company policy. Fate and all that."

"So, why do we all keep praying?"

"Beats me."

"Okay, long story short. All this time, I thought the reason Perfect and I weren't together was because he just wasn't a together kind of guy. Turns out he is. Just not with me."

"Well, what'd you expect? The guy's PERFECT! No jeans have ever adorned his long, lean legs that haven't been pre-creased in a wire hanger. No Hostess Twinkie has ever grazed his lips. He probably makes his bed, even as he's climbing out of it."

"And you're saying I'm a—?"

"Slob, no offense."

"None taken."

"Not a dirty slob, mind you. Just a sloppy slob. I mean, let's face it. You've got Elly May Clampett hair. You shop at Filene's SUB-basement. Your car's upholstered in dog fur. You gotta admit, you're a bit of a mess."

"But I thought Perfect and I HAD something. I mean, we talk, and talk, and..."

"Yeah? And about what? He reads, "The Berkeley Barb," and you read, "The National Enquirer." The only thing those two rags have in common is Jane Fonda. Perfect's fully informed on every subject. He makes well thought-out, educated decisions, whereas you plunge ahead, chasing every brain-fart like it was a Sign from God."

"But that's the problem. I can't tell the difference."

"Hey, don't look at me. I just work here."

Richmond, Virginia

I STARTED driving back toward Boston. Slowly, this time because there was nothing I really wanted to get back to.

Losing Perfect was like losing hope. I just liked knowing there was a guy out there somewhere who could make my heart go pitty-pat. And now, I feared my heart might never go pitty-pat again.

And even though Spring had finally come to Beantown and lovers were gliding around Frog Pond in swan boats; for me, it was a case of a little too little too late. And no amount of cute guys tossing frisbees around Harvard Yard was going to change that.

What I knew for sure was that I wanted out of Boston. Away from BellSouth Bobby, once and for all. I couldn't keep stringing him along. It just wasn't fair. I should've told him long ago that this so-called, "romance" wasn't going anywhere. But *nooo*. Instead, I just let him go on and on flapping his lips about his "feelings," all the time knowing I was only in it for the pizza.

Europe!

Yeah, Europe!

That's where I belonged!

It'd been my happy place ever since 1969 when it saved me from marrying my college sweetheart. And it had worked too. By summer's end, we'd been broken up three months already and he didn't even know it.

Yes, indeed, Europe had saved me once, and by golly, that sweet little continent could do it again. And if the American Youth Hostels wouldn't pay my way, then, dadgum it, I'd just finance my own friggin' bike trip. And I knew Babs would come along as well. After all, she had nothing to live for either.

Journey of a Teetotaling Virgin

And in the fall, yeah, I'd go home to Phoenix. But the very instant Mom was back from Kansas City, I'd be off to…to….to…to San Francisco! Of course, I would! San Francisco was the best-est city in the whole dang world.

San Francisco had *everything*. Cable cars clanging over Nob Hill. Bicycles zigzagging down the "Crookedest Street in the World." Fisherman's Wharf with its sidewalk crab stands. And Cost Plus' three stories of tchotchkes from all over the world. And then there was Chinatown, its Grant Street right out of *Flower Drum Song*. And Union Square, with its world class mimes. The Golden Gate Bridge. The Cliff House. Golden Gate Park. Even my next potential boyfriend, "The Human Juke Box," a bearded fellow who waited inside his cardboard box for folks to slide coins through a slot in its side, at which time he'd pop his head through, and play a tune on his trumpet.

Yes, indeed. It was San Francisco where I'd finally live out my Mary Tyler Moore fantasy. And just like her TV character, Mary Richards, I'd embark on a glamorous career of some sort. A receptionist in an advertising agency, maybe. Or a goffer at a television station. A shopgirl at a high-end department store. Somewhere—anywhere, really—where I'd be recognized for my Extraordinary Human Potential and promoted to secretary or some other lofty position. Of course, I'd have to learn to spell, but how hard could that be?

Yes, indeed, I just needed to get my Mary Tyler Moore on. That done, and life would once again be one big bowl of shimmering cherries.

Get thee behind me, Perfect!

Fay Faron

Chapter 17
The Second Comeuppance

April 8 - May 19, 1974

****Watergate:*** *64 White House tapes subpoenaed, Nixon sends heavily edited transcripts instead* ***In Other News:*** *SLA's LA safe house targeted by S.W.A.T. team* ***On TV:*** *Love American Style; How to Survive a Marriage* ***At the Movies:*** *The Lords of Flatbush; That's Entertainment!* ***On the Radio:*** *Elton John's "Bennie and the Jets;" Grand Funk's "The Locomotion"*

Boston, Massachusetts

"WE DON'T NEED no stinkin' AYH," I told Babs. "We can just bike around Europe on our own! And we don't need no gol-dern Eurail Pass either because that's why God invented hitchhiking."

"And" I continued, "we can eat for cheap 'cause I know where to find pasta for 28¢ in Venice, and paella for 32¢ in Pamplona, and Wiener schnitzel for 47¢ in Austria. Plus, London's got architecture right out of Dickens and 16th century moated castles they've turned into hostels. And the shopping in Florence makes Filene's Basement look like a boutique at the Ritz Carlton."

What really cinched it was, I told her about my trip to Europe in the summer of 1969. How I'd danced in the streets at the Running of the Bulls in Pamplona. And hitchhiked through Scotland with a bag pipe-playing boy in a kilt. And the most magical day of all, the one where I'd strolled through Venice with my two new best friends, one from Israel and the other from India. All of us in a saris. And how at St. Mark's Square, we were serenaded by four Spanish musicians dressed like the Three Musketeers.

And yeah, sure, I left out some of the hard parts. Sleeping on trains by night and walking around sleep-deprived all day. Not speaking "the language," including those in the British Isles that passed for English. And getting felt-up by every Tomas, Ricardo, and Henri in France, Italy, and Spain. But hey, by the time she figured that out, we'd be zipping around the Amalfi Coast on the backs of Vespas, so how mad could she be?

And just as I'd hoped, Babs bought it. We were going to Europe!

We gave notice on our apartment, informing the landlord we'd be out by May 15, which would allow me to work right up until Friday, the 17th and still give me plenty of time to catch my flight out of New York on the 20th. Babs would move in with Jodie in Salem until her teaching job ended mid-June, then join me for the Running of the Bulls in Pamplona, the first week of July.

Now, all I needed was another job to take the place of Polcari's.

THE AD READ:

WAITRESS WANTED
Durgin-Park
Apply in person to Mr. Kelley, 340 Faneuil Hall

Durgin-Park! I *looovvved* Durgin-Park. Durgin-Park was the oldest restaurant in all of Boston, beginning its history as a nameless dining room in 1742, serving up the same plentiful plates of New England comfort food as it continued to do today. And even when John Durgin and Eldridge Park bought the place in 1827, they carried out the tradition of hiring the same kind of tart-tongued waitresses who'd been verbally abusing fishmongers, sailors, longshoremen, butchers and local politicians for decades.

And while I agreed to wear the same white uniform, black apron, and nursing shoes, I really had to draw the line at the rhinestone reading glasses and the platinum and inky-black beehive hairdos favored by many of the middle-aged broads.

"What's on special, doll?" asked a fellow whose back-lit features were lost in the blinding light streaming from the arched window behind him. The only things I could make out were a halo of Ryan O'Neal, *Love Story* curls, and the word "Harvard," on his faded tee-shirt.

"What'da I look like, a menu?" I barked, sashaying off.

"Can I get some water?" he called after me.

"Get it yourself or pray for rain!"

The best part about working at Durgin-Park was that not only were you allowed to mouth off to the customers, you were actually encouraged to do so. In fact, the cleverest quips were tossed around the kitchen like folk lore, to be admired by all.

When I returned to his table, "Harvard" was puzzling over whether to order the prime rib, Boston baked beans, lamb hocks, Yankee pot roast, chicken legs or pot pie.

"What's a 'smelt?'" he asked, studying the menu.

"Little fishies with bones the size of toothpicks. You eat the whole thing, head, guts, tail and all."

"I'll have that."

"Nope."

"Why not? You out?"

"I have no idea. I'm just not gonna waltz around here with some random fish giving me the hairy eyeball. Order something without a face or leave."

"Uh, okay, lemme see. Steamers. Broiled scrod. Lobster rolls—"

"Look, I don't wanna spoil the ending, but the sooner you get to the Indian pudding swimming in molasses, the sooner you eat."

"Fish chowder?"

"Good choice, Harvard."

It was then I noticed the dog-eared copy of *Let's Go, Europe* open to the page on Pamplona.

"Got a date with a bull," he bragged.

"Yeah? Me too. Or I would, but sadly, girls can't run with the bulls."

"Yeah, they can. First year ever."

"Oh, well, that changes everything," I lied.

Fay Faron

"You stayin' at the free campground?" he asked.

"I am now."

"Maybe I'll see you there."

I peered into the featureless backlit face and wondered if Harvard was as cute as his Ryan O'Neal curls.

"Maybe you will, Harvard. Maybe you will."

FINALLY, I COULD put it off no longer. I had to break up with Bobby. I hoped he'd have taken the hint by now, given I was never around, and seldom answered the phone even when I was. Still, the guy kept coming around.

Taking a scene from my favorite movie, *The Heartbreak Kid*, I planned on dumping him in a public place, just in case he got all slobbery and whatnot. What I failed to remember was this technique hadn't worked so well for *Heartbreak's* Lenny Cantrow, when he broke the news to his bride that he was leaving her for a babe he met on the beach—especially since they were on their honeymoon at the time.

Still, for all his shortcomings, I'd never seen Bobby blubber, not even once. The most I expected was the same passive-aggressive sullenness he'd perfected in the year since we'd been going together.

The spot I chose for our uncoupling was one of our favorite North End eateries, a Chinese restaurant run by Italians, where plastic grapes hung from the ceiling and fat candles melted into Chianti bottles onto a red checkered tablecloth while delicacies like moo goo gai pan were delivered to your table by a chick named Sophia.

"Where were you all weekend?" asked Bobby, shouting over the 5-piece band playing, "When the Moon Hits Your Eye Like a Big Pizza Pie."

"I called you all weekend, and I didn't see your car parked anywhere in the neighborhood."

He was, of course, referring to my lost cause of a lost weekend pursuing my lost love in Durham, North Carolina.

"I went to stay with Jodie in Salem," I lied, turning my attention to the middle-aged lady who showed up every Friday night to dance around the tables, twirling a white handkerchief over his head, like she was second-lining in New Orleans.

"Really," he challenged me, giving me the hairy eyeball.

"Yup. Really."

"Really-really?"

"Look, if you don't believe me—"

"I don't believe you."

"Oh, yeah? Well, relationships are built on trust, so if you don't trust me, maybe we should just break up."

"Yeah, well maybe we should!"

"Okay, then, we're broken up!"

Just then, Sophia arrived with our flaming poo poo platter. She asked if we'd like another half bottle of Chianti and Bobby informed her we were celebrating our breakup, and to, "bring it on." And then, since neither of us had ever abandoned a poo poo platter in our lives, naturally we stayed for dinner.

"So," I said, casually, searing a spare rib over the tabletop hibachi. "Did I mention I was going to Europe for the summer?"

I looked up. Bobby was just sitting there gobsmacked. It was like it never occurred to him that once we were broken up, I might be moving on.

"What about me?"

"We're broken up, remember? Oh, and I'll be moving to San Francisco in the fall."

Bobby didn't even fight me for the last Crab Rangoon, which wasn't like him at all.

Well, that went well, I thought.

Brockton, Massachusetts

"WHY WOULD anybody shop here when they could go to Downtown Crossing?" I asked Mr. B., staring out the window of his Impala at Massachusetts' very first shopping mall, a rectangle building that looked like something designed by a kid with a Lego kit. It was our last trip to the branch stores, this one in Brockton, birthplace of the Department Store Santa.

"Everyone's moving to the suburbs," explained Mr. B. "People want to shop where they live, not take the train into the city and have to haul everything home. Another decade and The Big Three will be gone from Downtown Crossing. Mark my words."

Clearly, Mr. B. had lost his marbles. Jordon Marsh, Filene's and Gilchrist's were as much a part of Boston as the Old South Meeting House. They'd been around 100 years and they'd be around 100 more.

We'd just finished touring the lady's coat department when the boss asked if I'd like to see his house. I said sure. Who would not say sure?

We wove our way through several affluent neighborhoods to a typical New England home on a large corner lot with a manicured lawn. Mr. B. used some fancy gizmo to open the garage door and glided his Impala inside.

"Don't want the neighbors to think you're playing hooky?" I teased.

"Uh, something like that," he stammered.

We entered through a large eat-in kitchen with gleaming maple cabinets, wallpaper patterned with old-fashioned coffeepots, and a blue Formica countertop on which sat a row of cannisters marked, "Sugar," "Flour," "Coffee," and "Tea." Mrs. B.'s touches were everywhere, from the plastic-encased couch to the needlepoint pillows reading, "Home Sweet Home."

"Where's the missus?" I asked.

"Uh, it's her bridge day," said Mr. B. "Brew us some tea, will you? I need to get out of this monkey suit."

I filled the kettle and was pulling down a couple of Mrs. B.'s china cups when I heard him coming up behind me.

"Two sugars, right?" I asked, turning.

And there was Mr. B., standing there with his old-man alabaster belly protruding over a pair of white boxer shorts, the kind with little red hearts on them. Even more shocking was his gray wiry chest hair and scrawny white legs dangling beneath.

"Judas B. Priest!"

Mrs. B.'s china cup fell from my hand. I dropped to my knees and started picking up the pieces, cutting myself in the process.

"Holy Toledo, what are you doing? What if Mrs. B. saw you like this?"

"I just thought—"

"Well, you thought wrong, Mr. Man. Criminy! What the fork!"

I peeked up. The old guy was just standing there, legs crossed at the ankles, wrinkly hands folded over his private parts. I grabbed the screeching teakettle and slid it onto a cold burner.

"No tea for you," I scolded. But softly this time because I could see how embarrassed he was.

"You're not going to tell, are you?"

"Oh, please. Who would I tell? Just go back in there and put on your natty little suit and we'll never speak of it again."

And we never did.

NOW, NORMALLY, I'd have just quit. I mean, what else can you do when the boss makes a pass? But I couldn't change my flight, and besides, I still needed more money for Europe. And so, two people who clearly never wanted to see each other again were stuck in the same small office waiting for the clock to strike, "Go."

It was torture. Mr. B. and I were back to those first awkward months, but this time, there was an elephant in the room. An elephant I now knew wore white boxer shorts with little red hearts on them.

I mean, what the soap was the old guy thinking? It should be obvious to a person of a certain age, that another person of a whole other age, wouldn't want to see their lily-white, old-man self in broad daylight. Especially, when this other person was one-third their age and stone-cold sober.

People don't like that!

It was a couple of days later when Mr. B. slunk in with that stupid, happy smile guys get when they're about to do something nice for you that they know you're not going to like.

"I got you a job," Mr. B. announced.

"You're firing me?"

"No, no, no. A moonlighting job. Working Saturdays at the Woolworth's lunch counter."

What the frog?

Had he heard nothing I'd said about quitting Durgin-Park when my first (and last) day's tips came to $12 for an 8-hour shift? And Durgin-Park was a world renown eatery. I couldn't imagine what my tips at a five-and-dime counter would be.

Still, what could I do? I didn't want to hurt the old guy's feelings, any more than I already had. I mean, he was *trying* to be nice. *Trying* to make it up to me. Besides, it was only four Saturdays. I guess if volunteering to feed bargain shoppers—and bargain tippers—made Mr. B. feel better about himself, it was the least I could do.

And so on my lunch break, I trotted down to Woolworth's four-stories of plastic crap topped with five floors of parking, and there I met my new boss, Mr. Rosen.

"You Mr. B's girl?" asked the short, squatty man in the silly, white paper chef's hat, smelling of rotisserie chicken.

I was about to protest that I wasn't anybody's girl and certainly not Mr. B.'s, but the sooner I got hired, the sooner I could go back to my dreary little storeroom office and the boss who practically hid under his desk every time he saw me.

"Yup, that's me."

"Okay, but I'm only hiring you because Mr. B. said to. So, here's my rules. You're five minutes late, you're fired. You don't show up, don't bother coming back at all. Not even to pick up your paycheck."

I assured Mr. Rosen I was as punctual as Big Ben, and my Protestant work ethic would have Mother Theresa rethinking Catholicism.

And so, I was hired.

Journey of a Teetotaling Virgin

The first Saturday, I made $9.57 in tips for an eight-hour shift.

Oh well, only three more Saturdays to go. Then, no more lunch counter. No more Mr. B. No more blustery Boston winters. And, best of all, no more BellSouth Bobby.

Hang in there, I told myself. Just three weeks, and my reward would be a glorious summer in Europe.

IT WAS the second Saturday I was to work. Babs was spending the weekend with her mom in New Jersey, and I was ironing my uniform when the buzzer rang. Not the one downstairs announcing you had a visitor, but the one in the hallway, being leaned on continuously, making it perfectly clear your visitor wasn't going anywhere until you let them in.

I opened the door to find BellSouth Bobby weaving in the doorway, his hazel eyes rimmed with red. He looked like he'd been up all night, crying or drinking or possibly both.

"Hey, what's up?" I asked, loping backwards as I buttoned my blouse. "I got five minutes, so spit it out."

"Gotta use the can," he growled, pushing past me. He bounced his way through the narrow hallway, bypassing the bathroom entirely. By the time I caught up, he was in my bedroom, whizzing away into a potted plant.

"What the hell!"

Bobby looked around, confused.

"This ain't the crapper?" I watched as he surveyed the dozen or so half-packed boxes, a visual reminder that, once again, I was leaving. But this time, somewhere he couldn't follow.

"Hey, toss over my shoes, will ya?" I said, trying to distract him. I plopped down onto an overturned bucket and started pulling on my socks. "C'mon, Bobby. Chop-chop. I gotta go."

RING! RING!

I hopped up and headed for the phone. Bobby blocked my way. Then in one swift move, he shoved me backwards.

"Hey, watch it!" I said, trying again. He pushed me again. This time I hit the wall, sliding down onto the floor.

RING! RING!

Bobby lunged at me with his full body weight. He ripped off his sweatshirt and threw it over my face. The smell of stale beer was staggering. I was struggling to get free when I felt him yank down my panties, shredding them in the process.

RING! RING!

He leaned forward, shifting his weight onto his hands. One on my throat, the other across my mouth. Shoving himself inside of me, I felt like I was being scraped by a thousand razor blades.

RING! RING!

I felt my lower tooth bite into my lip and my mouth fill with blood. That's when I stopped fighting. Because I knew, for sure, there were only two ways this was going to end. I could either have sex—or I could get beat up and have sex.

I chose the former.

Pearly Gates, Heaven

There was a roll of barbed wire atop the gate, a new addition since my last visit. And a padlock that looked quite cut-able if only someone had thought to bring along a pair of clippers when they died.

"What's your bellyache now, missy?" asked Celeste, barely looking up from checking IDs.

"I'm having sex! Right now! And I don't wanna!"

"Oh, boo-hoo. Such a drama queen. So what if you're not in the mood? Buck up, little pony. Just lay back and enjoy it."

"But he's hitting me! And chocking me! And he doesn't look like Jon Voight anymore. He looks like Robert Mitchum in 'Cape Fear.'"

"Then stop making him mad! You haven't read the literature? You make 'em mad, they just might kill you. That's why they tell you not to resist."

"That's horrible advice. Anybody ever tell you you're a TERRIBLE therapist?"

"Look, Miss La-de-dah. I'm not the slutty little sexpot whose been having premarital shenanigans for over a year now. What were you thinking? That God wouldn't NOTICE?"

"Well, I never get to talk to God, now do I? Just you and Javier. Where is He anyway?"

"Javier?"

"No, God. And not the Old Testament one, either. I want the new, improved New Testament Almighty. Or, hey, let me just shoot for the moon here. Jesus even, okay? Where's Jesus?"

"Sorry, kiddo. Nobody gets in to see the Big Bosses without an appointment. I hate to break it to you, but there's a two-century wait."

"TWO HUNDRED FRIGGIN' YEARS TO TALK TO GOD????!!!! What am I supposed to do RIGHT NOW?"

"Oh, you're big-time fucked. What's happening to you now? TOTAL game changer. MAJOR traumatic event. You'll never marry. Or if you do, you'll be frigid, of course. Your husband will probably leave you for a REAL woman. You'll be that mother hiding her liquor bottles in the ceiling tiles. That little old lady peeking out through lace curtains at a world she's afraid of."

"Fuck city."

"Sorry, cookie," said Celeste, not sounding sorry at all. "I don't make the rules."

Boston, Massachusetts

I LAY THERE for hours after Bobby left, crying quietly in the silence of a phone that no longer rang. I never found out who called, let alone why.

No way was I in any shape to go to Woolworths now, acting like nothing happened. And what excuse could I give for being late? "Sorry, I was getting schtupped the time."

Then, it hit me. I was pregnant! Of course, I was. Because today was Judgment Day. It just made sense The Good Lord Almighty would throw in a baby as the ultimate kicker.

"That what ye sow, that also shall ye reap," said a premarital sex-hating God—who inexplicably spoke the King James English.

I knocked on my neighbor's door. As a student nurse, Lynn would know about this new Morning After pill I'd heard about on the news.

Lynn took one look at me, scanned the hallway for evildoers and yanked me inside. I told her all about what BellSouth Bobby had done. About how Mr. Rosen was sure to fire me. And how mad Mr. B. was going to be when he found out I didn't show up for the job he so kindly got me.

And that's when Lynn told me that not only was the Morning After Pill not on the market yet, it probably wouldn't be for at least a decade since that's how long it would take for FDA approval.

"*Jeeze.* The kid will be in the fourth grade by then."

"I know. It's not fair. Rape never is."

"Yeah, except it wasn't rape. He's my boyfriend. Or at least, he was. We'd done it before. Plenty of times."

"Holy Moley, girl. I gotta get you a subscription to *Ms. Magazine*. Anytime you don't consent, it's rape."

I thought about that a minute.

"What about New Orleans?" I asked her. I told Lynn about the first time. How I'd woken up, and Bobby was already inside of me. Lynn said that was rape too. That I wasn't "asking for it." That I couldn't have consented because I wasn't even conscious at the time.

I went back to my apartment and cried some more. Well, at least one good thing had come of it. Bobby would never have the nerve to come around again. It was finally over. This time for good. This time, he'd *totally* stepped over the line. And if he did show up, no more worrying about hurting his itty-bitty feelings. Finally, I had the excuse to banish him forever. He didn't deserve my forgiveness. And he wasn't going to get it either.

I would've cried some more, except Chum was prancing to go out. I opened the door to find myself face to face with Bobby. I pushed past him, trailing a cascading Chum down the stairs as my weeping ex followed. All the way to Haymarket, he kept making excuses about how sorry he was, but I just made him so darn mad sometimes.

Chum was trotting along, off-leash as usual. Bobby was still sniffling out his apologies when I realized something wasn't right. And it wasn't just his lame excuses either.

"Chum! C'mon, girl! C'mere, Chum!"

Don't do this, baby. Not today.

Bobby and I searched for hours, through the Saturday afternoon shoppers as plentiful as the colorful produce. But it was useless. My little pooch had disappeared without a trace. Head down, eyes too blurry to see the sidewalk beneath me, I stumbled back down Salem Street. This time, Bobby didn't follow.

Nor, sadly, did Chum.

MONDAY NOON, for whatever reason, I felt compelled to slink over to Woolworths to get officially fired.

Which Mr. Rosen did.

Brutally.

Cruelly.

By the time I got back to Gilchrist's, he'd called to "thank" Mr. B. for recommending "the most irresponsible girl" he'd ever met. And with that, things got even icier in our little storeroom office. And they stayed that way for the last three weeks I worked at Gilchrist's. And then, if things weren't depressing enough, our rent ran out on the 15th, five days before my plane left out of New York City.

Babs had gone off to stay with Jodie, and Lynn had gone home for the summer, so the 5th floor was completely vacant. And so, I decided to just camp out in the hallway outside our vacant apartment for a few nights.

God wasn't kidding this time, I thought. I'd gone off in search of earthly pleasures and now He'd smited me, Big Time.

And this wasn't just some divine little slap-on-the-wrist warning smite, either.

Nope.

Fay Faron

This was a Full-Scale, Zero-Tolerance, Holy Shit Comeuppance.

Chapter 18
The Back of Beyond

May 25 - June 3, 1974

***Watergate:** Impeachment hearings on live TV **In Other News:** Identities of slain SLA members not yet identified **On TV:** M*A*S*H*, Mary Tyler Moore & Alan Alda all win Emmys **At the Movies:** The Conversation; Inside Daisy Miller **On the Radio:** Steely Dan's "Rikki Don't Lose That Number;" Jim Stafford's "My Girl Bill"*

Cornwall, England

I HIKED the quarter mile footpath from Lands End Youth Hostel back to the single lane road lined with hedgerow. I drank in the sunshiny morning with its soft breeze whistling beneath the clanking of cow bells.

Spontaneously, I began to sing, "Oh, What a Beautiful Mornin'" from *Oklahoma!* Because it was indeed a beautiful morning and having just spent 40 pence—92¢ if you still thought in American money—for a restful night's sleep in a remote Cornwall cottage, it seemed as if all was right with the world.

I kept up my singing—or at least my lame imitation of it—until an old man in a hay wagon gave me a lift over the moors to the ancient village of Morvah.

Just beyond St. Bridget's Church, I followed a footpath through yellow buttercups to Chûn Castle. I climbed atop a perfect circle of boulders and gazed across the fields toward where the misty sky melted into the matching sea. Pulling open the 700-page gothic romance I'd been lugging around since London, I studied the map on the inside cover. The one on which author, Susan Howatch, had placed her fictional places in amongst the real ones in this sparsely populated corner of Cornwall.

Fay Faron

Penmarric is the tale of a 20-year-old country gentleman, Mark Castallack, and his obsession with his decade-older neighbor, Janna Roslyn. And here I was sitting atop the very same 2,500-year-old ruin that Mark had galloped past when wooing the lovely widow.

Across the fields of bluebells would be the fictional rectory at Zillan where Mark first spotted Janna leaving a spray of roses on her husband's grave. And *just there,* where the dove gray cottage stood—its roof scarred by rain, its windowpanes ground opaque by blowing sand—would be where her farm would have been.

From Chûn Castle, I took a miner's trail, cut deep in the saffron scrub from centuries of people passing, to the collapsed Levant Mine, where 31 miners died in 1919 when a moveable platform collapsed beneath them.

Settling on the bluff above Portheras Cove, I bit into my Cornish pasty and watched the inky ocean turn aqua as it washed onto the sandy beach below.

This place is so beautiful, I thought. So pristine. So historic. Cornwall was a wild and untamed country where gale force winds had forced many a seafaring vessel onto its unforgiving shores. A place where pirates' ladders still clung to the cliffs above smuggler's coves. Cornwall was the last piece of England the Mayflower passed en route to America, as well as the first glimpse of Great Britain Charles Lindbergh had spotted on his historic flight from New York to Paris.

For a minute there, I was almost happy. And then, I remembered—oh no, I couldn't be.

Because I was a rape victim.

A victim of rape.

A victim.

Doomed to a lousy sex life. Destined to drive my husband into the arms of another. Fated to become a mother who hid her liquor bottles in the ceiling tiles. And an old lady peeking through lace curtains at a world she's afraid of.

And I was angry about that. Although not at BellSouth Bobby. Sure, there was no excuse for what he did, but I couldn't deny I'd been a real shit to him. I'd taken his money, along with his heart, all the while knowing I didn't love him. Of course, there was no way I deserved to be raped, I'm just saying I was no saint either.

I'd expected the gloom to lift with the plane as it rose out of JFK Airport. Instead, it lay as thick as the gray clouds outside my window seat.

My foul mood only increased when I checked into the same Luxembourg hotel where my friend, Julie and I'd stayed in 1969. That night, we'd barely settled into our lumpy mattresses when there came the shrieking, the giggling, the crashing about of three boys and two girls chasing each other through the hallway just outside our room.

All went quiet around midnight, only to start up again as the party moved next door to us. Then came the thuds on our common wall. The shaking of our beds like thunder. The strange "meowing," like a cat in heat. The low mumblings of the two boys talking to each other, but never to the meowing girl.

At the time, I'd chalked it up to kids being away from home for the first time. College kids hyped up on jet lag, sex, drugs, and rock 'n roll. The next morning, Julie and I'd even had a good laugh about it. But now, I knew better. And that's because I knew something now, that I didn't know then.

That one is not always a willing participant at every event at which they are present.

What I knew now, was that girl was being raped. Gang-banged, in fact. And it broke my heart to think our only response had been to bury our heads in our pillows and try to sleep.

But what troubled me even more was that this was no longer some nameless, faceless, meowing girl.

Because I knew that girl.

I was that girl.

I TOSSED the crusts of my Cornish pasty to the gulls and hiked back to the road, continuing my quest to visit every place Susan Howatch wrote about in *Penmarric*. It was an hour before a car came by, and when it did, the yellow station wagon had a dozen young people already crammed inside.

"Where ya off'ta, luv?" asked the fellow hanging out the passenger window, his jaunty tweed cap pulled low over his eyes.

"St. Ives," I said.

(Where Janna discovered her young husband living with his second family by his mistress, Rose.)

"And where ya comin' from?"

"St. Just."

(Where Janna spent her childhood with the mysterious old crone, Griselda.)

"Blimey! The Colonist's got it all catawampus," the fellow called over his shoulder. Everyone laughed, which turned out to be an appropriate response, given I was standing on the left side of the road when I should have been standing on the right.

"We're off to Penzance, if ya' don't mind squeezin' in."

(Where Janna spent her Saturday mornings selling produce from her farm? Absolutely!)

The guy in the window seat scooted over onto the lap of the fellow beside him, and I squeezed in between them and a rattling door I feared might pop open at any moment. The driver shifted gears and the guy perched atop the shift knob let out a moan of sexual pleasure, sending ripples of laughter through the vehicle.

I peeked over. With his shaggy Beatle's cut, thick brown bangs, and cheeky Mickey Mouse tee-shirt, the moaner had the same craggy features as Mick Jagger.

Hmm. Not bad. Not bad at all.

The group turned out to be a hiking club out of Dorset on "bank holiday," one of eight days Great Britain sets aside each year which celebrates nothing, simply gives citizens a collective day to play hooky. The group was in Cornwall to hike between the Stone Age monuments. And so, with nowhere to go until Bab's plane arrived mid-June, when invited along, I happily agreed.

Bumping over roads so slim we had to back up whenever we met an oncoming car, we sought out every *menhir*, stone circle, and *quoit* Cornwall had to offer. Unencumbered by tourists, traffic and entrance fees, we explored ancient, abandoned villages and remnants of stone houses, their thatched roofs as long gone as the pigs, cows and goats once kept in their courtyards.

We tromped across gentle slopes of orchids and bluebells where centuries ago, farmers grew oats, barley, and rye. Along the way, we found dozens of massive stone structures, some used for burial rituals, some for religious rites, others with uses unknown.

By mid-afternoon, we were climbing aboard the Mermaid Pleasure Trips' charter boat, gazing back at old men pitchforking seaweed into horse-drawn carts along the beach. By the time we glided past St. Michael's Mount, the Mick Jagger-lookalike and I were one-upping each other with double-entendres, many of which I didn't fully understand, but which sounded vaguely risqué nonetheless.

Rhys, for that was his name, was a 29-year-old art director, who owned a home in a village so small the houses didn't have addresses, their mail addressed to the cottage named after its original owner. Equally intriguing, Rhys was a friend of the real Mick Jagger, even claiming to hang out with the rock star at Soho discotheques where they danced the frug and whatever else rock stars dance to.

What I liked most about Rhys was he had none of that James Dean swagger, American guys took on when they were trying to impress a girl. In fact, Rhys made no secret of liking me, which he demonstrated by snapping my photo every time my head turned. He laughed at my jokes and was charmed by my accent. Which was totally weird because I didn't have an accent, he did.

And then, just like in a fairytale, my prince and his court dropped me off at Pendennis Castle Youth Hostel, maybe not with True Love's Kiss, but with an invite to visit him in Dorset.

Not wanting to appear anxious, I hung around Falmouth a few days, hiking trails with jaw-dropping views of the rugged Cornish coastline, reading in the "Quiet Room," and playing Scrabble with kids from all over the world.

Evenings, we'd all tromp into town, frequent some quaint harbor-side pub for fish 'n chips doused in malt vinegar, and then, numbed by strong, dark ale, race back to make the hostel's 10:30 curfew, lest we find the 2-ton oak doors bolted shut, and no way to get inside short of scaling the 16th century ramparts.

For three nights, I lay on my bunk in the U-shaped army barracks, gazing out at the flood-lit castle built by Henry VIII, and dreaming of Rhys.

The guy just seemed so right.

So English.

So—dare I say it?—perfect.

But then, oops, I forgot. There would be no happy ending for me. And that's because according to The Divine Rulebook—and surely there was one, otherwise, where was everyone getting this stuff?—I was damaged goods.

A rape victim.

A victim of rape.

A victim.

Still, I felt like I'd been set up. This whole love/hate relationship I had with my sexuality existed because I'd been trying to dance between two Absolute Truths. That God created me as a sexual being while my fundamentalist upbringing demanded I couple up ASAP, regardless of the suitability of the match.

It wasn't fair. Not just for Christian kids, but for all of us raised in the optimistic, innocence of the 1950s. Our lives had always been a race between finding *The One* before our guilt-riddled, happy-at-last hormones sprinted over the finish line.

But why were we being held up to this unrealistic standard? How many young people ended up in bad marriages because they confused lust with love? How many had shunned birth control, only to be ambushed by their own unignorable desires? How many so-called, "good girls," upon finding their passion more powerful than their resolve, had been forced to choose between the heartbreak of adoption, the shame of abortion and the harsh life of single motherhood?

Frankly, I was exhausted by pretending I was never going to have sex again. Let alone trying to match up God's randomly doled out punishment with some transgression I'd committed weeks, even months before. I wanted out of this rabbit hole of fathomless guilt I faced every time I found myself unable to live up to rules I didn't even make.

And that's when I began to see the rape for what it was. One very bad Saturday in Boston. And now that my period had come and gone, whether there were lifelong repercussions was entirely up to me.

Bottom line, BellSouth Bobby had never had any influence over my life before this, why would I give him that power now?

What if I simply ignored, *The Devine Rulebook?* What if I faced the fact that I was going to have sex again—I didn't know when or with whom, but since marriage wasn't in my immediate future, it seemed pretty likely premarital sex might be. What if I stopped playing Russian roulette with my baby-making parts? Got myself some protection? What if I let go of the guilt, and started to actually *enjoy* sex?

What if I found a British boyfriend like the brooding soldier in, *Ryan's Daughter?* Or a handsome Spaniard like in, *The Pleasure Seekers?* And/or swarthy Italian, straight out of *Three Coins in a Fountain?*

My life would be like the Miss World pageant, except with guys. Each of my fellas would have his own beguiling accent, national costume and unique talent like bullfighting, bagpipe-playing, or yodeling. It would be like a human version of Puppy Paradise, except nobody would die and have to wait in the freezer until trash day.

Motcombe, England

IT WAS WELL past ten by the time I arrived at Rhys' thatch roof, Tudor style cottage with windows looking out on all four sides.

It was my dream house. Quite literally. The home I'd pieced together from Gram's *Better Housekeeping* magazines, collaging the front of one onto the backyard of another.

Rhys toted my backpack up to the pale pink, Laura Ashley-inspired bedroom across from his, and gave me a sweet, chaste, kiss goodnight. I brushed my hair at the dressing table, its spring flowers matching the curtains, bedspread, and even towels hanging above the clawfoot tub. Then I crawled into bed and slept like the princess I obviously was.

I awoke to the sound of hunting hounds trotting along the bridle path outside my window, and descended to find Rhys in his pale blue, paisley, Carnaby Street suit, cooking up a full English breakfast of fried eggs, bangers, black pudding and grilled tomatoes. Feeling very much the lady of the manor, I waved my new beau off to work in Salisbury.

I spent the morning drinking Rhys' fine English tea and eating apples off his tree. Mid-morning, I strolled down to the general store, passing a dozen thatched roof cottages, their backyards full of horses and chicken coops, their sunny doorsteps guarded by sleeping pooches. I picked out a postcard of Salisbury Cathedral for Jack Easley, then sauntered back for a mid-morning snooze in Rhys' easy chair beside the fireplace.

Could it be that Rhys was—*gulp*—*"The One?"*

Wouldn't it be killer if I showed up at Sunnyslope High's 10th class reunion, not only with my adorable British boyfriend, but his good friend, Mick Jagger, as well? And Bianca. She could come too, of course. And Mama Cass, if she was free that weekend. And David Bowie and Marianne Faithfull, if they were up for a bit of slumming.

By mid-afternoon, I was pushing aside the leather-bound copies of Dickens and Chaucer for something juicier to read. And then, I saw Rhys' journal of handwritten poems.

He said I could read anything...

I opened the cover to find a photo of Rhys deep in conversation with—who else?—Mick Jagger. So, he wasn't exaggerating, after all. They really did know each other. In fact, there seemed to be quite a bit of intimacy between them.

I turned my attention to the poems. Obviously, these were love sonnets of some sort, although certainly nothing Hallmark would print. Plus, it was difficult to follow the action, what with the boy-parts flying all over the place and nary a lady-part to be found.

Good golly, Miss Molly! Where were the lady-parts?

My hands shaking, I turned to the dedication. "To Mick. Always and forever. Love, Rhys."

Holy Toledo!!!!!
Eeekkkk!!!!!!!!!!
Major Flaw!!!!!!!!!!!

Yes, indeed. Yet another deal-breaker. I mean, I didn't like it when my boyfriends had girlfriends, but I really had to draw the line at my boyfriends having boyfriends.

And no, you don't get a pass, even if it is Mick Jagger.

Fay Faron

Chapter 19
The Newlywed Game

June 4 - 18, 1974

***Watergate:** Woodward and Bernstein's "All the President's Men" is published ***In Other News:** IRA bombs Houses of Parliament ***On TV:** Happy Days; Good Times ***At the Movies:** Herbie Rides Again ***On the Radio:** Paul McCartney & Wings' "Band on the Run"*

Dublin, Ireland

WITH ITS CATHEDRAL ceilings, stained glass windows and high-polished floors, the Dublin International Youth Hostel was as romantic a setting as one could get in a place where palm trees do not grow.

The convent's one-time chapel was now a cafeteria with two long community tables, at which sat dozens of college-age kids, their heads buried in dog-eared copies of *Let's Go: Ireland.* From the ceiling hung international flags representing every country in the world.

I slid my tray of coffee, juice, fruit, cereal, and toast across the table from a boy with Paul Newman eyes, a Dr. Zhivago mustache, a faint spray of Van Johnson freckles, and a traveling costume of Levi's, a sweater vest and jean jacket.

Sooo cute!

Alas, next to him, was a girl so similarly wholesome that if she wasn't his fraternal twin, she was surely his soulmate. Wholesome Girl wore a fuzzy pink sweater with a bulkier, burgundy one knotted around her neck, her breakfast all but forgotten as she sketched her diary around us.

"Fifteen bucks a day," muttered *Sooo Cute*, the denim darling across from me, his face folded into a year-old copy of *National Geographic*.

"Come again?"

"Says here for fifteen bucks U.S., you can hop in with a family of Gypsies, and tour Ireland for a week."

"Lemme see."

Sooo Cute slid the magazine across the table. The page was open to a photo of a woman in a headscarf, her face as rough as rawhide. At her feet were a gaggle of smudge-faced youngsters tugging at her long, flowered skirt. Behind them was a barrel-topped wagon, pots and harnesses hanging off its wooden wheels.

"Oh, crud," I said, scanning the article. "The stupid horse goes just fourteen miles a day."

"You shouldn't call the horse stupid," said Wholesome Girl. "He's probably just old and slow."

Sooo Cute and I locked eyes. After they stopped rolling.

This was just too danged easy.

"I CAN'T SEE you as a banker," I said to Dean, the French-Canadian cutie-pie, formerly known as *Sooo Cute*. We were sitting on a park bench beneath the Daniel O'Connell statue, still scarred from the 1916 Rising that liberated Ireland after 700 years of British rule.

"I'm not a teller," Dean was quick to explain, his words all but lost in the four lanes of double-decker buses, taxies, lorries, and tinkling cyclists swirling all around us. "I give people money. Like in *The Millionaire*, eh?"

"But they gotta pay it back, right?"

"At 9.19% interest. But no job's perfect."

Teaming up with a stranger—for a day, a week, a month—was pretty much a given in the hostel world. You found somebody going your way and off you went. As long as your itineraries coincided, you were best friends. And when you were going north and they were going south, you hugged goodbye, and found another new best friend, never to see your old best friend ever again.

From there, we wandered over to Trinity College to check out *The Book of Kells*, famous for the artistic penmanship of the 9th century monks who'd painstakingly copied the first four chapters of the New Testament.

Settling in the grass at St. Stephen's Green, we plotted every postcard-worthy site onto our tourist map, threading our way through Dublin's tree-shaded pools and fountains and across the ornate cast-iron pedestrian walkway known as Ha'penny Bridge.* From there, we proceeded to window-shop at the Irish linen shops on Grafton Street and then poked through the secondhand bookstores along the quay.

When we reached Lower Lesson Street, Dean stopped at a massive three-story brick building whose sign read, "Magdalen Asylum for Penitent Females."

"C'mon," he said, loping toward one of the long, arched windows. He cupped his hands, and I hoisted myself up and peeked into a large room, its walls flaking of plaster. Inside were a hundred women, many with shaved heads, all in shapeless, bulky, woven dresses. Some hunched over porcelain sinks scrubbing laundry by hand, others sorting socks and underwear, or folding sheets. Strutting between them were foul-faced nuns who looked like SS sergeants, scolding anyone who dared to so much as whisper.

"What are they, slaves?" I asked, slipping back down to earth.

"Fallen women," said Dean, making air-quotes.

"Prostitutes?"

"Not all. Some are unwed mothers. Others, victims of rape. And then there are the girls who were so pretty that their families put them here, lest they tempt a man to sin."

"You're kidding, right?"

Dean said there were dozens of these Catholic-run laundries all over Ireland. That they were set up 200 years ago to teach these so-called "sinful women" a trade. But then, realizing the hefty profits from these forced labor camps, the policy became to never consider anybody rehabilitated.

"So," said Dean, "unless they are rescued by their families, most of these women will be here until they die.

The irony was not lost on me. Had I been born in Ireland instead of America, I might very well have ended up here as well.

THE NEXT MORNING, Dean and I took a coach to the outskirts of Dublin where we joined a plethora of hitchhikers headed into the countryside. Inspired by a postcard of a farmwife with a plump duck trying to escape her fat fingers, we set our sights on what one postcard called, "the drowsiest, most magical, most Irish of Irish towns," Galway. It soon became apparent, we wouldn't be choosing our destination, it would be choosing us.

"The stupid horse is looking pretty good right about now," I groused, as thumb-bums disappeared all around us.

The girls were the first to go, the prettier, the less time their feet spent on the ground. Next came the guys, traveling alone. And last, assuming nobody arrived to replenish these first two groups, the couples would be picked up.

Giving up on getting rides together, we came up with a plan. We decided to break up into groups of one, and then whoever got to Kilkenny first, would find a place to stay, leaving a note in the lower left-hand corner of the main door of the main post office. It seemed foolproof since every town had just one main post office, and each post office had just one main door.

I hiked back a few hundred feet and stuck out my thumb. Thirty seconds later, a lorry driver picked me up. Thirty seconds after that, he and I were whizzing past Dean, looking sad and sorry.

"Bye-bye, Darling!" I yelled out the window.

"That bloke a mate of yers?"

"My husband. We're newlyweds. On our honeymoon, actually. But we can't get rides together so—"

Screech!!!!

Kilkenny, Ireland

"SO HOW MANY brothers and sisters do you have?" I whispered across the breakfast table at our first night's lodging.

I'd easily found a farmhouse that took in guests for £1 per night— roughly what Dean and I would be paying if we stayed in a hostel. Not wanting to end up in the Magdalena Asylum for Penitent Females, Dean and I kept up our honeymoon ruse. I soon found playing "married" while essentially on your first date was like showing up at *The Newlywed Game* with a guy you just met on the bus.

"Ye be likin' yer breakfast?" asked Mrs. MacCarthaigh, hovering over us in case we required more porridge, eggs, bacon, sausage, fruit or Irish soda bread slathered in butter and marmalade.

Dean waited until Mrs. MacCarthaigh had filled our teapot with more hot water and scurried off before asking, "Got a boyfriend?"

"I did almost sleep with a guy who slept with Mick Jagger," I admitted, already regulating BellSouth Bobby, and even Perfect, into the category of ancient history.

Dean turned out to be quite fun to play bride-and-groom with. In fact, in my first foray into Free Love, I experienced none of the guilt I'd been programmed to expect as an unrepentant sinner, let alone the frigidity I'd so easily accepted as the inevitable outcome of being a rape victim. Conversely, our lovemaking was soft and sweet—and so very quiet—given our Catholic host and hostess were sleeping just across the hall.

The Republic of Ireland

NOW WITH our fellow hitchhikers spread throughout the countryside, it was like Dean and I had Ireland all to ourselves. Occasionally, we'd run across a donkey cart or boozy Irishmen wobbling along on his bicycle, but with few cars on the road, we found ourselves hiking far more than hitching.

What hadn't occurred to either of us was that the Emerald Isle was called that for a reason. It rained every day. In fact, *most* of every day. And so, we'd find ourselves huddling in our flimsy rain gear, our backs pressed up against a crumbling castle, and us as drenched as the sheep burying their black faces in the mud behind the velvety, moss-covered, stone fences.

Given we had no map, Dean and I seldom had any idea where we were. We tried asking directions from some monks toiling outside a monastery, only to realize they'd all taken a vow of silence. We had no better luck with a gaggle of clear-eyed, rosy-faced school children, too shy to reply when spoken to and then running away like deer on their sturdy little legs, and muddy bare feet.

Late one afternoon, we paid 10p for a ride in a horse-drawn jaunting car to the nearest pub, where we shed our "wetties" by the fire, downed a couple of mugs of strong, dark ale, and watched the rain lash against the windowpanes. And then when we were nearly dry, we sprinted through the downpour to the nearest farmhouse to continue playing *The Newlywed Game* with our unsuspecting hosts.

Dingle Peninsula, Ireland

IT TOOK US five days to reach the east coast of Ireland, the same rugged countryside showcased in the 1970 film, *Ryan's Daughter.*

Set in 1917, Rosy Ryan, played by Sarah Miles, is the high-spirited daughter of an innkeeper, who marries a much older, widowed schoolteacher, (aka, Robert Mitchum,) only to be sinfully distracted by a handsome British soldier.

Now, four years after the film wrapped, the fictional town of Kirrary still stood, primarily because director, David Lean, had hoped to entice tourism to this most impoverished part of Ireland. But the destination was too remote and the journey too challenging for most tourists, leaving the three blocks of facades crumbling away in the wind and the rain.

And so, all alone, we walked the same cobblestone streets the mute "village idiot," (played by John Mills) had sauntered down. We peeked into the facade of Ryan's Pub, then hiked to the wide beach where Rosy had strolled in her long skirt and sun umbrella in the film's opening scene. We climbed to the hillside schoolhouse where her husband had spent his days, even as his young bride galloped off for woodsy dalliances. (The woods, by the way, we never found.)

The next day, we began hitching back toward Dublin, our route taking us through the most famous tourist trap in all of Ireland, the Blarney Stone.

We climbed the 120 dark and clammy stone steps up to the wind-whipped tower, where we proceeded to wriggle, face-up, through a hole in the wall, then arch ourselves backwards, dangling 83 feet over the earth, where we proceeded to plant our lips on a bit of limestone where thousands of lips had pressed before.

Lips with cold sores.

Lips with herpes.

Lips you'd never have kissed if they'd been the last lips on earth.

Yuck.

London, England

THE HOLLAND HOUSE Youth Hostel was nestled in Holland Park, the one-time 54-acre country estate of diplomat, Sir Walter Cope.

Built in 1605, "Cope Castle" was typical of the kind of massive homes showcased in *Upstairs, Downstairs,* a 1971 British TV series, depicting a landed-gentry way of life that had all but disappeared by the end of World War I.

Sir Walter Cope died without producing a male heir, leaving the Jacobean mansion and surrounding woods to his daughter, Isabel. Two years later, Isabel married the 1st Earl of Holland, and the name "Cope" disappeared, along with Isabel's claim to her inheritance.

London grew up around what was now called, Holland House, leaving the mansion and its surrounding parklands a green oasis in the midst of a bustling city. Mostly destroyed by bombs during the German Blitz, the mansion was retooled into a youth hostel in 1959, the ribbon-cutting presided over by Queen Elizabeth and Prince Philip. And now, the very place where kings and queens were once entertained, was a haven for up to 200 budget travelers, all paying 75 pence for a bunk, and another 55p for a full English breakfast.

For nearly a week, Dean and I galloped through London with the giddiness of actual newlyweds. We hung around the fountain at Trafalgar Square, trying to guess where people were from, based upon their accents, shoes and haircuts. We fed the pigeons at Piccadilly Circus, danced the polka at the Changing of the Guard, (much to the chagrin of the locals.) and strolled around St. James Park with a Pakistani man who'd driven overland from Ceylon, the telling of his journey taking far longer than the trip itself.

We drank "coffee regular" (i.e., with milk and sugar) in cafes without washrooms, because the buildings were built before indoor plumbing was invented. We feasted on fruit because it was delicious and nutritious, and milk because it was filling and just 10¢ a pint. We mused at how the English always told you how far somewhere was by how many minutes it took to walk there. And how everywhere was always 5, 10 or 15 minutes away, but never seven or eight. And we took the Tube everywhere, popping off at whatever stop was named after a tourist attraction.

Unlike the complicated and mysterious Perfect, the bilingual cutie-pie from Quebec was a sparkling fountain of sweetness and light. Kind. Funny. Adorable. Polite. Sweet. Thoughtful. Deep. Truly, the "boy next door." Or more accurately, "the boy from the country next door." It seems I'd finally met a guy I could take home to Mom and Dad, and not have them carve him up like tri-tip at a backyard barbecue.

Traveling with Dean was fun and easy, uncomplicated, and yet exciting. It was like we were movie stars and everybody else were just extras.

DESPERATE FOR NEWS from home, Dean and I had gotten in the habit of stopping by whatever libraries we happened to pass, checking out that day's edition of *The International Herald Tribune*, the English language newspaper available all throughout Europe. Given the newspaper's worldwide coverage, the U.S. got barely a page, and Canada, seldom even that. The only sources for in depth news were *Time* and *Newsweek*, the weeklies never reaching Europe until roughly two weeks after the events occurred.

Dean's obsession was the state of the 3-year marriage of Canada's prime minister, Pierre Trudeau, who at 48, had wed an 18-year-old flower child he'd met in Tahiti.

The top U.S. story was, of course, Watergate. And although the break-in of the DNC offices had occurred two years earlier, it now seemed to be culminating in the almost certain impeachment of President Nixon for his part in the coverup.

And then there was the story of the kidnapping of 19-year-old newspaper heiress, Patricia Hearst, taken at gunpoint from the Berkeley, California apartment she shared with her fiancé.

Kept in a closet for 57 days, the coed emerged as a full-fledged revolutionary, calling herself, "Tania," and joining her captors in a San Francisco bank heist. Three weeks later, in Compton, California, Patty was shooting up a sporting goods store as she provided cover for her shoplifting pals, Bill and Emily Harris. This rookie mistake alerted the fuzz to the gang's L.A. safe house, where the nation watched on live TV as the SWAT team's gas canisters ignited the gang's sizable arsenal, setting the house on fire, and killing everyone inside.

For three weeks, the world waited to see if Patty was among the casualties. That mystery ended on June 7th when she recorded a eulogy for her fallen comrades, including her lover, Willie Wolfe.

But now Patty and the Harris' were on the lam. And just as the world was waiting for another Patty sighting, I had to wait even longer for *Time* and *Newsweek* not only to be published but be shipped overseas.

SUNDAY MORNING, Dean and I wandered over to Speaker's Corner to witness whatever local citizens showed up in Hyde Park to pontificate on their latest brain-fart.

"Thou shalt cast out the Devil!" shouted a bearded, Rasputin-looking fellow atop a somewhat shaky kitchen chair.

"Now why would'ja wanna cast out the Devil?" heckled Dean, in a cockney accent no less. "God created the Devil, now didn't He? So why would'ja wanna cast him out?"

"I'm talking about Jesus Christ, the Son of God!" the monk screamed, making no eye contact with Dean, let alone anybody else. "You know why? *You know why???!!!* You go all over the world, you find tombstones of all these so-called, godly men. You go to Jerusalem, what do ya' find? An empty tomb! You know why? *You know why???!!!* Jesus Christ is alive!"

"Check it out," I said, nodding toward two men sitting on a nearby bench, their faces hidden behind newspapers as they slipped notes between them. "Bet'cha they're gay."

"Nah, I'm thinking IRA."

Dean would know. In fact, he'd been in Northern Ireland just before he and I met in Dublin.

Dean described Belfast as a war zone, with British soldiers in camouflage crouching behind bombed-out cars while IRA militants in ski masks only bothered to duck out of sight when a tank rolled by. He said the city center had been closed to all traffic except milk trucks, so the guerillas had begun planting bombs in the delivery vehicles and threatening to kill the drivers and their families if they didn't drive into the city, leave their trucks and run.

"The Troubles" were just the latest installment in a Catholic/Protestant feud that began when Henry VIII created the Church of England so he could divorce his wife, Catherine of Aragon, and marry Ann Boleyn. The country remained Protestant under Henry's son, Edward, then reverted back to Catholicism when he died at sixteen and Queen, "Bloody Mary," inherited the crown. It flipped back to Protestant under her successor, Queen Elizabeth I, daughter of Ann Boleyn. It was Elizabeth who declared it legal for her subjects to worship however they pleased.

But Dean said the fighting wasn't about religion at all. It was about discrimination. Jobs. Housing. And how the Protestant-run government was keeping the "poor" in "Poor Irish Catholic."

The Catholics had pretty much accepted their fate until—perhaps inspired by America's Civil Rights Movement—they began marching for their own civil rights. Protestant militants retaliated by fire-bombing Catholic pubs and cafes, even shooting civilians on the streets of Belfast and Derry.

By the 1970s, there were too many groups and splinter groups to count, all under the banner of either Protestant Loyalists—whose aim was to maintain the status quo—or the Catholic-led IRA, fighting to unite the two Irelands as an independent nation, free of British rule.

By 1973, the violence had breached Northern Ireland's borders, first with a car bomb outside London's Old Bailey Courthouse, then an explosion on a coach carrying British soldiers through northern England. And then, just a month before Dean and I met in Dublin, three bombs exploded there during the city's rush hour, killing 33, and wounding 300.

"I've got nothing against Americans!" bellowed a second speaker, in a white trench coat, atop a step ladder. "In fact, they make wonderful pets! Everyone should own one! But by God, you must keep them on a strong lead, otherwise they're prone to go wandering all over the place!"

I took a discrete glance over my shoulder, only to lock eyes with one of the suspicious characters who were either I.R.A. or gay, or possibly both. His newspaper sprung back into place, and seconds later, the two fled in opposite directions.

"Wonder what that was about," I said.

"Here's hoping we don't find out, eh?"

THE NEXT DAY was Monday, June 17, 1974. Dean and I had had our noses pressed up against the ornate, stained-glass windows at Westminster Abbey when we heard the sirens. Taking Peter Pan's advice to "never run from danger," we started loping in the direction of Big Ben. There we found bunches of "old boys" in white wigs flying past, proving to be quicker than one might suspect, when given a 6-minute warning to move their black-robed butts or get blown to smithereens.

The explosion that followed, delivered billows of smoke rising out of the Houses of Parliament. Dean and I passed a wary glance between us. Had we actually witnessed the planning of this event the day before in Hyde Park, or were we just victims of our own vivid imaginations?

In the end, we'd never know.

Journey of a Teetotaling Virgin

Chapter 20
The Sun Also Sets

June 19 - July 14, 1974

Watergate: John Ehrlichman convicted in Pentagon Papers case
In Other News: Nixon visits USSR; Mikhail Baryshnikov defects; Isabel Peron succeeds husband as Argentine president
At the Movies: Chinatown *On the Radio:* The Hues Corporation's "Rock the Boat"

Paris, France

I SAID GOODBYE to Dean in London and met Babs' plane at the brand-new Charles De Gaulle Airport in Paris. No easy task given she'd provided me with the flight number and arrival time, but not the airline.

We hung out a couple of weeks in The City of Lights, strolling the handsome boulevards, sunning ourselves in the meticulously manicured Luxembourg Park, sipping white wine alongside Sorbonne students on the Boulevard St. Michel, and dosing in the grass on the bank of the River Seine. Like the French, we lived our lives at the sidewalk cafes, nibbling on croissants and café au laits for breakfast, and ham and cheese baguette sandwiches for lunch.

And although Babs was charmed, I grieved for the "Gay Paree," I'd discovered back in 1969. Back then, Paris looked like it was supposed to look—just like it did in the travel posters lining the lilac walls of my childhood bedroom. This modern-day Paris had taller buildings, fewer open air markets, fewer old men in black berets shuffling along the Seine, and far fewer girls on the backs of Vespas swirling around the Arc de Triomphe.

I blamed television. In 1969, a local had asked me, "What's America like?" Now everybody knew—or at least thought they knew—what America was like. Sonny and Cher were a typical married couple. *The Dick Van Dyke Show's* Rob and Laura Petrie, an average middle-class family. *Happy Days,* an accurate depiction of America's youth.

Back then, I had told someone I was from Arizona, only to have him exclaim, "Oh! Cowboys and Indians!"

Yeah, like a hundred years ago.

Once American television had come to Europe, fast food quickly followed. Now, just five years later, McDonald's Golden Arches had invaded the Continent with Hitleresque aggression, drop-kicking charming little diners like Wimpy's to the curb in the process.

What hadn't changed were the "Continental Casanovas." With no laws to deter them, randy Frenchmen continued to pinch every curvy derrière on the Metro, catcall their sucky wolf whistles, and manhandle any breast unprotected by a can of mace.

And so, after a two hour wait for a free 15-minute tour of the Parisan sewer system, we exited the slimy, stone tunnel—lit by the swinging lamp of a man who pulled us through a river of sludge while bloated fish knocked belly-up against our boat—and happily headed for Pamplona.

Pamplona, Spain

THE FIESTA KNOWN as the Running of the Bulls began back in the 14th century with the tradition of using fear and excitement to hurry the cattle through the city streets on their way to the market. It wasn't long before the Basque boys began showing their bravado by running alongside the bulls, with the goal of making it all the way to the pen without being gored, trampled, or killed.

Las Fiestas de San Fermin was named for the town's patron saint, decapitated in the 2nd century, after being tied to a bull and dragged to his death. The red bandanas were a symbol of his martyrdom. The event remained an obscure Basque tradition until

Journey of a Teetotaling Virgin

Ernest Hemingway's 1926 novel, *The Sun Also Rises*, exploded the fiesta into the world's consciousness. By 1974, the nine-day event was bigger than Bastille Day. Bigger than Oktoberfest. Bigger even, than the 4th of July, which nobody in Europe even celebrated, if you can believe that.

In a city which swelled to five times its population every second week in July, hotels were booked months in advance, dooming most visitors to pay top dollar to stay with a local family, sleep ten to a room, or jostle for space on a barroom floor.

Babs and I settled in at the quiet, tree-lined, free campground I'd learned about from Harvard, my old Durgin-Park customer.

By the time we arrived, the meadow on the bank of the river Ar-ga was already littered with white canvas tents. And even though we arrived sans sleeping bags, we were welcomed in by anyone with a bit of space, or blanket to share.

Babs found a spot with two Irish lads, while I camped out beneath a canopy with Tex, a long, lean cowboy who wore alligator boots, straight-legged jeans, and a leather vest over his bare chest. With his dreamy drawl, and propensity to say, "Yes, ma'am," Tex could've easily qualified as my Pamplona boyfriend, except (a) he disappeared each day from sunup to midnight, and (b) his open-air canopy put the kibosh on canoodling.

When seven Australians turned up in a daisy-painted camper, they became Bab's and my new best friends. Embracing life with as much gusto as they did their Mason jars of homemade whiskey, these brawny, good-natured mates filled the campground with their boozy off-key singing, off-color limericks, bawdy humor, and ability to stay awake for super-human amounts of time.

I loved that they'd given each other amusing nicknames, based on their most obvious personality trait. There was Lollie, the sweet one. Hooligan, the rowdiest. Larriki, the prankster. Stiffy, the playboy, Knickers, because he was a bit on the effeminate side. Legless, the fellow who drank too much—even by Australian standards—and Mongrel, who even he had to admit, could be a bit of a dick.

Every day would begin the same, with ten or so of us hiking over the stone bridge, past the corrals where the bulls were kept, then up Calle de Santo Domingo, following the same route the mammoth creatures would take on the last gallop of their lives.

At the top of the hill was Town Hall, the plaza already awash in Basques in their traditional fiesta garb of white shirts and trousers, red scarves and sashes, and straw cowboy hats. Mingled amongst them would be hundreds of college students, most wearing blue jeans and tee-shirts touting the name of their university. And then there were the *gigantes*, 14' stilt figures, their papier-mâché bobbleheads bobbing in time to the nearest marching band, its drums crashing like artillery as they gathered dancers, Pied Piper-style, and headed for the bullring.

It was in the square where we'd part, the Irish off to find a lucrative corner for their fiddle-playing, the Aussies to choose a spot for that morning's run, and Babs and I in a never-ending quest for the perfect place to view the blink-or-you'll-miss-it action.

At 8 a.m., a rocket would fire, signaling the bulls had left the corral. They'd find their first crowd of runners at Town Hall, there for the thrill of watching the creatures come over the rise. The bulls would then slip and slide their way around a sharp right-hand corner and onto the cobblestones of Calle de Estafeta, the main artery through the old city.

It was in this urban canyon where the one-ton bulls would meet the majority of the *mozos*—young Basques with more adrenalin than sense—who'd proceed to swat at them with rolled-up newspapers, grab their horns, spank their butts as they whizzed by, or jump in front of them, only to leap aside at the last minute. Escape for some meant smashing oneself up against a wall, scrambling over a barricade, or diving into a gutter and playing dead until the danger passed.

The last set of runners would be waiting at the underground chute leading to the bullring. Their goal was to keep pace through the tunnel, then burst into the arena right alongside the bulls. But timing was everything. Arrive too soon and you'd find yourself jeered by 20,000 judgy spectators. Arrive too late, and you'd find the gate shut in your face.

After the run, the Irish, the Aussies, Babs and I would all meet up for *café con leche* and sugary churros in The Square. It was here, the Down-Unders would gush about how they'd come *this close* to being trampled or gored, felt the breeze of a horn grazing past them, or had a ton of muscle, horns, and hoofs leap over their backs. Then, it was back to the campground for a wash up in the chilly Rio Arga, followed by a quick dry on the hot rocks and a mid-morning siesta in a progressively warming tent.

Afternoons were reserved for bullfights—but not for Babs and me, since she was too much of an animal lover for such senseless bloodshed, and my innate fear of all things dead was exceeded only by my angst in observing the process. Those who did go returned with stories of exhausted bulls, and arrogant matadors with the cutest butts in Europe, (according to the girls.)

Dinner would be a late and lazy 4-course meal of soup, salad, fish and flan, available everywhere for about $1, a bit more with a decanter of local red wine.

At 10:30, the fireworks would signal the start of the all-night party. The sidewalk cafes along The Square would be chockablock with diners, the nearby bandstand competing with street corner bands, hard rock sharing the airspace with fandango. In the streets, senoritas in flouncing skirts would be pounding their heels to the beat of clattering castanets while we danced among them like the locals—hands over our heads, clicking our fingers to the beat of steel drums—as we passed a bota bag, Hemingway style, between us.

Finally, at 3 a.m., we'd take the long walk back to the campground. We'd sleep for a few hours, get up and do it all again. Between the tranquility of outdoor living, bookended by the run in the morning and the dancing at night, Las Fiestas de San Fermin had to be the best danged festival in the whole danged world.

Maybe even the galaxy.

DAWN WAS JUST breaking when I peered past the dusty vehicles to a lanky fellow with an Ichabod Crane nose, a scraggly Fu Manchu mustache, and a ball of springy hair billowing out from beneath his baseball cap. If it hadn't been for his faded tee-shirt, I'd never have recognized Harvard, my old, Durgin-Park customer.

After several cups of "cowboy coffee," prepared by a Rolf, a red-headed German who wore flowers in his beard, Babs, Harvard and I headed for the bullring, the only place that could accommodate a large crowd of spectators.

By the time we arrived, *taurine* clubs, all dressed in white trousers and colorful blazers, were tossing foot-long, foil-wrapped, ham and cheese sandwiches into the air, delighting as they came crashing down, kamikaze-style, into the grandstands, while vendors poured homemade sangria into the gaping mouths of anyone who could tilt their head back without throwing up from the previous night's partying.

At 8 a.m., the first rocket fired, signaling the bulls had left the corral. Thirty seconds later, came the second blast, proclaiming the last bull had left the pen. This lengthy lag time signaled the herd hadn't left in a pack, predicting a dangerous run, given the bulls would be spread out all along the route.

It was only a couple of minutes before the first bulls burst into the arena alongside a tsunami of *mozos*.

"¡Uno! ¡Dos! ¡Tres!" sang the crowd, counting out the bulls as they burst into the ring. The animals paid little attention to the men milling around, instead, dutifully following the steers into their new pens.

"¡Cuatro! ¡Cinco! ¡Seis!" everyone continued shouting. "¡Siete! ¡Ocho! ¡Nueve! ¡Diez! ¡Once!"

And then, the counting stopped.

"One to go," said Harvard, as if he was the only one who knew how to count in Spanish.

It was another full minute before Bull No. 12 galloped into the ring. The gate was pulled shut, the third rocket sounded, and the last bull galloped across the arena, following its guiding steer into the new pen. Only then, did the final rocket blast, signaling the barricades could come down and the streets reopened.

We watched as the *mozos* meandered around the arena, their adrenalin wafting upwards like mist rising out of a lake. A dozen or so crowded around the chute where the bulls had disappeared, jumping aside as one lone bull, his horns encased in leather, trotted back into the ring.

Galloping through the cast of thousands, the bull focused on one *mozo*, chased him down, then tossed him from horn to horn, until he fell like a rag doll. The boy lay lifeless until the others could distract the bull long enough for him to roll from beneath the pounding hoofs and sprint to safety. The bull then zeroed in on a second mozo, recreating the ghastly scenario.

This went on for three heart-stopping minutes until the handlers arrived with one lone steer. And then, as if lulled by some magic potion, the ballistic bull would docilely follow his pal back into the pen.

THE FIRST WE heard of the death of Juan Ignacio Eraso was at breakfast, the news waffle-balling from table to table, translated from Spanish, to English, to French, and then back again, as more details became known.

The 18-year-old Basque had chosen to run at the entrance to the chute leading to the bullring. He'd tried to keep pace through the tunnel with what he thought were the last two bulls, but left in their wake, he began walking back toward Calle Estafeta. It was in that long passageway where he found himself face-to-face with the last bull, Palmello.

Juan should've run, but he didn't. He should've dived into a gutter, but there wasn't one. He should have smashed himself against the wall, but he was paralyzed with fear. In fact, all Juan did to protect himself was cover his face with his arms, which, of course, did nothing at all.

Palmello charged, his massive horns piercing Juan, tossing him against one fence, and then throwing him against the other, where the bull continued to gore him until he was dead.

That was the thing about Las Fiestas de San Fermin. Everyone knew someone might die. But just like everybody else, Juan Ignacio Eraso never thought it would be him.

THAT EVENING, we all went to dinner at Café Iruña, Hemingway's old Pamplona hangout. The 19th century cafe still sparkled with casual, old-world elegance. Vast polished mirrors adorned the walls. Tall, white pillars rose into a gilded ceiling, and chandeliers twinkled above a black-and-white tiled floor scuffed by decades of chair legs scraping backwards.

We'd just ordered a traditional Basque family-style meal—pork pâté, sautéed tomatoes with peppers and onions, milk-fed lamb and flan—when the Aussies began their daily *tinto*-tinted debate over where they'd choose to run the next morning.

"I was havin' some coldies over at Bar Fitero," said Legless, "when I heard a bunch of gray-hairs—local blokes, they were, wood-chippers, long distance truckers, bogans, and the like—grinnin' like shot foxes 'cause of that morning's run at Calle de Santo Domingo."

"The steep uphill grade?" asked Mongrel.

"Deadset! Except these cobbers didn't run with the bulls, they run *through* 'em. Back to front! Busting dang through the dang herd like they got a gut full'a piss."

"Holy dooley!"

"Crikey! We should do that!"

"Gnarly!"

"Defo!"

Babs and I tried to talk them out of it. It was too dangerous, we argued. A boy had *died*, after all. A local, no less. In a far less dangerous place than the one they were proposing.

"He died a happy Basque," proclaimed Harvard.

Journey of a Teetotaling Virgin

"You outta your gourd?" challenged Babs. "Nobody wants to get trampled to death."

"Basques do," insisted Harvard. "The kid's going down in the history books. They'll be talking about him for years to come. Doesn't get much better than that."

"And what about the bull?" I argued. "I doubt he's thrilled to spend his last day on earth getting harassed by a bunch of schoolboys on his final gallop to meet his Maker."

The Irish claimed Babs and I didn't understand the culture. That Juan had died with honor. The Aussies praised the pageantry of the bullfight, as if it were a carefully choreographed ballet.

"It's like a sword fight between man and beast," said Mongrel.

"Where only one of them has a sword," I countered.

We were just birds, said Irish John.

Sheilas, said the Aussies.

Chicks, said Harvard.

The bill came to $16 for the twelve of us. The check was passed around, everyone tossing in their share, until it hit a snag at Harvard. He studied it just a moment too long and then leaned in and whispered, "What say we split?"

"We *are* splitting," I said, "Yours comes to—"

"Naw, I mean split-split. C'mon, none of these cats knows us."

"What'd the *dag* say?" growled Knickers, who made up in hearing what he lacked in testosterone.

"The *seppo's* talkin' 'bout takin' a walkabout!"

"Well, fuck me dead!"

"*Basta!*" yelled Larrki, rising from his chair like Vesuvius over Pompeii.

Babs threw down 200 pesetas and we hauled Harvard out of there just as Hooligan came crawling across the table, his mates gripping his biceps to hold him back.

THE AUSSIES LEFT the next day, along with Harvard and Tex, my long, lean canopy-mate, all headed to Paris for Bastille Day. That evening, finally partied out, Babs and I kicked in 50 pesetas each to share a pig, spit-roasted over an open fire all afternoon by German Rolf.

It wasn't until the fire was out that I remembered I had nowhere to sleep. Rolf offered his van, suggesting I claim a spot now, before the others returned from town. I crawled into the inky darkness of the van, bundled my jacket into a pillow, and drifted off.

Sometime later, the door slid open and a second sleeper slipped in.

"Ouch!"

"Sorry."

"It's okay. Hair grows back."

The fellow tossed his sleeping bag next to me and settled in.

"You came from town?"

"Yup."

"What's the mood?"

"Like it never happened."

We talked about Juan. About how awful it was that he died. And the bulls. And how awful it was that they died. And we laughed about how we ought to free the bulls into the Pyrenees so they could live happily-ever-after in a matador-free world. Okay, sure it would destroy six centuries of Spanish tradition, along with the economic engine of Pamplona, but who could put a price on the life of a bull?

Actually, I said most of this. My van-mate mostly drank from his soft, camel bota bag, albeit passing it freely in my direction.

"So, when are you scheduling this pen-break?" he asked.

"Well, maybe not tonight," I yawned. I shivered and snuggled into a ball. He unzipped his sleeping bag and threw it over the top of us, and we huddled together.

"I bet you're pretty," he said.

"I am," I lied.

"Lemme feel your face. I can always tell if somebody's pretty by feeling their face."

He felt my face.

"You feel pretty."

I felt his face.

"You feel pretty too."

And then, we both felt compelled to discover if the rest of us felt pretty, as well.

And we did.

I FELL into a dreamy sleep, vaguely aware of the soft mumblings of folks sliding in and out of the van. Dawn peek booed through the thin cotton curtains and I turned toward my new boyfriend, ready for a morning cuddle. But alas, there were a couple of girls already cuddling where my new beau should have been.

I exited to find everyone back from the run, washing in the rocky river. Babs was atop a boulder, her hair wrapped in a thin hand towel she'd thought to bring from home.

"I'm in love!" I gushed, plopping down beside her.

"Oh, really? Again?"

"We talked all night. Okay, not all night, wink-wink, if you get my drift. But he's *soooo* funny, and *soooo* sweet, and *soooo* animal activist-y. We're gonna save bulls together. It's going to be our life's mission. Anyway, I'm pretty sure he's *The One*."

"Which one is he?" Babs asked, scanning a dozen guys splashing in the rocky river.

I checked out the likely suspects. Like that'd help. It was only then occurred to me that I'd never seen his face.

"Okay, then," said Babs. "What's his name?"

"Didn't catch it."

"Where's he from?"

"Not a clue."

"Is he good-looking?"

"He *felt* pretty."

And so, Babs and I spent all day engaging strangers in conversation, only to realize my latest *The One* had fled like a thief in the night.

Fay Faron

Yes, indeed. Yet another Major Flaw. I couldn't identify the guy in a lineup.

Chapter 21
Masher of La Mancha

<u>July 15, 1974</u>

***Watergate:** All The President's Men" is bestseller ***On TV:** End of "The Sonny and Cher Comedy Hour" ***On the Radio:** George McCrae's "Rock Your Baby"*

Castile, Spain

"SO WHERE DO you live?"

"*¿Que?*"

"*¿Dónde esta vive?*" Babs tried again.

No answer. The trucker's eyes never left her breasts, such as they were, poor things. If he was a boob-guy, he'd surely have preferred mine, but I was on the far side, smashed up against the door, my arms folded protectively across them.

"*¿No Inglés?*"

Again, he didn't answer. Instead, Trucker No. 7 unzipped his pants, pulled out his ding-dong and started yanking.

"*¡Alto!*" Babs screamed, clamping her eyes shut and crushing against me. Trucker No. 7 looked confused, as had truckers *números uno* through *seis*, when we'd protested similar bad behavior on each of our previous rides through the sun-scorched desert south of Madrid.

Trucker No. 7 finished pleasuring himself while Babs and I squeezed our eyes shut and waited. Ten minutes later, he glided to the shoulder of the road, and we tumbled out into the 100+ degree middle of nowhere.

"*¡No está bien!*" scolded Babs, reaching up to slam the door in the trucker's laughing face.

"*¡Bad hombre!*" I screamed at the departing truck.

"What now?" Bab's sighed, plopping down beside her travel sticker-covered backpack.

"We wait," I said. "But cheer up, it's never for long."

Fay Faron

"Neither are the rides," she grumbled.

OUR DESTINATION was Torremolinos, a beach town on the Costa del Sol, site of the opening chapters of James A. Michener's 1971 novel, *The Drifters*. If fiction were to be believed, this tiny resort village would be brimming with beautiful young people from all over the world, half of whom, statistically, had to be guys.

Set in present day, Michener's characters were our exact ages, facing our same social issues, struggling to navigate out of the safe and predictable world of the 1950's into the chaos of the 1960s and '70s.

"These are our peeps!" I gushed to Babs, making my case that we should recreate their journey from Torremolinos to Marrakesh.

"Yeah, sure. Except for the draft-dodging, LSD trips and merry-go-round of sexual partners. Oops! No offense."

"None taken."

Truthfully, I never considered my Pamplona dalliance to be anything akin to Erica Jong's "zipless fuck," made famous in her bestseller, *Fear of Flying*. I had to be in *looove*. Or at least think I was. And having seen a lot of movies, I knew it was quite possible to go from meeting someone to marrying them in the time it took to wolf down a tub of popcorn.

Okay, it hadn't happened this time, but I was through beating myself up every time I made a romantic mistake, let alone sit around waiting for God to dish out another Holy Shit Comeuppance. My new company policy was to just forgive myself and move on.

A BIG RIG appeared in the distance, floating over a hazy mirage wafting off the scalding pavement. Babs and I bounced up and down, waving to get the driver's attention. We needn't have bothered. There wasn't a trucker in Spain who'd passed us by.

The semi stopped, and a pleasant-looking man, fortyish, with a deeply lined face and striking dark-brown eyes, motioned us to climb inside.

"*¿Cómo te llamas?*" asked Babs, settling between us.

"Jose."

"*Yo Barbara. Mi amiga, Fay.*"

"*¡Encantada!*"

Babs was the Spanish-speaker of the group. Actually, she wasn't, but I was even less of one. Given she had two years of high school French, we agreed she would be our translator in Paris, while I, having grown up in Arizona, would take over communications in Spain.

At least, that was the plan. Except, as it turns out, Spanish is not a communicable disease. It does not, in fact, waft through the air like influenza, inflicting everyone within a 200-mile radius of Mexico. And so, in the end, Babs became our designated foreign-speaker for the entire trip. My job became how to strategize getting us the farthest piece down the road without having to leap out in the middle of nowhere. Which, as it turned out, I was no better at than speaking Spanish.

We tried everything. If we were friendly, our chattiness was seen as flirtatious. If we appeared sullen, we ceased to be seen as human beings with basic human rights. We even tried acting batshit crazy—Babs twitching like she had cooties, me rocking back and forth speaking in some tongue that would've confounded even folks who spoke in tongues. And yet, every ride ended in overt sexual advances. It didn't matter if we were nice or mean, sane or deranged. In a truckers' world, the only reason a couple of chicks would be out in the blistering La Mancha desert was that they were hot-to-trot. Eager for a little slap-and-tickle. Ready to do the horizontal tango.

"*¿Familia?*" asked Babs.

"*Mi mujer, Maria,*" said Jose, speaking to her chest as if that's where she kept her ears. "*Siete niños.*"

"*¡Buen padre!*"

Well, this was going well, I thought. So far, at least. Actually, things always went well until they didn't. Still, it was encouraging that we'd been in Jose's truck for nearly an hour and we hadn't even seen his penis.

For the first time, I began to relax enough to take in the magnificent monotony of the sprawling plains of La Mancha. There was the "Imperial City" of Toledo,' moated on three sides by the Tagus River. And Castile's arid plateau, named for the many castles erected to defend Spain from a Moorish invasion. There were clusters of sunbaked houses, vines cascading off their red-tiled roofs, shepherds prodding their sheep across the roadway, and donkeys teetering under stalks of hay.

But best of all were the windmills, the same ones made famous in Cervantes' 1605 novel, *Don Quixote*, along with the 1972 film it spawned, *Man of La Mancha*. For the mad knight, Don Quixote, these whitewashed towers with their steel-blue conical hats were monstrous giants with menacing rotating arms, but in reality, they were Dutch-designed grain mills, still very much in use.

In fact, not much had changed along this straight-as-a-ruler highway lined with olive groves and vineyards since that 15th century super-couple, King Ferdinand and Queen Isabella, ruled here during the Spanish Inquisition.

This very countryside had been Ground Zero for the Spanish Civil War, considered by many a dress rehearsal for World War II. After the conflict, poverty-stricken Spain remained internationally isolated until U.S. aid arrived in the 1950s. And even now, under the dictatorship of 81-year-old Francisco Franco, Spain was the most underdeveloped country in Europe.

Jose kept smiling even as Babs continued asking about his family, in the naive belief that proud fathers could not also be philanderers. Meanwhile, I kept flying under the radar, silently praying, please, Lord, let us ride this one all the way to the coast.

Amazingly, for once, my prayers seemed to be working. Could it be that Jose—who admittedly looked more like James Coco's Sancho than Peter O'Toole's Don Quixote—might be our very own knight-errant? A truly chivalrous and gallant gentleman who wanted nothing more than to deliver his Dulcineas to their destination?

"*¡Comida!*" Jose announced, pointing to a black plastic bag beneath my feet. I peeked, and then recoiled at the sight of a greasy leg of lamb that could've fed ten schoolchildren for a week—and then sent them to the hospital for food poisoning.

Jose glided the big rig over to the shoulder of the road, grabbed the bag and a large earthen jug and motioned us to follow. With no polite alternative, we trotted behind the burly man in the white pleated embroidered shirt, corduroy trousers and wide-brimmed hat, down a gravely slope into a steamy gulch.

Jose lay his blanket out beside a mud-blistered creek bed and pulled the mutton from the bag. The trucker retrieved a machete from his sash and—*chop!*—off came a hunk of meat as big as his beefy hand. Smiling shyly, he passed the fly-covered slab to Babs, who sat stone still, giving it the hairy eyeball.

Jose held the jug high, and a stream of scarlet liquid flowed from the side spout down his throat. When Babs tried the same, the wine dribbled down her chin and onto her white peasant blouse. I tried as well, with similar results. Still, it hardly mattered, since it turned out Jose was the thirstiest.

"I hope this isn't like home where once a guy feeds you, he expects sex," I whispered.

The words were barely out of my mouth before Jose ripped off his shirt, revealing a pudgy torso resplendent with black wiry hair. He lunged at Babs, pushing her backwards into the dry, cracked creek bed.

"Jose! No!" I screamed, climbing onto his back, even as Babs tried wriggling out from beneath him. I picked up a rock and gingerly bashed it against his head, taking care not to do any real damage since even in my woozy state, it seemed clear that offing a proud papa in a male dominated dictatorship would not end well.

Jose's beefy arm slung me backwards, tossing me aside like a rag doll. I grabbed another rock, climbed back on and started poking at his head. Seemingly oblivious, the trucker continued wriggling out of his trousers. I yanked his machete out of the lamb and stood over him, his corduroy trousers now down around his knees.

"¡*Halt!*" I screamed.

When Jose ignored me, I sliced a thin line down his back and watched in horror as bubbles of blood oozed out.

"¡¡¡¡*Arrrggg!!!!!*" screamed Jose, turning to give me a look that would've killed, had he had the machete instead of me. Still, it gave Babs time to scramble out from beneath him and sprint for the rock wall, losing her shoes in the process. Meanwhile I kept air-stabbing at Jose, always stopping short of actually hitting him.

"Ouch! Ouch!" Babs cried as she hopped across the hot pebbles. She was halfway up the hill when I flung the machete into the creek bed and ran. Jose took the bait and followed the knife.

I scrambled past Babs and reached back for her, only to find Jose had grabbed her ankle.

"Jose! Let go of that girl!"

The trucker smiled, an eerie sight given the knife was clutched between his teeth.

And then in a case of fright giving way to flight, Babs turned, stared Jose down, then took her free leg and kicked him square in the face. The machete sliced into his mouth, he shrieked, and slid backwards into the gulch. Together, we scrambled out of the ravine.

Babs sank onto her butt, sobbing as I ran into the roadway. A big rig rolled to a stop, and Trucker No. 9 leaned out, his dark eyes taking in the scene. Jose's empty truck idling beside the road. One girl yelling, the other crying and rocking herself in a fetal position. Both of us dirty, our clothing disheveled, smelling of strong red wine.

I followed the trucker's eyes to find Jose lumbering over the cliff. His shirt was open and blood was dripping from his mouth onto his matted chest.

"¡*Bad hombre!*" I yelled, just in case Trucker No. 9 wasn't getting the picture. I ran to Jose's truck, climbed inside, and tossed our backpacks onto the ground.

"No more hitching!" Babs cried, as I reached down to help her up.

"*What??!!??* How else can we get outta here?"

"I'm not doing it! And you can't make me!"

Oh crap, she's gone bonkers.

"Babs," I said, kneeling beside her. "We gotta, okay? Just to the nearest train station. Promise."

"Pinky-swear?" she sniffled, blinking up through her tear-stained lashes.

By then, Trucker No. 9 was off talking to Jose, hopefully giving him a good tongue-lashing. We climbed into his big rig, Babs huddled up against the door, and I laid down on the long bench behind the driver's seat. When our Good Samaritan didn't immediately arrive, I peeked out to see Trucker No. 9 sharing a giggle with Jose.

The engine's low grumble lulled us to sleep. Sometime later, I awoke to find my jeans unzipped and Trucker No. 9's hand on my stomach, working its way south. I swatted him away and he just chuckled. I glanced over at Babs, and she was out cold, her left breast glinting in the afternoon sun.

"Bad hombre," I muttered and went back to sleep.

Fay Faron

Chapter 22
Road to Morocco

<u>July 16 - 21, 1974</u>

Watergate: *Articles of Impeachment Prepared* ***In Other News:*** *Inflation rampant 3 years after Nixon takes U.S. off gold standard*

Gibraltar, Great Britain

"SORRY, MISS, Brits only," said the bobby, checking my passport at the cable car station leading up to the Rock of Gibraltar.

"But I gotta meet my friends," I said.

"English blokes?"

"Aussies."

"Aye, that counts. But'cha not be meetin' 'em up top, miss, you being a Yank 'n all. Best you run along now, luv."

I wandered down to the harbor, but the Aussies' banana-yellow van wasn't in the line leading to the Tangier ferry. The closest I found to my funny, exuberant friends were the golden-brown, tailless, Barbary apes climbing onto car roofs, nibbling rubber off their windshield wipers, and tugging at the pockets of any traveler smelling of peanut.

As for Hemingway's Torremolinos, Babs and I found no one near as exquisite as the characters depicted in *The Drifters*. Instead, we were horrified to find the place was little more than a dozen high-rise hotels. Worse still, the beach too far across the traffic-y Malecon to risk your life over.

Conversely, nearby Málaga was resplendent with broad boulevards, well-kept parks, bougainvillea-draped villas, open-air fruit and vegetable markets, and even a few battle-scarred historic sites. So, that's where I left Babs, white zinc oxide smeared across her pretty nose, contentedly scarfing down whatever seafood didn't have a face, far too traumatized to take the Aussies up on their offer of a lift to Marrakesh.

As for me, I stuffed a few essentials into a knapsack and headed off to meet them in Gibraltar.

As it turned out, the bus didn't go all the way to the British territory, ending its route five miles short in the Spanish town of La Línea de la Concepción. And that was because in 1969, Spain closed its border in retaliation for the Brits' building a harbor on the small isthmus of land the two countries had been squabbling over for twelve centuries.

As the nautical gateway to Africa, Gibraltar had always been an important strategic military outpost, as well as a natural harbor for importing, exporting, trading, selling, and storing goods.

Closing the border hurt both countries and helped neither. Cafes, shops, and casinos in both La Línea de la Concepción and Gibraltar lost half their customers. Mail between the two had to first travel 2,200 miles to London to be processed. Families could only communicate by shouting across a barren strip of no-man's land between security fences, their newborns visible to relatives only via high-powered binoculars.

While once there were 1,500 cars per day crossing, now there were just thirty, the wait between two hours and two days. As for me, I was lucky to catch a lift with some day-laborers. Still, I watched as one traveler stood helplessly by while guards pried open his trunk with a crowbar, prodded the hood with a screwdriver, probed the upholstery with a rifle butt, and poked a coat hanger into every possible crevice.

With most of the peninsula taken up by the Rock of Gibraltar, there was nowhere to build an airport runway except the roadway between La Línea de la Concepción and Gibraltar, leaving vehicles to have to wait to cross between take-offs and landings.

As for Gibraltar, clearly it couldn't decide if it was British or Spanish. Flags of both nations fluttered from wrought iron balconies while bobbies strolled past newsstands carrying both *The London Times* and Madrid's *ABC*. Red phone booths lined Spanish plazas and sidewalk cafes served both paella and afternoon tea. Pesetas and pounds were both considered official currency, and residents often began a sentence in English and finished it in Spanish.

In short, Gibraltar was a land of cricket and bullfights. Of crumpets and gazpacho. Of flamenco and the frug. It was like an international city where the world consisted of just two nations.

But it wasn't Gibraltar I'd come to see. The real draw was Morocco, 56 miles across the strait.

Tangier, Morocco

"WHAT'DA YA WANT, buster? Nice young girl, very clean?" "Boy-bar? Girl-bar? Dirty picture show? Kif? Cookies? Bong?"

The sing-songy chorus of offers rang out from a gaggle of boys swarming the Port of Tangier Med, come to peddle any place offering them a commission. Ignoring them, I followed the crowd aboard a blue shuttle headed to the city. At least I hoped that's where we were going. It was hard to tell when all the signs looked like scribbled signatures on a prescription pad.

From across the Strait, The Rock of Gibraltar's iconic half-dome looked more like a sleeping St. Bernard puppy, its nose pointed out to sea. All along the roadway, caftan-clad bodies strolled the highway like it was a sidewalk, baskets of straw spilling off their donkeys almost to the ground. Casbahs dotted the land like giant sandcastles, ticky-tacky houses tumbled down the hillside and mangy dogs dozed in the shade of skinny palms.

Forty-five minutes later, we arrived at a forgettable corner in Tangier where I exchanged a $10 traveler's check for 42 dirham. I wandered around until I stumbled across the keyhole-shaped entrance to the market known as the Grand Socco.

Really?

Was this the same glittering portal that had graced my childhood travel poster? How had Tangier gone from the glamorous, decadent international hotspot of the 1920s, '30s, '40s and '50s to somewhere with all the charm of a Mexican border town?

Tangier's tawdry reputation began in 1924 when seven European nations—and later, Great Britain and the U.S.—began jointly governing the Tangier International Zone. Or more accurately, hardly governing at all.

Being a mere two-hour ferry ride from Europe, "The Zone" was a place where everything was for sale, even young boys and pubescent girls of a half dozen races. It was somewhere homosexuals could live freely without fear of incarceration. Where millionaires, diplomats and spies met openly in pornographic cinemas and boy-brothels. Where artists sketched naked men frolicking in fountains, and woozy high-on-hashish literary geniuses scribbled tomes at sidewalk cafes.

In 1956, The Zone was given over to the newly formed nation of Morocco to govern. Wanting no part of the wild and wooly town, the conservative Islamic nation left Tangier to implode under its own sinful devices.

And implode it had. Now, its once blindingly white sun-bleached plaster walls had flaked away to expose the sandstone bricks beneath. The glittering plaza was now awash in young girls in cheap cotton dresses, babies clinging to their limbs. Small boys carried brass trays on their heads while old, bearded men exchanged coins faster than their eyes darted about. Old women in mismatched garments shuffled along, their stick canes clicking on the faded cracked tiles. Through them came the tourists following their loud-mouthed guides, the husbands snapping Polaroids of a crumbling St. Andrews Church while their wives slipped coins into the palms of pleading children.

"Come wiz me to ze casbah, lady?" came a smarmy whisper uncomfortably close to my ear. I turned to find a dusty fellow in a tunic, his greasy brown hair tied back in a ponytail, a lethargic snake wrapped around his neck.

"Harvard!"

"How's it hangin', Durgin?"

"I thought you were in Paris."

"Caught a flight to Tangier," said my old campground buddy, unwinding the snake from his neck, and slipping it back to the charmer. "Iberia even threw in a free hotel room."

"Get out!"

"You don't read *Let's Go?*"

"Not until its irrelevant."

I followed my disheveled friend to a small cafe, deep within the souk. My sugary mint tea arrived in a small brass bowl, and Harvard's skinny glass water pipe came on a brass platter ringed with what looked like piles of cremated human remains.

"This shit may be illegal," said Harvard, "but in Morocco, hash's as common as a medina alley cat." I looked around. It must be okay, I thought, since every man in the joint was sucking the same white smoke through the same sort of long, flexible tube.

"No way, Jose," said Harvard, when I told him of my plans to catch the Marrakesh Express, the train made famous in Crosby, Stills and Nash's 1969 hit of the same name.

"And why not?"

"'Cause it's illegal for ladies to travel alone in Morocco. If you'd bother to read, *Let's Go,* you'd know that."

"I got this far, didn't I?"

"Only because you boarded the ferry in Gibraltar. You're in a whole new world now, kiddo. Or more to the point, a whole new Old World. Nobody'll sell you a ticket. And even if you do bribe your way onto a bus or train, you'll be raped and pillaged long before you ever reach Marrakesh."

Shitzola on a stick! I HATED getting raped and pillaged.

"As luck would have it," said Harvard, "I, myself, am en route to Marrakesh. I just gotta make a stop in Fes first."

"Isn't fes a hat?"

"It's also the spiritual heart of Morocco. In the rest of the world, it's the 20th century. In Fes, it's still the Middle Ages."

And that's all it took for me to hop the train with Harvard to Fes.

Big mistake. Huge.

Fay Faron

Fes, Morocco

WE WEREN'T EVEN out of the train station before Harvard began negotiating with a child of seven for a place to stay. And although every hotel was cheaper than the last, my French-speaking companion continued haggling until the plucky cherub threw out a figure that would make a youth hostel blush. And with that, we trekked two miles downhill to the old walled part of the city dating back to 800 AD.

Everyone in Fes wore some variation of a long flowing robe, the only difference was their station in life. The Bedouins looked like they'd just stumbled out of the sand dunes, still smelling of camel while the wealthier men wore their white, gray, and black tunics with the swagger of Peter O'Toole in *Lawrence of Arabia*.

As for the women, the young girls wore long skirts and jackets with *hijabs* encircling their hair and necks. The oldest and poorest of them wore *chadors*, dark, shapeless, hooded cloaks hand-held together in front. Others were draped in long loose garments called *abayas*, some with *niqabs*—a veil covering their entire face except for their eyes—others left to view the world through the dark mesh grille of a *burka*.

Once inside the Fes el Bali—the largest vehicle-free zone in the world—we threaded our way through a maze of alleyways, some so narrow you had to press up against a wall to let a donkey pass. Stopping at a bright blue door across from a butcher shop with a stuffed camel's head in the window, the boy knocked, and a pair of wrinkly eyes peered through the iron grille like the Great and Powerful Oz.

Mohammed led us up a steep, dim stairwell to a wooden hatch which opened up onto a blue-tiled roof ringed by a hip-high wall, beyond which loomed the mountains of the High Atlas. Mohammed and Harvard exchanged a few words in French, and then my travel buddy turned to me and said, "Six dirham."

"For sleeping on a roof?"

"It's a quarter, for Chrissake. C'mon, cough it up. I'll get tomorrow. Besides, that includes the bodyguard."

"That guy?" I asked, nodding toward the old man lugging two futons across the tiles. "He's guarding us from what? Pigeons?"

"White slave traders. Oh, and Mohammed needs your passport. Shitty Moroccan bullshit. C'mon, chop-chop."

And just like that, my identity disappeared along with my funds.

Our octogenarian bodyguard, Jamail, locked the hatch door behind us, then went over to the low wall and fell asleep. Harvard folded himself into a cross-legged position, rolled some kif into a stubby cigarette, pulled out his guitar and started strumming. As for me, I bedded down on my lumpy futon and gazed off into the starry Arabian night, dreaming of the next day's ride on the Marrakesh Express.

I AWOKE with the Morning Call to Prayer, one of five times a day Muslims are summoned to the mosque to pray. This first one was being billowed out before dawn and continued on until the sun lit the full width of the sky

"Cock-a-doodle-do!" I crowed to Harvard, nudging him with my toe. The disheveled lump of caftan shivered, grunted, and rolled onto his emaciated side.

"C'mon, upsy-daisy! Get the lead out!" I was met with a snort and a silence so unarguable I gave up on Marrakesh and went out to explore the vast and ancient medina all by myself.

My first stop was to purchase a *hijab,* in an effort to meld my blonde woofiness into the populace. The saleslady showed me how to wrap it so my hair and bare shoulders were covered. This, coupled with my appropriately lowered blue eyes, rendered me nearly as invisible as the ladies in *burkas* who floated through the souk like black ghosts.

I spent the day exploring the medina's 9,000 alleyways. Canvas sacks of grain and root vegetables spilling out the doors of the small shops. From their walls hung copper pots, plastic totes, clothes, scarves, and soft pointy "genie" slippers. In the alleyway, laundry fluttered from the windows above, adding an extra barrier to the thin reed roof blocking the blistering Moroccan sun.

Late afternoon, I returned to find Harvard deep into extreme yoga. I sat cross-legged on my straw mat and watched as he twisted himself into a vertical pretzel, reached for his toes, walked his hands out, then hopped one leg up in a quick jerk over his shoulder. It was really quite impressive.

By the time Mohammad arrived for that night's rent, Harvard was in a full backbend, from which he sprang into a standing position, only to drop his head down and peer at me from between his knees.

"Your turn to pay," I said, meeting his gaze.

"Sorry, toots. Didn't get to the bank." Harvard rocked back and forth in a long, slow stretch, then repeated the process on the other side.

"Okay, but it's Marrakesh tomorrow, right?" I said, counting out my dwindling stockpile of dirham.

"Hmmm," he answered, the sound somewhere between a "yes," and a mantra.

Mohammed left, and Harvard spent the rest of the evening strumming his guitar and nibbling on *mahjoun* cookies—a sticky mixture of hashish, cashews, pistachios, almonds, dates, and honey—while I stared up at the Arabian night, praying that somewhere, somehow, Omar Sharif would come find me and carry me away on his big white horse.

Hopefully to Marrakesh.

THE NEXT MORNING began the same, with Harvard sleeping through not only the un-ignorable Call to Morning Prayer but the sun prickling his emaciated, comatose frame. I tried shaking him, zapping him, even kicking him. Nothing worked. I'd have thought him dead except the dead don't sweat.

Once again, I spent the day exploring the medina. This time, I ventured off the narrow, crowded lanes into the courtyards and mosques. I stumbled across the University of al-Qarawiyyin, the world's oldest college. I found another part of the souk that sold copper goods and another that peddled only leather products. And

Journey of a Teetotaling Virgin

from one spacious second-floor factory, I peered into a courtyard where permanently stained young men sloshed about in vats of red, blue and yellow dye, stuffing animal skins below the surface with long, wooden sticks.

I found small groceries, their countertops piled high with chestnuts and figs. Apothecaries with every kind of medicine, none requiring a prescription. Community ovens where people came to bake their bread and lamb. There were goldsmiths and rug merchants. Metalworkers and shoemakers. Storytellers and water-sellers. People who wrote letters for those who could not write. Holy men who recited the Koran for those who could not read. There were shops selling kabobs, baklava, and honeyed breads. Dark cafes where a bowl of greasy stew cost 12¢. Bakeries serving mint tea and doughnuts caked with chewy sugar. And 150,000 residents, more humanity crammed into one square mile than seemed humanly possible.

I returned to find Harvard lost in a haze of hashish, far too lethargic to consider anything as taxing as extreme yoga. His guitar-strumming no longer produced notes that connected to each other in any melodic way. Likewise, his nonsensical word patterns tumbled out of his mouth as if falling from a broken kaleidoscope.

When he made any sense at all, Harvard spoke so slowly it was like he could only think ahead one phrase at a time.

"If there was…. one piece of information…I could pass on to future generations…" Harvard took a hit off his hand-rolled cigarette, dropped the hashish, found it, shook off the dust and jabbed it around his face until he found his mouth. "It…. would…. be……………. that… in… the… same way….. you remember the past…. you can remember the future………… And you can pull that future….. into the present."

The longer he talked, the more space between words, as if he could no longer compose an entire phrase at a time. Finally, he just stared into space, fixating on something only he could see. He smiled vaguely and mouthed some soundless words, then nodded, as if the heavens had answered him.

Criminy. What the fork?

Back in Pamplona, and even Tangier, at least the feral creature had been speaking in sentences. When I didn't understand something, I just accepted that he knew more than I did, was smarter than me. But this was like I was hanging out with Howard Hughes in his final unkempt/ recluse/ Las-Vegas-hotel-penthouse stage.

Talk about your Major Flaw.

THE NEXT MORNING, I awoke even before the Call to Morning Prayer. Often when something troubled me, I would work it out overnight, waking with a clear, concise plan of action.

That morning's epiphany was that I had to leave. If not with Harvard, then without him. Marrakesh was out, of course. If it was illegal for me to travel alone, I'd be lucky to make it back to Tangier without ending up in a third world hoosegow without benefit of a second-rate public defender. The far end of the country seemed an impossible dream.

I sat on the low wall and watched the sun spread a thin layer of light across the city. For one brief moment, I felt like I was atop a magic carpet that could float me over this jumble of cement blocks, back across the Strait of Gibraltar to the safety of Europe. But alas, my rooftop abode was no hot-air balloon out of Oz, but an open-air dungeon where I was imprisoned by my third-class citizenship.

The Call for Morning Prayer blanketed the dim city like fog. I turned to see Jamail billowing into an upright position with astonishing agility for a man his age. He stretched, picked up his satchel, and headed for the hatch. I grabbed my knapsack and followed him out, just as I had every morning. Jamail paused long enough to lock Harvard away from would-be robbers and rapists, and together we descended the dark, stone steps.

We were almost out of the hotel before I remembered my passport. I waved Jamail on, then backtracked to Mohammed's empty office. I rummaged through the papers on his desk. Finding nothing, I attacked the only locked drawer with a bobby pin plucked from beneath my *hijab*. I stuck it in, twisted it around, and just like in the movies, the drawer slid open.

Inside were two passports, both a comforting American navy blue. I grabbed mine, and then as a final "fork-you," slipped my bobby pin onto the cover of Harvard's.

Good riddance to bad rubbish.

The medina was as deserted as the hotel, made even eerier with the Call to Morning Prayer echoing through the empty alleyways. I hurried along, my heart beating faster than a prison escapee. I had little hope of finding the exact gate we'd entered upon our arrival since in all my wanderings since, I'd never stumbled across it, not even once. But any of the eleven portals would do since once outside, I'd simply follow the wall until I found the long, steep uphill street that led to the train station in the New City.

I came to a mosque with hundreds of men inside, all facing the far wall in silent meditation. Some were sitting cross-legged, others kneeling, others standing. I watched as those upright bent forward, folded onto their knees, pressed their foreheads to the tile floor, then sat back on their haunches.

I hurried on.

Finally, I found a gate leading out of the medina. And not just any gate but Bab Bou Jeloud, the one Westerners called the Blue Gate. And there I found a line of busses with signs sporting exotic names like Rabat, Casablanca, Marrakesh and—*yes!*—Tangier.

I elbowed my way through the pushers-and-shovers, waved a wad of dirham at the ticket-seller and cried out, "*Billet de bus, Tangier!*"

The ticket-seller looked up and gasped. I felt for my *hijab* and realized the silk scarf had slid off my indecently exposed blonde curls. Add that to my wild-with-fright, bright blue eyes and I was anonymous no more.

"*Je parle français?*"

"Me no speakenze foreign. Me! Tangier! Go!"

I shoved my dirham through the barred cage, gesturing he should take whatever he liked, including a hefty bribe, for all I cared. The man scribbled out a ticket and slid it through the bars, along with some extra dirham that went above and beyond the cost of the ticket, and perhaps, the bribe.

And then—for God knows what reason—I handed him my passport.

The ticket-seller looked genuinely puzzled. He politely opened it and his eyes swam between the photo of the 20-year-old girl with the Gidget flip and my 25-year-old woofy-haired self. He chuckled softly and handed it back. I reached for it, only to find it intercepted by a random Bedouin. The man studied it, shook his head and passed it to a third man for inspection. This fellow had the very same bewildered reaction to my two very different selves. As did Fellows No. 4, 5 and 6.

"C'mon, guys! I'm the same girl, okay! Who among us does not have hair that grows?" My gibberish did nothing to quell the men's curiosity as they continued passing my passport around.

"So, what if I've got no husband?" I blathered on, my eyes chasing the cherished document like it was a nut in a shell game. "What'cha gonna do, arrest me?"

And even when I lost sight of it completely, did I stop babbling? *Nooo.* How could I when any fool could see the bus to Tangier was filling up.

"I know what you're thinking! Nobody even knows I'm in Fes, right? Who's coming to rescue me? Nobody, that's who! You can do whatever you want and no one will know. Rape and pillage me right here and right now! Is that what you're thinking? *Huh?!!!??? Well, is it?!!!???*" I demanded of no one in particular.

Gee, not until you mentioned it.

Then one of the dark ghosts—a woman dressed entirely in black, her face obscured by a *burka*—nudged me with her hip.

I turned to give her the hairy eyeball, but her dark, mesh grille put the kibosh on that. It was then I saw her slide my passport out of her sleeve. She silently pressed it into my hand.

But there was no time for thanks. Nor need, given she obviously didn't want to acknowledge her part in my sneaky little getaway. And so just like that, I turned, walked, and then ran for the coach marked, "Tangier."

High Atlas Mountains, Morocco

THE BUS CLATTERED through 275 miles of Morocco's dry, inhospitable, treeless ridges. We passed tribesmen in vibrant local dress leading donkeys across ancient stone bridges. Through valleys of lush oasis villages and past women pounding their laundry on rocks in the river.

Every half mile or so, we'd pull over to pick up somebody beside the road. The bus filled up, and zz then filled up further since the armrests folded down to create two additional seats in the aisle. Meaning every time someone wanted off, everyone in their path would have to get off the bus and back on.

Still, the biggest surprise was the number of women traveling alone. Okay, not *alone*-alone, given the children and farm animals attached to their limbs, but unaccompanied by the required male escort.

So, it'd been a bluff! It wasn't illegal at all for women to travel alone in Morocco. Not at all.

What else had Harvard lied about? That nobody'd sell me a ticket? Well, I'd gotten one, now hadn't I? That I'd be raped and pillaged before reaching my destination?

Come to think of it, I didn't even know what pillaging was. Bottom line, here I was, wedged between a blonde, blue-eyed Berber and a blue-black Sudanese, both speaking neither French nor Arabic, but the local language of Tamazight. And shockingly, neither man seemed the least bit interested in raping and pillaging me. Maybe they didn't know what it was either.

In fact, the deeply religious Islamic men of Morocco were proving to be far more respectful than the Continental Casanovas of Spain, France and Italy who'd pinched my hinny black-and-blue at every opportunity.

Harvard's lies had cost me a trip to Marrakesh. Worse still, they created a tsunami of angst as I scurried through the medina, fearful the entire male population of Fes had been deputized to come capture me.

And that's when I realized that when all one's information comes from a single source—and that source turns out to be an unreliable narrator—then everything you've learned has been built on lies.

I couldn't believe how easily I'd bought into Harvard's worldview. That people who looked different than me couldn't be trusted. And yet, it was the most foreign-looking person of all—one of the faceless "black ghosts" in a thick mesh grille—who had proved to be my savior.

For centuries, we women had accepted our second-class citizenship as easily as our gender. If our bosses got randy, we quit. If our men-friends wanted sex, we gave in or got beat up. If a fellow offered us lunch at the bottom of a Castilian gulch, we dutifully followed him, rather than risk offense. And if some Ivy League yogi/ hippie/ druggie told us we couldn't travel alone in Morocco, we stayed with him until the fear of the known usurped the fear of the unknown.

It's what we, as women, had been programmed to do. We weren't feminists, after all. Feminists wrote soaring lyrics like Helen Reddy's, "I Am Woman." Feminists wrote inspiring books like Betty Friedan's, *The Feminine Mystique*. Feminists like Gloria Steinem went undercover as Playboy bunnies to hand Hugh Hefner his fuzzy tail back to him on a silver platter.

The rest of us didn't burn our perfectly good bras. We didn't march for equal pay or fight over control of our reproductive rights. We didn't tattle on our bosses every time they made a pass.

Let alone scream "Rape!" if our boyfriend's sexual demands trumped our need to get to work on time.

What we did do was to stand up for each other, most especially when we couldn't stand up for ourselves. We went on double dates with our gay friends even though we feared lesbianism might be contagious. We lectured our pals about birth control, even when they insisted they were never having sex again. And we sliced open the backs of Spanish truck drivers when they wouldn't take, "No, Jose!" for an answer.

So, maybe we were feminists after all. Foot soldiers in the Women's Movement, striding together in a long, slow march toward Equal Rights. Quietly uniting against men who so effortlessly controlled us, as much through lies, fear and intimidation as brutality.

And marching alongside us was my sweet Moroccan sister who'd managed to outsmart some cocky menfolk so that I might escape 12th century Morocco—even though she knew she never would.

Fay Faron

Chapter 23
A Broad Goes Abroad So You Don't Have To

July 22 - August 21, 1974

Watergate: *Nixon resigns ahead of impeachment* ***In Other News:*** *Philippe Petit walks tightrope between WTC's Twin Towers* ***On TV:*** *Name That Tune* ***On the Radio:*** *Roberta Flack's "Feel Like Makin' Love;" Paper Lace's "The Night Chicago Died"*

L'Abri, Switzerland

IT WAS ONLY upon reaching the controversial mountain-side Christian retreat of L'Abri that the fish tacos Babs and I'd consumed in Málaga sent us sprinting across the horizontally challenged meadow to the woodside latrine.

Known for taking in far worse sinners than we ever aspired to be—lesbians, divorcees, heroin addicts, unwed mothers, and evildoers so unrepentant they snuck out in the night to smoke pot and have sex in the woods—L'Abri's American founders, Francis and Edith Schaeffer put us up in a tent outside their grand chateau, and to their credit, charged us nothing for our stay.

Traditionally, Born-Agains largely ignored the hippie element, given heathens were notorious for scarfing down free snacks and then backsliding with a hit of weed in the church parking lot, leaving proselytizers with nothing to show for their efforts but an empty plate of Rice Krispies Treats.

Let's just say the snack-to-soul ratio was not good.

The Schaeffer's were different. Fran Schaeffer even *looked* different. The stocky 62-year-old wore his craggy face in a perpetual scowl, the bags under his eyes reaching nearly to his white goatee, his scraggly black hair grazing the collar of his Nehru jacket, and his knickers laying bare his tree-trunk, Alpine-climbing legs.

By the time we met Fran, the hippie guru had authored four books, all bestsellers in religious circles. And yet, largely unnoticed by the secular world since the New York Times Bestsellers List does not count books sold in Christian bookstores.

But it was his work-in-progress, a book and film series, *How Should We Then Live? The Rise and Decline of Western Thought and Culture* which would galvanize evangelicals to get up out of their pews and demand an end to legalized abortion.

Producing the film was Fran's 21-year-old son, Frankie, who having fathered a child at sixteen, was making it his mission to overturn Roe v. Wade. His collaboration with Republican Congressman, Jack Kemp, would eventually lead to the movement known as the Religious Right.

When Babs and I finally recovered enough to hike up to the lavishly cozy chateau, we were served breakfast in five-star hotel manner with candles, white linen and fine china by Edith herself. Afterwards, we dutifully attended Fran's workshop on how Bob Dylan's lyrical philosophy mirrored Biblical theology. We scooted out before the inevitable "Come to Jesus" moment—the core of every gracious gesture of Christian hospitality I'd ever known—only to be intercepted by Edith with the command, "Let's pray!" This turned out to be a 45-minute sermon masquerading as a prayer, the giveaway being that she kept informing God about stuff He already knew, but which she sensed we did not.

Heidelberg, Germany

BABS AND I were lugging our backpacks across an 18th century sandstone pedestrian bridge in one of the few German cities spared from Allied bombings, when two young soldiers asked if we needed somewhere to stay. They offered us lodging in Mark Twain Village, military housing for Campbell Barracks, the European headquarters for both NATO and the U.S. Army.

Journey of a Teetotaling Virgin

For three days, it was like we were back in America. We watched reruns of *Gunsmoke,* enjoyed hearty breakfasts at the canteen, and replenished our dwindling supply of peanut butter at the commissary. Our soldier admirers took us on a tour of Heidelberg's cobblestoned streets, treated us to a funicular ride up to the castle, and escorted us to a local casino where I won $3 in dimes and Babs $8.50 in nickels at the slot machines.

Hanging out at Mark Twain Village made me homesick for The Real America. And by "home" I meant San Francisco, the next and perhaps final destination on My Grand Adventure. I might even get a *real* job, something that didn't involve carrying coffee. I had no idea what this new, exciting career might be, but since I'd majored in practically everything, my options seemed limitless.

Conversely, Babs wanted to stay a year in Switzerland, get a job as an au pair, maybe brush up on her French. The irony was her non-changeable return ticket left on August 21st whereas mine was open-ended, good for a year. And so, problem solved, we decided to swap tickets. This seemed a simple process since there was never a station—ticket counter, immigration, gate, nor customs—where you were asked for both your passport and airplane ticket.

The bigger hiccup was the bike I'd brought from Boston. Thus far, it had cost me nothing since it had traveled as my free baggage allotment, not only on the Greyhound to New York, but on the Icelandic flight to Luxembourg. I lasted just three days in the hilly countryside before taking it to the Frankfurt Airport with the intention of shipping it home. Only then did I find out that unaccompanied, my bike was no longer considered, "baggage," but now considered "freight." A hundred dollars' worth of freight.

And so, I pedaled back into the countryside, found a friendly farmer and talked him into storing it in his barn until I flew home in September. At least, I think that's what we agreed. I don't speak German, you know.

But now that Babs and I were off to the British Isles, it was time to deal with the bike. And so, I retrieved it from the friendly farmer, rode it to Frankfurt Airport, approached the cutest guy in the ticket line *(natch)* and asked if he'd might (a) check it as his free luggage allotment, (b) retrieve it from baggage claim in Boston, (c) tote it home in a cab, (d) carry it up however many flights to his apartment, (e) walk around it for a month or so, and then, (f) if he wasn't doing anything, maybe come pick me up at the airport.

Although, I doubt I went into that much detail.

The English Channel

ON MY FIRST trip to Europe, I'd taken the grueling Night Train, leaving Victoria Station at 11 p.m. and arriving at Paris Gare du Nord at 5:38 the next morning.

In theory, one could sleep the entire way since the compartment's benches pulled together to create a giant bed that "slept" eight. That was if you could ignore the stifling heat, the train cars clanging together, and the scraping of chains that kept the vehicles from rolling about on the deck below.

But this time around, I was a hitchhiker, not a Eurail-passer, and so for the first time, I took the Day Train across the Channel. When a lorry driver suggested I pose as his wife and ride across the Channel for free, I leapt at the chance. This worked so well, I did the same thing when crossing back to meet Babs in Paris. By the time she and I headed to the British Isles, I was an expert stowaway, and mentoring my very own protégé.

It wasn't until we arrived in London that I discovered I'd lost the silver bracelet my dad bought from Navajo Indians at a roadside stand. Mentally retracing our route, it seemed likely I'd lost it in the woods outside Brussels where Babs and I'd found ourselves stranded for the night.

I left my friend to explore London and hitched back across The Channel to find my precious bangle. Crossing over into France was easy. Finding my bracelet proved impossible. I even posted a $50 reward at the Brussels police station, giving my parents' address in Phoenix. Nothing came of it, of course.

It was my return trip that proved my undoing. I was scarfing down beans on toast when I was unceremoniously goose-stepped into the captain's tiny office.

The captain turned out to be an upper-crust British chap of about 50, sharply dressed in a crisp white uniform, his silver sideburns framing his tanned, handsome face. (Think Christopher Plummer in *Sound of Music*.)

He proved to be an impressive orator, giving me a stern lecture on how I was a charming girl, but if I continued stealing rides from the SS Twickenham Ferryboat Company, he'd have no choice but to throw me in the hoosegow.

Banned from The English Channel. It doesn't get much more bad-girl than that.

Wemyss Bay, Scotland

REUNITED WITH Babs in London, we hitchhiked to the Firth of Clyde where we spent three days with her 91-year-old Aunt Jean, and her roommate, "Grandpa." It was here we heard Nixon had resigned rather than become the second president in U.S. history to be impeached.

Truthfully, thinking about Watergate hurt my heart. Not because I had any great love for, "I Am Not a Crook" Nixon, but because I knew my dad's whole "Republicans-can't-be-wrong" groupthink had to be imploding.

In Scotland, the news barely made a ripple. Aunt Jean was far too old to worry about Nixon and far too Scottish to care. She lived in a two-bedroom, too-warm apartment decked out with lace doilies, old-lady tchotchkes, three cats and Grandpa, who at 87 was as spry as a man of sixty.

I could never figure out the relationship between the two and neither could Babs. It seemed unlikely they were husband and wife, or even boyfriend and girlfriend, since Grandpa showed more than a passing interest in my grandmother, "Jessie Redhead" Malcolm, 86, and also Scottish. He even said he'd like to visit her in Phoenix, maybe take her to Disneyland. All this in front of Aunt

Jean, who didn't bat an eye. But then, she was rather hard of hearing.

Aunt Jean drove us slowly around the village—Grandpa had lost his license due to an impressive rap sheet of speeding tickets—and pointed out the all-glass ferry and train station, said to be the most beautiful terminal in all of Scotland. Babs and I were all set to take the romantic sounding, "Sea Road to Rothesay," until we got push-back from our elders.

"Ye canna be goin' that way," warned Aunt Jean.

Or, "Feck! Yer aff yer heid!" as Grandpa so colorfully put it.

As it turned out, the many waterways between Wemyss Bay and Malcolm territory could only be traversed by passing through numerous lochs and canals, or meandering miles out of the way to skirt them. And so, Babs and I hitched 25 miles back to Glasgow, then headed north through County Argyll, where there were more Malcolm's than in all of South Missouri.

At the end of a very long day, we reached Duntrune Castle, the oldest continually occupied castle in all of Scotland. It was also home to 72-year-old Lt. Col. George Ivan Malcolm, my relative so distantly related that even my genealogy-obsessed mother couldn't find him on the family tree. Alas, Uncle Lt. Col. was away at the Edinburgh International Festival overseeing the Military Tattoo, the musical showstopper he founded in 1950.

Rather than welcoming us into the 12th century ghost-infested fortress, the games-keeper's two young sons nixed our request to peek inside the 6-foot-deep stone walls, instead sending us off to find other lodging for the night. Still, we left a letter for Mrs. Uncle Lt. Col., asking her to please drop a note to Mom so they could get better acquainted. She never did, of course.

Paris, France

AUGUST 21st finally arrived, the departure date for Bab's use-it-or-lose-it return ticket to Boston. We arrived at the six-month-old Charles de Gaulle Airport, having planned our ticket-switcheroo with the precision of a bank robbery. Our scheme was for Babs

Journey of a Teetotaling Virgin

to use her ticket to check my backpack, and then slip the ticket to me. I'd then flash my passport at Immigration, then pull out her ticket to board. Since there was no station which compared your ticket with your passport, our plan seemed foolproof.

If, perchance, there was a hiccup of some sort, my descent down the escalator would be Babs' cue to race to the rescue. As for what this act of heroism might entail, we hadn't a clue. We did, however, agree there'd be no eye contact. If caught, we'd serve out our sentences in the Charles de Gaulle Airport Prison, discretely passing coded notes between our adjoining cells.

I waited inside the duty-free shop, my nose buried in *Ms. Magazine* until Babs arrived to slip her ticket behind Cicely Tyson's smiling face. We blinked a tearful goodbye, and I proceeded up the escalator to Immigration and the gate. Except Immigration wasn't at the gate where it belonged, but downstairs by the ticket counter, where it clearly didn't belong.

And so, with no alternative except to descend the escalator—which, if you recall, was the signal for Babs to race to the rescue—I met her midway down. I shook my head violently in the universal signal to "Abort!" only to find Babs was taking the no-eye-contact edict far too seriously.

I hung around Immigration awhile, but when she didn't show up, I made a beeline for the plane.

Fay Faron

Chapter 24
You're Never Too Old for Late-Onset Teenage Angst

October 1 - November 5, 1974

Watergate: *1st term Democrats, dubbed "Watergate babies," sweep Congress **In Other News:** Randolph Hearst withdraws reward for Patty's safe return **At the Movies:** The Texas Chain Saw Massacre; Airport 1975 **On the Radio:** Olivia Newton John's "I Honestly Love You;" Dionne Warwick and The Spinners' "Then Came You"*

Paradise Valley, Arizona

"THIS IS WHO I am now, and this is what I do," I muttered to myself. It had become my mantra ever since returning home to a house I'd never lived in, my way of reminding myself that my current situation would eventually pass.

"What's that, hon?"

"Nothin' Pops," I said, waving to Mom as she backed out the mesquite-flanked driveway, the first leg of her 1,200-mile journey to Kansas City.

"Come back soon!" called Gram, probably as much in dread of missing my mother, as my so-called cooking. She was right to be concerned. Truthfully, I'd never taken care of another human being in my life, and why they'd entrusted me with the wellbeing of these two was anybody's guess.

Dad plopped down at the square oak table, poured over the morning edition of *The Arizona Republic,* and waited for his bone-dry scrambled eggs and burnt toast.

"Cereal's fine!" called Gram. "I'm sure you don't know your way around this kitchen yet, dear!"

"Nor any kitchen," muttered Dad, with his usual smirk.

He was right, I didn't. Still, the bright, yellow-wallpapered kitchen in our new house was a far cheerier place to overcook and undercook in-edibles than in our old Sunnyslope abode. In fact, everything about this new house was better. Certainly, the posh Paradise Valley neighborhood where McMansions towered over our cul-de-sac of modest ranch style homes. Our new house had a view of Camelback Mountain from the front, and Mummy Mountain from the back, and although our quarter-acre lot was worth more than the structure, Dad had no intention of cashing in on his $26,000 investment because this was to be their "forever home."

Hermetically sealed against the elements, the residence was devoid of energy, lulled into a monotony of white noise by the low drone of the air conditioner. In my parents' world, home was where I was expected to be, by default, unless some necessity—Tums for Dad, meds for Gram, Tampons for me—arose for which I had to venture out into the Big Bad World. And even then, my ETA would be evaluated against the time it took to complete the task. There'd be no stopping at the Red Pony Saloon for Happy Hour, that was for sure.

Once again, I was a Child in the House of Dad, an infidel in a place where there existed no tolerance for sluts who imbibed in an umbrella drink now and again.

"Fay's Room," was the official resting place of the teakwood bedroom set I'd picked out in seventh grade because it looked like something Cricket from *Hawaiian Eye* would have in her room. And although I'd never actually slept there, Fay's Room remained christened that in anticipation of the short window of time between when I arrived home and found a husband.

But for now, Gram was happily ensconced in Fay's Room while I camped out on the pull-out couch in the den, the only room with a television. Between Gram's daytime soaps, Dad's 6 o'clock news, *Meet the Press, Marcus Welby, M.D., McMillan & Wife*, and the golf games Dad slept through on weekends, my only real privacy came when the white snow replaced *The Tonight Show* at midnight.

Still, I did not envy Gram the cool blue tile beneath her slippers, nor the spacious bath where she applied her nightly Noxzema. And that was because my modest digs continued to remind me that my stay was of limited duration.

This is who I am now, and this is what I do.

THIS ISN'T IN Wikipedia or anything, but my father actually invented Right Wing Republican. I only wish he had trademarked it so I could get a cut off Fox TV.

Back in 1960 when John F. Kennedy was elected president, I was surprised Pops didn't have a cow right then and there. This could not possibly be God's will! Everybody knew God was a Republican!! With a Democratic Catholic Pagan in power, surely this was the end of civilization as we knew it!!!

The Book of Revelations became a checklist of current events to be ticked off as the world's population marched toward the Rapture. When the Cuban Missile Crisis happened in 1962, the only issue was whether Jesus could get down to Earth in time to take Us Believers up to Heaven before we all got blown to smithereens, along with the idiot heathens who'd voted for Kennedy in the first place.

Now you'd think with just a few more days to live, I'd get to stay home from school, right? But *nooo*. Instead, I had to go learn how to crawl under my desk so I'd be the last one in my class to die. None of this, cautioned Dad, would be happening if Nixon had been elected.

When President Kennedy was assassinated, our TV droned on for days, just like in every other household in America. But there were no tears in my family. My family would not gloat, but neither would they mourn.

Dad's unshakable sense of right and wrong extended to everything. When I went to the movies, other kids got to call home, let the phone ring twice and hang up, as a signal for their parents to come fetch them. My brother and I weren't allowed to do this because that would be stealing from Ma Bell.

I recall once when a couple came to our house and brought a bottle of wine, which was considered the thing to do in polite society. After they left, Dad declared the man a drunkard who couldn't get through a meal without taking a nip. Well, I'm guessing our guest didn't have one that night because our family didn't own a corkscrew.

Dad's hubris developed in me an uncontrollable urge to get his goat either by (a) coming up with something I knew that he didn't, or (b) failing that, make him admit he was wrong about something, or (c) failing that, get him to actually change his mind. Since I couldn't compete in Biblical doctrine nor politics, my never-ending quest to best him took the form of good-natured pranks, a language we both spoke fluently.

Like the time my friend and I decided to push Dad's car out of the driveway and around the corner, and then tell him it'd been stolen. We'd let him panic awhile and then fess up just before he called the police. We put the Buick in neutral, effortlessly glided it down the driveway and then laboriously pushed it around the corner. Once it was safely out of sight, we raced back to breathlessly report the news.

"Dad! Your car's been stolen!"

Without looking up, my father said, "Fay, please push the car back into the driveway." Like he was asking me to take out the trash or something.

Then there was the time I decided to call him out on his decade-old promise that I could get married when I turned sixteen. Of course, there was no way he was going to let me do that. Obviously, I was anxious to see how he'd wriggle out of it.

My Sweet Sixteen came and went with the usual hoopla, leaving me far too excited to be thinking about marriage. But then a few days later, I grabbed Teddy from next door—a year older and nowhere near marriage material—and hauled him home. (Teddy, of course, was in on the joke.)

"Pops, you remember Teddy? Well, guess what. We're getting married!"

"No, you're not."

"Oh, no! You said I could, remember? You said I could get married when I was sixteen, and I'm sixteen so I'm getting married!"

"Nope. Sorry."

"Oh, yeah? Are you telling me you were *wrong????* Or that maybe you've *changed your mind????*" I really had him this time. There was no way out.

"Now, Faysie, if you recall, I said you could get married *the day* you turned sixteen. You turned sixteen three days ago. You could have gotten married on Saturday. But *nooo*, you were too busy with your Sweet Sixteen. Now, Teddy, you run along home. And if you two still want to get married when Fay turns 21, I'd be pleased to welcome you into the family."

Teddy laughed himself out the door.

When I was three, I got so sick everybody thought I was going to die. Mom kept vigil all night as the doctors pumped fluids into me, trying to stem a case of severe dehydration. Early the next morning, Dad came to relieve her. When I finally awoke, there he was, holding my cup as I sipped orange juice through a straw, the first liquid I'd kept down in days.

From then on, I was declared, "Daddy's girl." At least, that's how Mom told it. And Dad was only too happy to believe it. In truth, it was my mother who'd always been my savior. Ever since I was a toddler, I had only to climb into her lap to know that nothing bad could happen to me. And that included incoming missiles from Cuba.

Dad, on the other hand, was a bit pricklier. He doted on me as well, but his master plan for crafting me into an exemplary human being was to spank me for the slightest infraction. And there were so many infractions, not because I was ornery but simply because I was a kid and I didn't know the rules. And Dad wasn't kidding with the spanking either. It hurt. A lot. For a time there, I think he spanked me every day. Finally, I pleaded with him to just tell me what I was doing wrong and I wouldn't do it anymore. I don't think he ever spanked me again.

When Dad got wound up, Mom would quietly support him and then talk sense into him behind the scenes. Mom was the buffer between Dad and the world. I don't know if he knew that, but she was.

By the time I entered college, my father considered my brother and I pretty much raised and turned his attention to fixing the rest of the world. The first rung on his ladder was Arizona State Representative. Pops had always been the go-to guy if you were unclear on the difference between right and wrong, and now for the first time, he had the power to make the world do right simply by making everything that was wrong, actually illegal.

Dad took to politics like an Emperor to his throne. People were starting to know who he was and curry his favor. He liked that. He also liked all the hoopla that came with the job.

One day, Dean Rusk—the (Democratic) Secretary of State under (Democratic) President Lyndon B. Johnson—came to town. The reception was at the Westward Ho Hotel, a historic landmark in downtown Phoenix. Late in the afternoon, Dad called and told Mom to put on her best dress and meet him at the function. (Dad was not, apparently, above fraternizing with the enemy if free hors d'oeuvres were involved.)

"Oh Al!" said Mom, which she said a lot. "My hair is filthy, and I haven't got a thing to wear."

"Come anyway." he commanded her.

Mom took a shower and put her hair up in those pink little foam rollers so popular at the time. She drove downtown with the windows rolled down, which was a pretty common thing to do in Phoenix where the dry heat trumped a hair dryer pretty much any day of the year.

As Mom waited for Dad in the hotel lobby, she couldn't help but notice everyone was smiling at her, nodding, and laughing. I must be looking pretty good today, she thought. Dad strolled over, smiled his little side smirk, and led her past the red velvet ropes to the V.I.P. section. They approached Secretary Rusk, where he was speaking with a small group. When Secretary Rusk finally turned to greet them, the Secretary of State (!) of the United States of America (!!) graciously took my mother's hand, leaned in close and whispered, "Mrs. Faron, did you know you have rollers in your hair?"

"Oh, Al!"

And there was Dad, checking out the ceiling tiles for water damage.

Pops never came clean as to whether he really hadn't noticed Mom had rollers in her hair, or just thought the giggle would be worth it. With Dad, you never really knew.

FINALLY, THE BIG day arrived. I'd fulfilled my month-long duty to take care of Dad and Gram, Mom was coming home, and I was free to go live life as I pleased. By the time she drove up the long backyard driveway, I had Mrs. Turner gassed up and ready to go.

That night, we were all having dinner around the oak table as I prattled on about my new life in San Francisco. How I had $80 saved, enough for gas and a hotel room until I found a job and saved enough for an apartment. How I'd drive straight through—it was only 17 hours, after all—and if I got sleepy, I could always nod off in Mrs. Turner.

I couldn't help but notice Dad looked like he'd swallowed a tarantula, Mom like she was about to cry, and Gram with her fingers in her ears, trilling, *"la-la-la-la-la."* Okay, not really, but you get my drift.

Still, I figured it was the French-fried hot dogs—weenies on a stick swirled in a combination of Bisquick, barbecue sauce and mustard, and fried in lard—a recipe I got from Mom's *Anita Bryant Family Cookbook*. But *nooo*. It turned out to be something else entirely.

"You can't leave on Sunday," said Dad, pushing his pork and beans around on his plate. "You'll get stuck in the desert with no gas stations and no place to eat."

"C'mon, Pops. Gas stations are open on Sunday. Even in the desert."

"No, they're not."

"Yes, they are."

"No, they're not."

Obviously, there was no way out. The King had spoken. Meaning even if gas stations were open in the desert, they would now close in deference to his wishes. Worse still, with tomorrow being Sunday, I'd have to go to church.

Again.

And it wasn't just any Sunday, but the most dreaded Sunday of the month, Communion Sunday.

Communion Sunday was where the rubber met the road. Put-up-or-shut-up time for Getting Right with God. It wasn't that I wasn't a Christian anymore. It's just that I was more of an expatriate, a Christian living in a country outside the church. And I can't say I missed the coma-like peacefulness of the hallowed sanctuary that quashed my spirit and numbed my soul. The praying and *wah-wah* hymns were bad enough, but on Communion Sunday came the ritual where you had to "drink of Jesus' blood and eat of His flesh." But only if you were right with God.

And I so wasn't right with God. Not at all.

I mean, sure, I'd sinned. Truth be told, quite a lot, as of late. In fact, I could hardly wait to get out of Phoenix, so I could sin again.

As such, the honest thing to do would be to let that silver tray glide on by, publicly confessing my transgressions for all to see. But if I did that, the preacher's hairy eyeball would surely be trained on me. Alternatively, if I partook, God might smite me then and there. And even if He didn't, Pops would undoubtedly smite me on His behalf. Either way, I was getting smit.

COMMUNION SUNDAY started out like every other Sunday. We Faron's sitting in the long, hard pew while the dreary hymns droned on and on, everyone giving us the hairy eyeball because there wasn't a Faron on God's Green Earth who could carry a tune.

Then came the preacher *blah-blahing* about how Moses wandered around in the desert for forty years, searching for the Promised Land like he was on some kind of scavenger hunt. Then came the story about the Ten Commandments, which made me wonder why they weren't in a museum somewhere. Then, even more "true" Biblical stories. Seas magically parting. Jesus walking on water, turning H2O into wine, making fishies multiply like bunny rabbits. Jonah getting gobbled up by a whale and getting spit out, unharmed and undigested. Lazarus rising from the dead, only to be seen by a couple of people for a couple of days, and then disappearing before he could explain how "everlasting life" wouldn't necessarily be occurring on this particular planet.

It was about then, I nodded off.

Pearly Gates, Heaven

Nothing much had changed since my last visit except Hitler was now inching his way up in the Express Line, appearing suddenly at someone's shoulder, causing them to wonder if he'd been there all along.

"Hey, toots!" called Javier, jovial as always. "Wazzzup?"

"Well, I do have a few questions, as it turns out. See, I've been out in the world a while now, and some of this Biblical stuff just isn't adding up."

"Yeah? Like what?"

"Okay, let's start with the biggie. Does God love me?"

"What?"

"I'm asking if He loves me. Like personally."

"Abso-fuckin'-lutely! God loves ALL his creatures, big and small. Even the little birdies in the trees."

"Yeah, but does He love ME? Like, take a personal interest in MY every thought? MY every whim? MY every movement? MY every step?"

"Get a grip, girl. Who do you think you are, Cher? Give The Big Guy a break. God doesn't even know you."
"Aha! Just as I suspected."
"Think of God as Elvis. Elvis loves his fans, right?"
"Yeah."
"And why? Because THEY love HIM."
"So, basically, God just loves being loved?"
"Don't we all?

Church

I AWOKE just in time to join the time-honored story of Abraham and Isaac. In case you're unfamiliar, this is the tale where God tells Abe to slaughter his favorite son, Isaac, just to prove that he, Abe, loves Him, God, more than he, Abe, loves Isaac. And Abe goes, "Sure God," as if this is a perfectly reasonable request on God's part. And then, just as Abe's chasing Isaac around with a machete, God goes, "Kidding! Just wanted to see if you'd do it."

So, this story supposedly has a happy ending because (a) God shows He's the boss, (b) Isaac escapes bludgeoning, and (c) Abe doesn't have to explain to Mrs. Abe why Isaac won't be home for dinner. Anymore. Ever.

I looked around and everybody was just lapping it up. Like they didn't get that murder is *not okay*, even if God tells you to do it. You think if Abe pulled that stunt today, the judge would just say, "Oh, sorry, I didn't realize God told you to do it!"

As amusing as all this was, I found myself dropping off again.

Pearly Gates, Heaven

"So, Javier, fess up. Prayer's just a giant waste of time, right?"
"Well, it makes people feel better, so there's that."
"How do I know there even IS a God? After all, my parents lied about Santa Claus, so there's precedent."
"Of course, there's a God. Or simply, "God" as we call him. In fact, He's off playing golf on Planet 201, even as we speak."
"There's ANOTHER planet???!!!"

"Duh! You think Earth's the best The Almighty could come up with?"

"But Planet Earth's so beautiful. The plants and the trees—"

"Oh, all that's fine. It's the people that suck."

"But God created them—"

"Well..."

"No?"

"Well, He did, and He didn't. Right there in the atom stage, God realized the whole Free Will thingamajig was a really cruddy idea. But rather than go back and extract it, he left Planet Earth to gurgle up in a Petri dish while He started over with Planet 201."

"So, He never checks in on us at all?"

"Why would He? God gave you everything you'll ever need way back there in the Petri dish stage. A sense of right and wrong. Of justice. A moral compass. A craving for community. For family, whatever that turns out to be."

"And all this 'God works in mysterious ways' is just something people tell themselves when their kid gets cancer, or their dog dies, or the other team wins the Super Bowl?"

"Pretty much."

"So, you're saying life is random? There's no cause and effect? No getting smit because of something you did or didn't do?"

"Like the bumper sticker says—or will someday—'Shit Happens.'"

Church

I AWOKE just in time to see the silver tray sliding down the aisle, its six-sided oyster crackers spread out so not one of them touched another. All around me, heads were bowed in prayer, including Mom and Dad's, although they were undoubtedly peeking out to check to see if I was right with God.

I took a wafer and held it between my forefinger and thumb, staring at it like it had the power to blow up the world.

"This is my body, given for you," said the preacher. "Do this in remembrance of me." He placed the wafer in his mouth, a signal for us to do the same.

What if I was wrong? What if there *was* a Personal God, lying in wait, ready to bring the hammer down for my numerous escapades, most of them involving premarital sex? And even if I escaped The Almighty's wrath, there was always Dad, who'd now have proof positive I wasn't Right with God and ground me until menopause.

I put the cracker in my mouth, letting it melt on my tongue, nervously waiting for lightning to strike.

Nothing happened.

"You shall know the truth and the truth shall set you free," said the preacher.

Amen.

THAT NIGHT, I was in my little den/bedroom packing up for my morning exodus, when Mom knocked softly.

I should've known right then and there, something was up since normally my mother would burst into my room screeching, "Fay!" as if I was about to crawl in the bathtub with a toaster for company. No wonder I never did anything wrong. There was never any time for a coverup.

"Dad wants to talk to you."

"Uh, okay."

"In the living room."

Uh-oh.

The living room was for serious conversations. This was to be no mere den talk.

Mom and I sank into the blue paisley couch, facing the fireplace that had never seen a fire. Dad was in his Easy Boy chair, a fitting throne for the King. Grandma had gone off to bed, wise woman that she was.

"You're not going to San Francisco," said King Al.

"What? I am so! I'm packed and everything!"

"It's time you settled down. You're not a kid anymore."

"I am so a kid. Plus, I *am* settling down. In San Francisco."

"What's wrong with Phoenix?"

There wasn't time for a discussion about what was wrong with Phoenix. I was leaving first thing in the morning.

"It's not safe there, what with the SLA—"

"C'mon, Dad! They're not even into kidnapping anymore. They rob banks now, remember?"

"You could've been in that bank. It could've been you that got shot."

"I don't have any money! What on God's green earth would I be doing in a bank?"

Finally, a question he didn't have an answer for.

"Discussion's over. Go to your room."

"I don't have a room. Plus, I hate to break it to you, Pops, but, *duh*, not an heiress!"

Dad said nothing. Just popped another Tums.

"Mom?" I turned to her, desperate for an ally. She had to see how ridiculous this was.

"Al?" said Mom, tentatively. Dad's eyes reached for hers, but his face kept looking at me. "How ya gonna keep 'em down on the farm after they've seen Paree?"

Leave it to my mother to come up with the perfect World War I anthem.

I crossed and knelt at my father's feet. I knew that my dad loved me, and this wasn't about the Symbionese Liberation Army, or even security at Hibernia Bank. My father had grown used to having me around. He was going to miss me. I took his sun-spotted hand, the one with the big silver and turquoise ring that I hated by design but loved because it was his. His blue eyes gazed down at me, steady as always.

"Pops," I said, "I want a life of adventure. I don't see that happening in Phoenix."

Dad looked away, silently chewing his Tums.

"I'll call all the time, promise. I'll be home for Thanksgiving, Christmas, Easter. All the holidays."

My father swallowed hard and withdrew his hand from mine.

"No wonder nobody'll marry you."

"What???!!!"

"Nobody wants a woman who won't do what she's told."

I stumbled to my feet.

Is that what he thought? That I wasn't married because nobody *wanted* me? What about what I wanted?

I waded through the quicksand-colored Berber carpet toward the den.

"You're not taking the car."

I turned and searched my father's face. Dad might see things in black and white, but never was he this unreasonable. It was my car. Sure, Mrs. Turner was registered in his name, but I'd been making payments faithfully for two years. In just two more months, it would be paid off completely. Beyond that, the little red hatchback was my security blanket, giving me a safe place to sleep for the night. Moving to San Francisco without my best car-friend would be like bungee-jumping off the Golden Gate Bridge without a bungee cord.

"That's not fair. And you know it."

"Young lady, you're not too old to spank."

Yeah, but you're too old to catch me.

We just stared at each other, a true case of dueling hairy eyeballs. And that's when I knew for sure, what I'd suspected for some time. That my parents and I would never be adults in the same room, at the same time. That I'd always be their child, forever in need of training.

I'm going, Dad. If I can't take the car, I'll take the bus. If you won't drive me to the station, I'll hitchhike. If you break my kneecaps, I'll crawl down the driveway, pulling my backpack behind me.

But like it or not, I'm not your little girl anymore.

And I'm going.

OF COURSE, I didn't say any of that. If I had, I wouldn't be alive to be writing this. But that didn't mean I wasn't going to get out of there by any means possible.

That night, I dreamt I was taking a nap in my parents' house, only to awake decades later like some modern-day Rip Van Winkle, wondering why nobody was wearing bellbottoms anymore.

I awoke—this time, for real—with a plan. I'd ride my bike to the station, taking whatever I could carry in my saddlebags, then take Greyhound to San Francisco, even though the ticket would eat up most of my savings.

Was I really going to do this? Run away from home like some kind of Huckleberry Finn, my belongings tied up in a red handkerchief?

Still, what else could I do? I simply wasn't who my parents wanted me to be. *Demanded I be.* And while I might be able to fake being a good little Christian girl for a month, I could already feel my slutty self struggling to break free. And if my parents knew who I *really* was, it'd break their hearts far more than me leaving with their illusions intact.

I waited until dawn, then crept down the darkened hallway to Fay's Room. Gram was asleep, her bedside light still on, her glasses resting on her nose, her Bible open on her chest. Quietly, I pulled the quilt up to her chin and kissed her goodbye.

I checked for a light beneath my parents' door. I hated to sneak out without saying anything, but it was the only way I could think of to escape.

It occurred to me just then, that this was how I dealt with things. I was non-confrontational by nature, a product of my 1950's fundamentalist Christian upbringing. "Wives, submit to your husbands," sayeth the Lord. Subliminally stated was that even if it wasn't your husband, it was best to get in a little practice submitting to anyone with a penis in preparation for the real thing.

I'd snuck out on Perfect when I found him living with somebody in North Carolina. From Rhys, my English almost-boyfriend, when I realized he considered me more beard than bride. On my shady Appalachian boss, when I could take no more of his phony sewing machine-selling scam. On Harvard in Morocco. And thinking back, I probably should've left for Europe without telling BellSouth Bobby, but I didn't—and look how that turned out.

And now, I was going to slip away from my beloved father. But, what else could I do? I couldn't out-think him. I couldn't out-argue him. And I certainly couldn't out-spank him.

I wasn't so worried about Mom. My mother was the glue that held the world together. She was the one who softened Dad's rough edges and provided the charm that soothed the air between him and a universe he couldn't always control. No doubt my mom could do anything, including coping with a daughter who she'd find easier to love from afar than with the reality of who she really was.

Ironically, it was my seemingly invincible father who was the fragile one. The king, soon to be left without a kingdom. The *Father Knows Best* dad whose daughter had had sex on two continents, yet provided not even a hint of a grandchild.

I slipped into the dining room only to find the kitchen light on. *Uh oh.*

"I take it you've not outgrown peanut butter and mayonnaise sandwiches?" said Mom, slathering up a half dozen of them. "Oh, and your car keys are on the counter. Dad's already loaded your bike onto Mrs. Turner."

Was this really happening?

"Where is he?" I asked tentatively.

"Front lawn."

I knew what that meant. For a man who didn't drink, didn't smoke, watched golf on TV but never played it, mowing the front lawn—the hotter the Arizona sun, the better—was Dad working off stress. Hardly very effective, given the number of Tums he ingested on a daily basis.

"What if he changes his mind?"

"Too late," said Mom. "He's already hit his quota for the year."

Mom kept sniffling the entire time I backed onto Invergordon. I swung right onto Lincoln Drive, and then took the first right onto 63rd Place. And there was Dad, his broad back pushing the gas mower along to create another straight line of short grass.

I stopped the car and sat waiting for him to turn around. When he did, we stared at each other, neither of us making the first move. I watched as he, well frankly, I didn't know what he was doing. At first, I thought he might be having a heart attack. But no, my 57-year-old father—no longer a scrawny young man, now middle-aged with skinny legs who carried his weight in his belly—struggled to get down on one knee.

It was a gesture we both knew. It began when I was six and he took the family to see *Hit the Deck,* at the Starlight Theater in Kansas City's Swope Park. The musical was about three sailors who found love on weekend leave. And while the play was forgettable, one scene captured my father's Navy's man heart. The one where the sailor dropped to one knee, called out, "Step in, sister!" and his girlfriend came running, jumping into his lap.

This sweet gesture became a ritual between my daddy and me. Every evening after work, Pops would come through the door, drop to one knee, call out, "Step in, sister!" and I'd come running.

And now, in my much-older dad, I saw the father who applauded wildly as I rolled down the grassy hill beside our house. Who helped me capture fireflies and imprison them in glass Mason jars. Who traded a refrigerator for the first Chum-dog, whose job it was to lead me home each evening at dusk. And now, here he was. Still handsome for a man in his fifties, down on one knee, arms wide open.

"Step in, sister!" he called. And I came running, just as I had when I was a little girl, flying off to hug him with all my might.

Where Are They Now?

If you're wondering, "Whatever happened to the characters in this book, now you can find out. **For Free!**

All you have to do is to review ***Journey of a Teetotaling Virgin,*** post your review to Amazon, Goodreads or both, send me a copy at Fay@FayFaron.com and I will send you a PDF file by return email. (Just a line or two is fine.)

And be sure to visit the "PIX" page at FayFaron.com for a gallery of over 300 "back in the day" photos of both people and places.

Please Review This Book!

It really helps. Not in the ranking on Amazon, but in persuading others to read the book once they find it. So, if you liked this book, please let your friends know. And your strangers as well!

ABOUT THE AUTHOR

Fay Faron first came into the national conscienceless in 1982 when she founded The Rat Dog Dick Detective Agency in San Francisco. In 1991, her advice column, "Ask Rat Dog," was syndicated by King Features, leading to appearances on virtually every major TV talk & news show of the decade, including Oprah (3 times), Larry King Live and Good Morning America.

Faron has authored three books ("Missing Persons" & "Rip-off," published by Writer's Digest; and the self-published, "A Nasty Bit of Business") and been the subject of "Hastened to their Graves," a true crime by Edgar award-winning author, Jack Olsen.

In 2001, Faron sold her detective agency and moved to Louisiana, where she was named "Ferrygodmother of New Orleans" in 2012 for saving the local ferry system. In 2020, she was awarded Marquis Who's Who Lifetime Achievement Award" for her investigative endeavors and community activism.

"Journey of an Ex-Teetotaling Virgin" is a memoir of her traveling years right out of college.